Humorous Texts: A Semantic and Pragmatic Analysis

Humor Research 6

Editors
Victor Raskin
Willibald Ruch

Mouton de Gruyter
Berlin · New York

Humorous Texts:
A Semantic and Pragmatic Analysis

by
Salvatore Attardo

Mouton de Gruyter
Berlin · New York   2001

Mouton de Gruyter (formerly Mouton, The Hague)
is a Division of Walter de Gruyter & Co., Berlin.

⊚ Printed on acid-free paper which falls within the guidelines of the
ANSI to ensure permanence and durability.

Die Deutsche Bibliothek — Cataloging-in-Publication Data

> Attardo, Salvatore:
> Humorous texts : a semantic and pragmatic analysis / by Salvatore Attardo. — Berlin ; New York : Mouton de Gruyter, 2001
>   (Humor research ; 6)
>   ISBN 3-11-017068-X

© Copyright 2001 by Walter de Gruyter GmbH & Co. KG, D-10785 Berlin
All rights reserved, including those of translation into foreign languages. No part of this book may be reproduced or transmitted in any form or by any means, electronic or mechanical, including photocopy, recording, or any information storage and retrieval system, without permission in writing from the publisher.
Cover Design: Christopher Schneider, Berlin.
Printing: Druckerei Hildebrand, Berlin. — Binding: Lüderitz & Bauer, Berlin.
Printed in Germany.

"This has to be the least funny book one has ever read"
(Opening sentence of a review of Attardo 1994)

To Gaia

Preface

This book presents a methodology to extend the analyses of the General Theory of Verbal Humor to all texts, regardless of length. It also presents a number of more or less long and comprehensive applications to texts taken from a variety of literatures, media, situations, and historical periods. It is also an update of the GTVH, a decade after its first proposal.

The book has existed in many forms. In 1997, I used a collection of work-in-progress pieces in a course on "humor on television" . These were reworked in an early draft for a seminar on humorous narratives in the spring of 1999. Part of the seminar consisted of the analysis of some sections of Wilde's story, in ch. (8). It was radically overhauled over my year-long sabbatical at ITC-IRST, in Trento.

This work is certainly not the last word on the issue of "long texts" in humor research. Its goal is to explore some aspects of this field, hopefully setting some markers that will be used by other researchers to further our knowledge. The same goes for the actual analyses. I say this because so much in what follows is tentative, hesitatingly put, or plain speculative that I considered changing the title to *Out on a Limb*. However, in a sense I knew what I was doing; this is the lot of those who venture outside charted areas: they run into lions.

0.1   A cautionary tale

In 1966, Violette Morin published—in the famous issue of *Communications* which popularized the structuralist analysis of texts—a short article on jokes, in which she postulated a tripartite organization of the joke text. This approach gathered a substantial following among European scholars (see Attardo 1994: 85-92). However, ulterior research showed that, far from being unique to jokes, a tripartite structure is common to all narrative forms. Therefore, instead of having discovered a defining feature of jokes, Morin had merely rediscovered the truism that jokes are narratives (consider that a good definition of *joke* could be "a short narrative text which is funny"). This is not to say that all humor is narrative, but merely that jokes are a type of text that is a subset of narratives (in French, this is clearer as *joke* translates as *histoire drôle*, i.e., funny story).

The moral of the story above is that one must be very careful about what one is studying, because just looking at one's object of study and analyzing any of its given features may or may not result in a fruitful avenue of research. Let me emphasize again that no one is claiming that Morin's work wasn't interesting; but only that it was interesting as an analysis of narratives, not as an analysis of jokes.

The present work is faced with the same problem, insofar as this work is concerned with narratives (not exclusively, in fact, as we will see). I set out to investigate humorous narratives (and by that I mean other than jokes, taking length as a defining feature of this genre; see Attardo and Chabanne 1992). However, I intend to analyze not narratives *per se* but only narratives as they are humorous. In other words, I am interested in how and why certain narratives are humorous and others are not. The focus of the analysis is on the humorous nature of the texts, not on their narrative status.

In this sense, this work is not a standard narratological work. However, obviously enough, the narrative structure of the text itself may be humorous, and therefore we may have to cross over into the domain of narratology proper to investigate that aspect of humorous narratives. Furthermore, some aspects of the narrative structure of the text (first and foremost, its plot) will be relevant to the establishment of that humorous nature of the text; and, in this sense, this is then a work within the purview of narratology. I believe this work to be a sound application of linguistic (primarily semantic and pragmatic) methodology to the field of humor research and secondarily of narratology. As with all sound applications of one field to another, the applied field (here, linguistics) provides the methodology, while the fields applied to (here, humor research and narratology) provide the questions.

The central question that this book tries to answer is precisely the one mentioned above: how do narrative texts longer than jokes function *as humorous texts*? The chapters in the book work up to the answer. Chapter one presents an introduction to the linguistically based humor research applied in the rest of the book, namely the Semantic-Script Theory of Humor and the General Theory of Verbal Humor. The second chapter is a review of the scant literature on the topic of humorous narratives. Chapter three introduces the semantic and pragmatic tools necessary to model the text, while chapter four begins to work up to long texts by considering "intermediate" texts that share some of the features of longer and short texts. Chapter five introduces the tools specifically needed to handle the humorous aspects of long texts.

The next chapter deals with diffuse disjunctors, i.e., humorous texts that do not have a clear cut punch line. Irony and register humor are the examples chosen to illustrate this type of humor. Finally, the book is capped off by two chapters collecting a number of case studies that exemplify the method described in the text (ch. 7), as well as a longer analysis of an Oscar Wilde text (ch. 8). They range widely across genres (poetry, short stories, novels) and somewhat across languages (English, French, Italian) and historical periods (1600 to date). The last chapter sums up the discussion and opens a new venue in the quantitative analysis of text: a look at the frequency of humor within the text. It is a new approach, which may have some significant outcomes.

The texts analyzed in the book and not just quoted in passing are referred to with four letter codes, listed below:

CAND	Candide (Voltaire)
CBTD	Chuckles Bites the Dust (Mary Tyler Moore Show)
HEHA	Headlong Hall (Thomas Love Peacock)
NIAB	Nightmare Abbey (Thomas Love Peacock)
HRCI	Han Rybeck ou le coup de l'étrier (Alphonse Allais)
KUGE	The Kugelmass Episode (Woody Allen)
LASC	Lord Arthur Savile's Crime (Oscar Wilde)
MDMT	A Merry Discourse of Meum and Tuum (Henry Peacham)
ROSE	Il nome della rosa (Umberto Eco)
TSTF	The System of Dr. Tarr and Dr. Fethers (Edgar Allan Poe)
TRAN	Transformations (Anne Sexton)

Some informative notes are given for the authors. These should be intended as helpful hints for those not familiar with the given author, not as exhaustive treatments of their literary significance. With the more famous authors, the notes are minimal, since widespread knowledge of their work is assumed.

0.2 Acknowledgments

0.2.1 Publications

The discussions of the linguistic tools for the analysis of humor and the literature review are largely based on my previous treatment of these issues, updated as necessary. In some cases, the revisions have been major and the present text supersedes previous treatments of the same subject. This is especially significant in the treatments of script oppositions and logical mechanisms.

The precursor of much that appears in this book was an invited paper I presented at the first conference on the computational treatment of humor. It appeared as "Humor Theory Beyond Jokes: The Treatment of Humorous Texts at Large," in J. Hulstijn and A. Nijholt (eds.) (1996), *Automatic Interpretation and Generation of Verbal Humor.* Enschede, NL: University of Twente. 81-94.

The material discussed in section 4.2 was presented at the 1988 International Congress of Anthropological and Ethnological Sciences in Zagreb, at the 1993 Georgetown Roundtable on Language and Linguistics, Pre-session on Discourse Analysis: Written Texts, and at the First Symposium on Humor and Linguistics, at the 1994 International Conference on Humor Research, in Ithaca, NY.

Parts of section 6.2, on irony, appeared originally in the *Journal of Pragmatics* (2000: 32). A small part of the Peacock case studies in chapter 6 appeared in Attardo

(1994). The analysis of the Voltaire passage appeared first in Attardo (1986), then in Attardo (1994), and in Attardo (2000b), the proceedings of the stylistics conference held in Opole, Poland, the previous year. Each version is slightly different (hopefully better). The analysis of Peacham's text was presented in March 2000 at the University of Bergamo. In fact, I owe my interest in that text to that occasion. The analysis of the Mary Tyler Moore episode in 7.1 appeared in *HUMOR: International Journal of Humor Research* 11:3. 1998. 231-260. The analysis of Alphonse Allais' tale was originally my presentation at the first conference on Allais, held in 1996 in Liège, Belgium. A fragment of the tale was already analyzed in Attardo (1986). It later appeared, in French, as "Mécanismes linguistiques de l'humour d'Alphonse Allais dans 'Han Rybeck ou le coup de l'étrier'" In J.M. Defays and L. Rosier (eds.) *Alphonse Allais, Ecrivain. Actes du premier colloque international Alphonse Allais.* Saint Genouph: A.G. Nizet, 1997. 77-87; it too has been seriously revised. The analysis of the poem *Cinderella*, by Anne Sexton, is part of a forthcoming paper co-authored with Cynthia Vigliotti.

0.2.2 People

I am much grateful to the following individuals: Steven Brown, Donald Casadonte, Wladyslaw Chlopicki, Catherine Davies, Christie Davies, Jean-Marc Defays, K. Anders Ericsson, Giovannantonio Forabosco, Julia Gergits, Rachel Giora, Jennifer Hay, Christian Hempelmann, Susan Herring, Barbara Karman, Helga Kotthoff, Marvin Minsky, Craig McDonough, Franco Mele, Jodi Nelms, Don L. F. Nielsen, Anton Nijholt, Neal Norrick, John Paolillo, Victor Raskin, Laurence Rosier, Michele Sala, Justyna Skowron, Oliviero Stock, Cynthia Vigliotti, Peter Wenzel, Francisco Yus, and Anat Zajdman. I also wish to thank Youngstown State University for its support in different phases of the work, but mostly for granting me a sabbatical during which I finished the book. I especially wish to thank Victor Raskin and Willibald Ruch, who served as editors, as well as Victor Raskin (again), Wladyslaw Chlopicki, and Giovannantonio Forabosco for reading several versions of the text while it was being written and discussing it with me (not to mention remaining friends, after the experience) and Oliviero Stock, for having made possible a most conducive working environment at IRST, during my sabbatical. Cynthia Vigliotti hand-tagged all the index. My parents also contributed to my well-being in more ways than I can count. Cynthia Vigliotti contributed to this work in many ways, but mostly by seeing me through its writing. Needless to say, none of the individuals or institutions above is responsible for (or even necessarily agrees with) what I say.

Povo (Trento), June 2000

Contents

Preface   **vii**
    0.1   A cautionary tale vii
    0.2   Acknowledgments ix
          0.2.1   Publications ix
          0.2.2   People x

1   Preliminaries   **1**
    1.1   The SSTH 1
          1.1.1   The SSTH's Main Hypothesis 1
          1.1.2   Scripts 2
    1.2   The Structure of a Semantic Theory 9
          1.2.1   Formal Semantic Analysis 9
          1.2.2   Inferential Explosion 15
          1.2.3   Is this a formal analysis? 16
    1.3   The Semantic Theory of Humor 17
          1.3.1   Overlapping 17
          1.3.2   Oppositeness 18
          1.3.3   The Doctor's Wife Joke 21
    1.4   The GTVH 22
          1.4.1   Language (LA) 22
          1.4.2   Narrative Strategy (NS) 23
          1.4.3   Target (TA) 23
          1.4.4   Situation (SI) 24
          1.4.5   Logical Mechanism (LM) 25
          1.4.6   The KRs: Script Opposition (SO) 26
          1.4.7   The Joke, According to the GTVH 27
    1.5   Outline of the Theory 28
    1.6   Methodological and metatheoretical issues 30
          1.6.1   Competence, not performance 30
          1.6.2   Semiotics, Text, Narrative 32
          1.6.3   The role of intuition in humor research 33

2 Literature Review   37
2.1 The Expansionist Approach   37
2.1.1 Chlopicki   38
2.1.2 Kolek   39
2.2 The Revisionist Approach   41
2.2.1 Holcomb   41
2.2.2 Wenzel   42
2.2.3 Palmer   44
2.2.4 A digression: Jolles on jokes   45

3 Semantic Analysis and Humor Analysis   47
3.1 Semantic and Pragmatic Tools   47
3.1.1 Storage Area   47
3.1.2 Contents of the Storage Area   48
3.1.3 Scripts   53
3.2 How is information added to the storage area?   54
3.3 The Text World   57
3.4 Surface structure recall   58
3.5 Summing up   59

4 Beyond the Joke   61
4.1 Narrative vs. Conversation   61
4.1.1 Stand-up routines   62
4.1.2 Joke telling contests   65
4.1.3 Conversation   66
4.2 Joke cycles   69
4.2.1 Definition of Joke Cycle   69
4.2.2 A little history   70
4.2.3 Two generations of jokes   70
4.2.4 Recapitulation   78
4.3 Conclusion   78

5 A Theory of Humorous Texts   79
5.1 Method of analysis   79
5.2 Narratives   79
5.3 Lines and their Configurations   82
5.3.1 Jab lines   82
5.3.2 Punch lines   83
5.3.3 Strands   83
5.3.4 Repetition   85
5.3.5 Stacks   86
5.3.6 Intertextual jokes   87
5.3.7 Bridges and Combs   87

5.4	A typology of line position		88
	5.4.1	No line	88
	5.4.2	Final punch line	89
	5.4.3	Episodic	90
	5.4.4	Mere sequence of jab lines with final punch line	91
	5.4.5	Bathtub placement	91
5.5	Humorous Plots		92
	5.5.1	Narratives Structurally Similar to Jokes	92
	5.5.2	Metanarrative Plots	94
	5.5.3	Plots with Humorous Fabulae	97
	5.5.4	Plots with Serious Fabulae	98
	5.5.5	Humorous disruption and realistic illusion	98
5.6	Humorous Techniques		99
	5.6.1	Coincidences	99
	5.6.2	Hyperdetermined	100
5.7	General Considerations		101

6 Diffuse Disjunction   103

	6.0.1	Discrete or diffuse disjunctors	103
6.1	Register humor		104
	6.1.1	Literature Review	104
	6.1.2	Register Humor in T. L. Peacock	106
6.2	Irony		110
	6.2.1	Principle of least disruption	112
	6.2.2	A contextual-appropriateness theory of irony	114
	6.2.3	Reasons for using irony	119
	6.2.4	Irony and Humor	122
	6.2.5	A Passage from Voltaire's *Candide*	123

7 Case Studies   127

7.1	*Chuckles Bites the Dust*: the opening sequence.		128
7.2	Sexton's *Cinderella*		134
	7.2.1	Graphs	139
	7.2.2	Stacks	141
7.3	*A Merry Discourse of Meum and Tuum*		142
7.4	*Il nome della rosa*: Analysis of one strand		148
	7.4.1	A text with more than one model reader	149
	7.4.2	A Serious Novel with a Humor Strand	149
7.5	*Han Rybeck ou le coup de l'étrier*		150
	7.5.1	Overall Analysis	151
	7.5.2	Schematic representation of HRCI	155
	7.5.3	The text of Han Rybeck ou le coup de l'étrier	157
	7.5.4	English Translation of HRCI	160

8	**"Lord Arthur Savile's Crime" by Oscar Wilde**	**163**
8.1	CHAPTER I	163
8.2	CHAPTER II	174
8.3	CHAPTER III	176
8.4	CHAPTER IV	185
8.5	CHAPTER V	188
8.6	CHAPTER VI	199
9	**Further Perspectives**	**203**
9.1	A quantitative look at LASC	203
9.2	General Conclusions	206
9.3	Limitations of the Model	207

Primary Sources   **209**

Works Cited   **211**

Index   **226**

List of Tables

1.1	*List of known LMs*	27
1.2	*Hierarchical Organization of the KRs*	28
4.1	*The Canonical LBJ in the GTVH*	73
4.2	*Hierarchical Organization of the KRs (= Table 1.2).*	73
4.3	*Para-Jokes in the GTVH*	75
4.4	*Meta-Jokes in the GTVH*	76
5.1	*Text Vector Notation*	90
7.1	*List of Jab Lines in Peacham's The Merry Discourse of Meum and Tuum*	145
7.2	*List of Jab Lines in Peacham's The Merry Discourse of Meum and Tuum; continued.*	146
7.3	*Some of the anachronistic/intertextual jabs of ROSE.*	148

List of Figures

1.1	*The Lexical Script for* DOCTOR	3
1.2	*A Small Fragment of Semantic Network*	8
7.1	*Graph for Cinderella: SOs.*	139
7.2	*Graph for Cinderella: select LMs.*	140
7.3	*Graph for Cinderella: a select NS.*	140
7.4	*The Merry Discourse of Meum and Tuum by Henry Peacham, Jr.*	144
7.5	*MDMT segmentation chart*	147
7.6	*Han Rybeck ou le coup de l'étrier by Alphonse Allais*	156
9.1	*LASC segmentation chart*	204

Chapter 1

Preliminaries

This chapter provides the reader with the background information about humor research in linguistics which is assumed in the rest of the text. The novice humor researcher will find here a summary and introduction to the theory of humor adopted (and developed) by the author. No claim is made that this approach is the only one (or even the best one, although the author happens to believe this). A review of the field of humor research in linguistics can be found in Attardo (1994). No attempt is made to define such concept as *humor, funny*, etc. See Attardo (1994) and Raskin (1985) for discussions and definitions.

1.1 The SSTH

We start out with the Semantic Script Theory of Humor (SSTH) developed by Raskin (1985). What follows is largely based on the SSTH, thus a good understanding of the workings of the theory is an inevitable starting point.

1.1.1 The SSTH's Main Hypothesis

For ease of exposition, the main hypothesis of the SSTH will be presented immediately in (1), and will be followed by a discussion of the relevant semantic tools used by the theory. A summary of Raskin's analysis of a sample joke will follow.

(1) A text can be characterized as a single-joke-carrying-text if both of the [following] conditions are satisfied:
i) The text is compatible, fully or in part, with two different scripts
ii) The two scripts with which the text is compatible are opposite (...). The two scripts with which some text is compatible are said to overlap fully or in part in this text (Raskin 1985: 99)

It may be useful to recall that, in the meaning current in generative linguistics, a formal theory is an abstract device which manipulates abstract objects on the basis of explicit rules and, given a set of primitives and a set of rules, will generate a set of objects distinct from the set of primitives. This generation is intended in a purely logical sense and is equivalent to analyzing the output of the manipulations and reconstructing how they have been generated from the primitives. Another way to conceptualize the working of a generative theory is for the theory to pass a judgement upon any object as to its generability on the basis of the theory's primitives and rules.

Consequently, providing a formal theory of humor may be seen as either of two tasks: generating a humorous text out of its elements, or recognizing a humorous text when presented with one. From the point of view of the first task, a formal theory of humor must describe how one can generate a funny text by manipulating objects that are not funny taken separately. From the point of view of recognition, the theory must provide the necessary and sufficient conditions that a text must meet for the text to be funny and an algorithm for checking whether a given text is funny or not. As explained above, the two tasks are logically equivalent, and the two procedures differ only in emphasis.

1.1.2 Scripts

The notion of "script" comes originally from psychology (Bartlett 1932, Bateson 1955: 186-189), Goffman 1974) and was incorporated by Artificial Intelligence (AI) (Charniak 1972, Schank 1975, Schank and Abelson 1977) and by linguistics (Fillmore 1975, 1985, Chafe 1977, and Raskin 1981). The papers collected in the 1985/86 roundtable edited by Raskin in *Quaderni di Semantica* (Raskin (ed.) 1985 and Raskin 1985d) provide a good overview of the complexities of the field.[1] Scripts are (perhaps more commonly) also known as "frames;" other terms (scenarios, schemata) have also been used. A review of these terminological discussions can be found in Andor (1985: 212-213) and (Fillmore 1985: 223n). Raskin chooses "script" to designate the unmarked term for this type of cognitive structure. We will follow this use.

A script is an organized[2] complex of information about some entity, in the broadest sense: an object (real or imaginary), an event, an action, a quality, etc. It is a cognitive structure internalized by the speaker which provides the speaker with information on how a given entity is structured, what are its parts and components, or how an activity is done, a relationship organized, and so on, to cover all possible re-

---

[1] See also Lehrer and Kittay (1992) and Mandler (1984).
[2] Even in the weak definition of script (Abelson 1981: 717) the information in scripts is not completely unstructured. Abelson's fitting example is that of a circus performance: clowns may come before or after the lion tamer. However, we may add, the lion tamer may not leave the cage first and let the lions fend for themselves, nor may the clowns fire the cannon before someone has been lodged in its barrel (except of course for humorous purposes).

1.1. THE SSTH

lations between entities (including their consituents). Needless to say, this definition is impossibly vague. We will make it more specific in what follows.

What is in a Script?

Most definitions of script agree that it contains information which is prototypical of the entity being described, such as well-established routines and common ways to do things and to go about activities. At the simplest level, a script is equivalent to the lexical meaning of a word.

It should be noted also that Raskin insists on the fact that scripts, in his definition, are immediately related to, and evoked by, lexical items. Therefore, each script will have a lexematic "handle" which causes its activation. This is an important distinction because in psychological literature, as well as in AI, there is a tendency to consider scripts as merely experiential/cognitive objects.[3] Figure (1.1) will clarify what type of information a script may contain.

```
Subject: [+Human] [+Adult]
Activity: > Study medicine
          = Receive patients: patient comes or doctor visits
                              doctor listens to complaints
                              doctor examines patient
          = Cure disease:     doctor diagnoses disease
                              doctor prescribes treatment
          = (Take patient's money)
Place:   > Medical School
         = Hospital or doctor's office
Time:    > Many years
         = Every day
         = Immediately
Condition: Physical contact
```

Raskin (1985: 85). Note that "> " stands for "in the past," and " = " for "in the present."

Figure 1.1: *The Lexical Script for* DOCTOR

The psychological reality of scripts has been established, e.g., Abelson (1981), Andor (1985), or Tannen (1985). Typical tasks used in experimental research involve the recall of events in a story or the recall of a story with events in a different order than the usual one. Speakers tend to recall events that are in a script even if they

---

[3] Scripts without a lexematic handle may exist, but they will not be considered in what follows.

did not occur in the actual story, as well as reorder events according to the script's canonical order.

Hierarchy of Scripts

In general, there are various definitions that try to establish hierarchical structures within scripts. In this respect, typical examples are Schank and Abelson's "scripts" which are more specific than "plans:"

> A plan is (...) the repository for general information that will connect events that cannot be connected by use of the available script or by standard causal chain expansion (Schank and Abelson 1977: 70)

In turn, plans are more specific than goals: "A plan is a series of projected actions to realize a goal" (Schank and Abelson 1977: 71).

Fillmore (1985) and Raskin (1985b) both refuse the idea of denoting the hierarchical organization of scripts by different terms, in the Schank and Abelson mode, but Raskin introduces the idea of "macroscript," clusters of scripts organized chronologically, and "complex script" i.e., scripts made of other scripts, but not organized chronologically. A good example of macroscript would be the famous RESTAURANT (macro)script (see Schank and Abelson (1977: 42-50)), which consists of several other scripts linked chronologically (DRIVE UP TO THE RESTAURANT, BE SEATED, ORDER FOOD, etc.). An example of a complex script could be WAR, which presupposes other scripts such as ARMY, ENEMY, VICTORY, DEFEAT, WEAPON, etc.

The macroscript should not be confused with the metascript. A metascript is an abstract, minimally specified script, which may be realized in different ways (Abelson 1981: 725). For example, HELPING OUT or DOING A FAVOR are metascripts, that can be instatiated by WASHING THE DISHES, for example. The issue of underspecified[4] scripts brings forth the issue of within-script variation. For example, PREPARING A MEAL may or may not include MAKING COFFEE depending on the culinary tastes/habits of the people eating. Abelson (1981) lists eight aspects of script variability:

1. equifinal actions, i.e., different actions that have the same outcome. One may open a plastic bag with scissors or with a knife.

2. variables, i.e., the actual events instantiating a given slot.

3. script paths, these are branching points within a script, for example asking for the check may be accomplished by saying so to a waiter, or with a gesture.

4. scene selection, corresponds to the weak script concept illustrated in note (2).

---

[4]No ontological difference should be read in this definition. Metascripts are just a special kind of script.

1.1. THE SSTH

5. tracks, similar to paths, but more complex, for example, if the restaurant one is going to is a fast food, then the path in the RESTAURANT script for ordering at the table is precluded, while the one for ordering at the counter is activated.

6. interferences, i.e., things that go wrong in the instantiation of a script, for example, being served the wrong food.

7. distractions, events that interrupt the progression of a script, e.g., the entrance of armed bandits in the restaurant.

8. free behaviors, activities that may freely take place concurrently to a script, but are not part of it, e.g., reading while eating cereals.

Encyclopedic Knowledge

Another related issue is that of the difference between "linguistic" (lexical) and "encyclopedic" knowledge. Simply put, many speakers know that the chemical formula for water is H_2O, but many others don't. The latter are not hindered in their understanding or use of the word "water" at all; therefore, this seems to be grounds for excluding the fact that the chemical formula for water is H_2O from the meaning (script) for the word "water." This knowledge is then said to be encyclopedic. Since Katz and Fodor's (1963) claim that encyclopedic knowledge falls outside of the boundaries of linguistic semantics, a heated argument has ensued on the issues of how much of the knowledge of speakers about a word/extralinguistic entity designated by that word should be represented in the lexicon. Raskin and other frame-semanticists convincingly demonstrate that a large amount of contextual information has to be stored in the lexicon to be accessed during the processing of sentences. Consider the following example:[5]

(2) John stacked the beer in the fridge.

Unless the lexical item "beer" is capable of activating the knowledge that the given liquid comes packaged in containers of stackable shape and dimensions such as to fit in a refrigerator, the above sentence would be impossible to parse, given the semantic inconsistency between "beer" ([+LIQUID]) and "stack" which subcategorizes for a [−LIQUID] direct object.

This type of argument brings up the issue of distinguishing between the information pertaining to words (i. e., lexical knowledge) and pertaining to the world (i.e., encyclopedic knowledge). According to Raskin, the difference between lexical and encyclopedic knowledge is not so much qualitative, but rather quantitative in relation to the closeness of association of the scripts. Consider the information which this writer happens to have, and that presumably not many other speakers share, that Belgian brewers produce a special type of beer flavored with cherries, called *Kriek*

---

[5] Attributed to Fillmore.

Lambic. Where would this type of information appear? According to Raskin, it would not appear directly in the lexical script BEER, but it would appear in another type of script, a "restricted knowledge" script, linked to the lexical script, but distinct from the latter (on the lexical/encyclopedic debate, see the recent collection of articles edited by Peeters 2000).

How much information goes into a script?

Clearly, this issue is complex, but it does provide evidence for the falsifiability of the concept of script, and hence deserves particular attention. Essentially, one can never know that a given script is complete, since the next sentence one processes may include a new bit of information that was previously unavailable to one. It is simple to imagine a dynamic system which updates its knowledge banks whenever it encounters a bit of information it was not aware of (and which is consistent with its prior knowledge). This is, in fact, what humans do: faced with a new bit of information they revise their scripts. So, for example, if we read an article about doctors which mentions that they have to be certified by a board, we would have to add this information to the script in figure (1.1).

While this may seem to be problematic, since it is tantamount to claiming that scripts are open-ended, in fact it is evidence of the falsifiability of the concept. Basically, we can consider a script as an hypothesis on the semantic content of a given lexeme[6] which is disproved if a bit of information not included in the script surfaces. At that point, the script is revised and the revised version then takes the place of the original hypothesis, only to be further tested by new texts. If the script is viable, after a few revisions it will become stable, i.e., few if any changes will be required.[7] However, as we know from Popperian epistemology, this does not *prove* that the script is complete, but it is merely the best available construct that matches the empirical reality.

Static vs. dynamic definition of script

There are two approaches to the definition of scripts (in the broad sense we are using): a static and a dynamic one.

Both approaches largely overlap and agree that a script contains information about the lexematic handle (or about a concept). They differ in that the static approach sees a script as an (abstract) object, stored in memory, whereas the dynamic approach sees scripts as segment of the overall semantic network, dynamically defined by activation levels. In this writer's mind, the two approaches are equivalent and differ only in emphasis. Cf. section (3.2) for further discussion, and an example of how the process may work.

---

[6]The same can be said for other types of scripts, but we need not explore these complexities here.

[7]There is evidence from L1 acquisition that this is the process whereby speakers acquire the lexicon of their native language(s).

1.1. THE SSTH

The static approach sees scripts as ready-made objects, which consist of slot-filler relationships. This is the standard way in which the concept is used, however this is not the only way of seeing scripts. Let us return to Raskin's definition:

> every script is a graph with lexical nodes and semantic links between the nodes. In fact, all the scripts of the language make up a single continuous graph, and the lexical entry of a word is a domain within this graph (1985: 81)

From this definition, it is clear that scripts can also be seen as objects created on the fly, dynamically, to match changes in saliency, which distorts the graph, or new information, which changes it. Kintsch and Mannes (1987) have provided evidence for the emergent (i.e., dynamic) nature of scripts (see also Kintsch 1998: 82-86).

Attardo (1996a) introduced to humor theory the possibility of classifying scripts which lies in the way in which they are activated: a lexical script is activated by having its lexematic handle instantiated as a token in an utterance (i.e., if a sentence using the word "cat" is uttered, then we consider the script CAT to have been activated). An inferential script instead can be activated inferentially: suppose that a given text activated in rapid succession the scripts

(3) HUSBAND - LOVER - ADULTERY - PRIVATE EYE - WIFE - LAWYER - COURTROOM

then a reasonable inference will activate the inferential script DIVORCE. Essentially, what is being suggested is that the sum of weak activation upon DIVORCE caused by the activation of the related scripts in (3). Structurally lexical scripts and inferential[8] scripts are not different, and indeed the mere mention of "divorce" in the text would activate the script DIVORCE. To highlight the substantial identity between lexical scripts and inferential scripts, we will refer to both as "scripts," and distinguish between them only when necessary.

The use of the "inferential script" term is useful as a mnemonic device to remind us that inferential scripts are activated during the semantic/pragmatic processing of the text and can differ significantly from the surface manifestation of the text. It should also remind us that the interpretation of the text (be it that of the hearer/reader or of the analyst) is necessarily always a construct of the interpreter. Finally, it should also serve as a reminder of the fact that the larger the scripts activated in a text, the more other scripts may fill their slots.

Semantic Network

As we have seen, formally, a script is a subgraph of a very broad graph linking all the semantic nodes (= scripts) of a culture. Let us consider a simple example: in English there exists a word "mother" (itself the handle for the script MOTHER) which has an

---

[8] In psycholinguistics this is called explicit and implicit presentations of scripts (Bower et al. 1979).

hyponymy relatioship with the word/script PERSON.[9] So, the scripts MOTHER and PERSON are connected by a semantic link "hyponymy" (traditionally called ISA). The graph mentioned above is the sum total of all these links and nodes.

The issues above bring up a final concept that must be introduced in order to understand the SSTH, namely that of "semantic network." Scripts, lexical and non-lexical, are connected by links. The links can be of different semantic natures (synonymy, hyponymy, antonymy, etc.), and correspondingly labelled. Significantly, links may have different lengths, which reflect the fact that certain nodes may be less accessible than other nodes.[10]

The set of scripts in the lexicon, their links, plus all the non-lexical scripts, their links, and all the links between the two sets of scripts form the "semantic network" which contains all of the information a speaker has about his/her culture. The idea of a semantic network was prefigured by Peirce (1931-36; see Eco 1979: 26-49) and introduced into AI by Quillian (1967). It should be noted that the global network of all scripts and their links is very large and multidimensional (i.e., not limited to the three dimensions customarily used in geometrical representations). Figure (1.1.2) represents a small fragment of a semantic network.

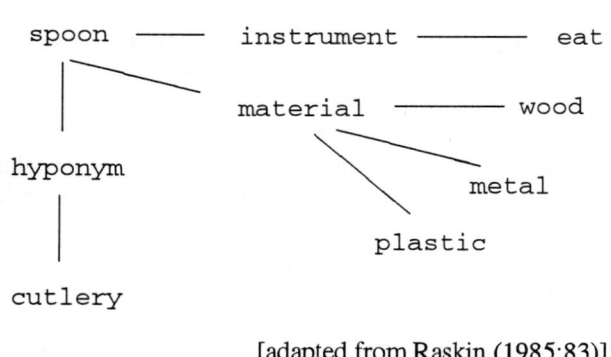

[adapted from Raskin (1985:83)]

Figure 1.2: *A Small Fragment of Semantic Network*

---

[9] It is common practice to indicate a script by its lexematic handle, so the word "person" is the lexematic handle for the script PERSON; for short, we say "the script PERSON"

[10] From the vantage point of a given node, of course. All nodes are accessible from any other node, by definition; however, the ease of access will vary.

1.2 The Structure of a Semantic Theory

In Raskin's view, a semantic theory must consist of the following (abstract) objects: the set of all scripts available to the speakers (along with their labeled links) and a set of combinatorial rules. The combinatorial rules correspond to Katz and Fodor's (1963) "amalgamation rules" and to their current notational variant known as "unification" (e.g., Shieber 1986). Their function is to combine all the possible meanings of the scripts and discard those combinations that do not yield coherent readings. Those combinations that yield coherent readings are stored and incorporated with other successful combinations until all the elements in the text have been processed. If there is (at least) one coherent, well-formed interpretation, that interpretation of the text is licensed as "the meaning" of the text, and the semantic theory classifies the sentence/text as "well-formed." Needless to say, the semantic interpretation is then passed on to a pragmatic "module" which draws inferences, implicatures, etc. (Raskin 1985: 80). It should be noted that Raskin does not separate semantic and pragmatic processing, as I am doing here for expository clarity. I will continue to do so for the rest of the exposition.

1.2.1 Formal Semantic Analysis

In this book, I assume that we have available a perfect semantic/pragmatic interpreter, capable of producing a literal interpretation/representation of the text and of drawing all necessary inferences from the text.

Needless to say, we do not in reality have such a tool available.[11] The issues involved in its building are of daunting complexity, as they involve both combinatorial and inferential explosion. An idea of the issues at hand can be gathered from a short discussion of two relevant sources in the humor research literature.

Combinatorial Explosion

Raskin (1985) considers the number of combinations of the various meanings of a simple five-word sentence.[12] Raskin posits that there are 12 scripts which can activated in the sentence, yielding 64 potential combinations. Of these all but 25 are ruled out by combinatorial rules (i.e., the disambiguation process). This still leaves us with a 25-way ambiguous sentence.[13]

In general, the number of potential combinations of meanings in a sentence is equal to the product of the number of scripts/meanings of each morpheme in the

---

[11] Nor do we have a complete syntactic description of any language. That has never stopped syntacticians, so why should it stop us?

[12] The sentence is *The paralyzed bachelor hit the colorful ball*. The meanings of the determinative articles are not considered; doing so would increase the number of combinations by a factor of nine: it is generally accepted that articles have three meanings in English.

[13] In fact, it does not, because context takes care of getting rid of most of those 25 meanings; however, the point remains: semantics is hard work.

sentence. Suppose we have a sentence S, made up of the following sequence of morphemes (M)

$$S = M_1, M_2, M_3...M_n$$

then, assuming that we mark with a variable (indicated with a lowercase Greek letter) the number of scripts listed in the lexicon under that morpheme, the number of potential combinations (PC) for

$$S = M_\alpha, M_\beta, M_\gamma...M_\omega$$

is

$$PC = \alpha \cdot \beta \cdot \gamma ... \cdot \omega$$

In order to give an idea of the harsh realities of semantic analysis, I will proceed to analyze the first sentence of the Wilde text (LASC) that will be discussed in ch. (8). While I will not *fully* analyze the sentence, I hope to give an idea of the complexity of the work involved.

A sample sentence

The sentence goes:

(4) "It was Lady Windermere's last reception before Easter, and Bentinck House was even more crowded than usual."

The lexematic handles of the following scripts are activated:

- IT = neuter referent to be found from antecedent text
- WAS = past tense of "be"
- LADY
- WINDERMERE = proper noun
- 'S = possessive (assumed monosemic)
- LAST
- RECEPTION
- BEFORE
- EASTER = proper noun
- AND = conjunction (assumed monosemic)

1.2. THE STRUCTURE OF A SEMANTIC THEORY

- BENTINCK = proper noun
- HOUSE
- WAS = second token of "was," as above
- EVEN
- MORE = comparative marker (assumed monosemic)
- CROWDED
- THAN = comparative marker (assumed monosemic)
- USUAL

The following are the senses of the lexemes involved taken from *Webster* (1913) and heavily edited, with integrations from *Wordnet* (Fellbaum 1998).

1. **it**
   (a) As a substance for any noun of the neuter gender; as, here is the book, take it home.
   (b) As a demonstrative, especially at the beginning of a sentence, pointing to that which is about to be stated, named, or mentioned, or referring to that which apparent or well known.
   (c) As an indefinite nominative for a impersonal verb; as, it snows; it rains.
   (d) As a substitute for such general terms as, the state of affairs, the condition of things.
   (e) As an indefinite object after some intransitive verbs, or after a substantive used humorously as a verb; as, to foot it (i. e., to walk).

2. **was** (past form of "be")
   (a) To exist actually, or in the world of fact; to have existence.
   (b) To exist in a certain manner or relation, – whether as a reality or as a product of thought; to exist as the subject of a certain predicate, that is, as having a certain attribute, or as belonging to a certain sort, or as identical with what is specified.
   (c) To take place; to happen; as, the meeting was on Thursday.
   (d) To signify; to represent or symbolize; to answer to.
   (e) To occupy a certain position or area; be somewhere.
   (f) Be, occur, happen or come to pass.
   (g) Equal, be identical or equivalent to;
   (h) Be, work, follow.
   (i) Embody, be, personify.
   (j) Spend or use time.
   (k) Be alive.
   (l) Cost, be – (be priced at.)

3. **Lady**

    (a) A woman who looks after the domestic affairs of a family; a mistress; the female head of a household.

    (b) A woman having proprietary rights or authority; mistress; – a feminine correlative of lord.

    (c) A woman to whom the particular homage of a knight was paid; a woman to whom one is devoted or bound; a sweetheart.

    (d) A woman of social distinction or position. In England, a title prefixed to the name of any woman whose husband is not of lower rank than a baron, or whose father was a nobleman not lower than an earl.

    (e) A woman of refined or gentle manners; a well-bred woman; – the feminine correlative of gentleman.

    (f) A wife.

    (g) The triturating apparatus in the stomach of a lobster.

4. **Reception**

    (a) The act of receiving; receipt; admission; as, the reception of food into the stomach; the reception of a letter; the reception of sensation or ideas; reception of evidence.

    (b) The state of being received.

    (c) The act or manner of receiving, esp. of receiving visitors; entertainment; hence, an occasion or ceremony of receiving guests; as, a hearty reception; an elaborate reception.

    (d) Acceptance, as of an opinion or doctrine.

    (e) A formal party of people; as after a wedding

    (f) Quality or fidelity of a received broadcast

    (g) The act of catching a pass in football.

5. **Last**

    (a) Being after all the others, similarly classed or considered, in time, place, or order of succession; following all the rest; final; hindmost; farthest.

    (b) Next before the present; as, "I saw him last week."

    (c) Supreme; highest in degree; utmost.

    (d) Lowest in rank or degree.

    (e) Farthest of all from a given quality, character, or condition; most unlikely; having least fitness.

    (f) Immediately past.

    (g) Occurring at or forming an end or termination.

    (h) Not to be altered or undone.

    (i) In accord with the most modern ideas or styles.

    (j) Occurring at the time of death.

6. **before**

    (a) On the fore part; in front, or in the direction of the front.

    (b) In advance.

1.2. THE STRUCTURE OF A SEMANTIC THEORY

    (c) In time past; previously; already.

    (d) Earlier; sooner than; until then.

7. **house**

   (a) A structure intended or used as a habitation or shelter for animals.
   (b) Household affairs; domestic concerns; particularly in the phrase to keep house.
   (c) Those who dwell in the same house; a household.
   (d) A family of ancestors, descendants, and kindred; a race of persons from the same stock; a tribe; especially, a noble family or an illustrious race.
   (e) One of the estates of a kingdom or other government assembled in parliament or legislature.
   (f) A firm, or commercial establishment.
   (g) A public house; an inn; a hotel.
   (h) Astrological term.
   (i) A square on a chessboard, regarded as the proper place of a piece.
   (j) An audience; an assembly of hearers, as at a lecture, a theater, etc.; as, a thin or a full house.
   (k) The body, as the habitation of the soul.
   (l) The members of a religious community living together.
   (m) Play in which children take the roles of father or mother or children and pretend to interact like adults.

8. **even**

   (a) In an equal or precisely similar manner; equally; precisely; just; likewise; as well.
   (b) Up to, or down to, an unusual measure or level; so much as; fully; quite.
   (c) As might not be expected; – serving to introduce what is unexpected or less expected.
   (d) At the very time; in the very case.
   (e) In spite of; notwithstanding.
   (f) To a greater degree or extent; used with comparisons.
   (g) To the full extent.

9. **Crowd**

   (a) To push, to press, to shove.
   (b) To press or drive together; to mass together.
   (c) To fill by pressing or thronging together; hence, to encumber by excess of numbers or quantity.
   (d) To press by solicitation; to urge; to dun; hence, to treat discourteously or unreasonably. [Colloq.]
   (e) To crowd out, to press out; specifically, to prevent the publication of; as, the press of other matter crowded out the article.
   (f) To crowd sail. (Naut.), to carry an extraordinary amount of sail, with a view to accelerate the speed of a vessel; to carry a press of sail.

10. **Than**

    (a) A particle expressing comparison.

11. **Usual**

    (a) Such as is in common use, in ordinary practice, or in the ordinary course of events.
    (b) Customary.
    (c) Ordinary.
    (d) Habitual.

Needless to say, the dictionary definitions probably significantly reduce the level of ambiguity present in natural language, not to mention that we are deliberately ignoring collocations, which on the one hand, reduce the ambiguity level combinatorially, since they prevent a large number of combinations from occurring, but on the other hand complicate the work of the syntactic-morphological parser which has to operate with multi-word units.

It should be noted that I have also reduced the ambiguity level by removing crosscategorial ambiguity; thus, for example *even,* besides the adverbial meanings listed has meanings as a noun (*even numbers*) and as a verb (e.g., *even out*). I have also not considered archaic and obsolete meanings.

Let us assume, for the sake of simplicity, that the lexicon contains entries for proper names, so that the syntagms "Lady Windermere" and "Bentinck House" are recognized as proper names and no further interpretation of "lady" and "house" is attempted (since presumably the lexicon/encyclopedia would have the information that the former is a name of a person and the latter of a building). The lexicon/encyclopedia would also presumably have a entry for "Easter." Let us assume also that a syntactic parse is available, such that it is capable of determining that the two stretches of text before and after the "and" are sentences and that the coordinating conjunction is coordinating them.

From the activation of the lexemes, and with the simplifications just mentioned, the combinations of the lexemes give rise to a possible 40.642.560 combinations. The staggering figure is easily explained; here is the sentence with the number of meanings indicated for each lexeme token:

(5) "It$_5$ was$_{12}$ Lady$_{7/1}$ Windermere's$_1$ last$_{12}$ reception$_7$ before$_4$ Easter$_1$, and$_1$ Bentinck$_1$ House$_{13/1}$ was$_{12}$ even$_7$ more$_1$ crowded$_6$ than$_1$ usual$_4$"

Therefore the potential combinations of meanings are

$$5 \cdot 12 \cdot 1 \cdot 1 \cdot 12 \cdot 7 \cdot 4 \cdot 1 \cdot 1 \cdot 1 \cdot 12 \cdot 7 \cdot 1 \cdot 6 \cdot 1 \cdot 4 = 40.642.560$$

Of course, the combinatorial rules discard those meanings which violate selection restrictions and subcategorization rules. For example, the Zodiacal sense of *house* (sense *h*) would have been discarded since none of the twelve houses of the Zodiac is called Bentinck. The mollusc-related meaning of *lady* would have been

1.2. THE STRUCTURE OF A SEMANTIC THEORY

similarly rejected as being unable to host a reception, in sense *e* (party); the nautical meaning of *crowded* would have been rejected on the incompatibility of sailing and of the rest of the text, etc.

We now move on to the pragmatic analysis.[14] Pragmatically more meanings can be ruled out: assuming that the first sentence is relevant (Grice 1989) to its coordinate, it follows that the first sentence is providing some information such that the meaning of the second is affected by it. This rules out the meanings of "reception" which are not social gatherings, since it would be pragmatically ill-formed to say that "since it was the last occasion in which Lady Windermere received critically something, a house was crowded."

Note a few implicatures: since we are to assume relevance between the two coordinates, it follows that there must be some relationship between Lady Windermere and Bentinck House. In fact, the text will actually never come out and say explicitly that Lady Windermere owns it; this is an implicature left entirely to the reader. Furthermore, we are to assume an even stronger (causal) relationship between the first and the second coordinate: i.e., the reason why Bentinck House was more crowded than usual is that the party the author is referring to happened to be the last one (for the year, scalar implicature from the maxim of quantity) before Easter. Here we presumably accomodate to the text and assume that there is a general rule that the last party before Easter is generally more crowded than others.[15]

Thus we arrive at the following tentative interpretation: the party [held by] [a woman named] Lady Windermere that occurred closest to the [Julian calendric point] Easter was taking place and [because of this] [a house called] Bentinck House was fuller of people than it was normal.

Note that the RECEPTION script, in its "party" sense, immediately primes the reader for other components of the script, such as guests, entertainment, food, decorations, etc. Indeed, the rest of the first paragraph discusses a number of guests, without having to specify who those people are and/or what their relation to Lady Windermere might be.

1.2.2 Inferential Explosion

Note that from what we have said it follows that we face another problem, possibly even worse than combinatorial explosion, namely inferential explosion: for example, McDonough (1997) calculated that roughly 60 presuppositions or inferences were activated in a simple 4 lines joke. More significantly, those were only the inferences and presuppositions demonstrably "useful" in the decoding and humorous functioning of the text. If we tried to calculate all presuppositions of a short text the number would probably be in the hundreds. Inferences are open ended and thus potentially

---

[14] As pointed out above, the sequential analysis presented here is only for expository purposes. Semantics and pragmatics are deeply enmeshed (cf. Raskin 1985: 80 and passim).

[15] It is possible that the encyclopedia of a contemporary of Wilde would have provided him/her with this information.

infinite, hence there is no upper boundary to the calculation of those. Therefore it would follow that, even if we manage to cut down the combinatorial explosion of the semantics of the text, we would still be faced with the problem of determining which of an infinite set of inferences are those intended by the author/speaker and/or interesting for the hearer/reader.

Luckily, as we saw exemplified above, pragmatic principles, such as the maxim of relevance (Grice 1989; Sperber and Wilson 1986) constrain the generative power of the speaker and direct the search heuristics of the hearer. We will not address in this context the exceedingly difficult question of the exact procedure involved in recognizing the relevant inferences and discarding the irrelevant ones, although it is fairly clear that they are, at least in part, abductive.[16] We limit ourselves to the fairly obvious consideration which we have already seen, that the cooperative principle is central to the process as are some generic constraints (e.g., in a detective story we expect clues to be present in the text towards the identification of the culprit).

There is considerable psycholinguistic evidence in favor of this model of textual processing. Kintsch's construction-integration model (Kintsch 1998) similarly starts with the construction, i.e., the activation of all the senses of a word[17] and the calculation of inferences, bridgings, etc. to create a textbase (a set of propositions). The integration phase weeds out all the contextually inappropriate propositions and integrates the propositions in a coherent, hierarchically organized textbase. (Kintsch 1998: 93-120).

1.2.3 Is this a formal analysis?

It may be argued that since as of today there exist no formal methods for extracting the semantics of a text, let alone for dealing with the cloud of implicatures that arise from it, or segmenting the text on a semantic/pragmatic basis, the point of proposing a (semi-)formal theory of the narrative aspect of humor is perhaps futile? After all, if the building blocks of a theory cannot be formalized, the theory itself can hardly be called formal.

The point is well taken, but it confuses the two different activities of creating a theory and creating an interpretation of a theory. In this sense theory building is indistinct from the creation of a calculus in algebra. Suppose that we have a

---

[16] Abduction is a kind of inference that follows the form

D is a collection of data (facts, observations, givens)
H explains D (would, if true, explain D)
No other hypothesis can explain D as well as H does

Therefore, H is probably true (Josephson and Josephson 1994:5)

On abduction, see also Eco and Sebeok (1983).

[17] This somewhat counterintuitive fact has been established beyond doubt in psycholinguistics: between 100 and 350 milliseconds of reading/hearing a word all its senses are activated. The contextually inappropriate senses never make it above the threshold of consciousness.

(minuscule) theory claiming that $n_{even} = n \cdot 2$. The theory is essentially empty until we instantiate (interpret) it using a number (say, 3) and we verify that indeed $3 \cdot 2 = 6$ and 6 is an even number. However, under another interpretation, if we admit fractions (decimal numbers) among the members of the set from which n is taken, then the theory makes incorrect predictions (e.g., $1.5 \cdot 2 = 3$).

Thus a theory may be perfectly formal(izable) but its interpretation may not be so (suppose for example that we could not define formally the concept of even number). I want to suggest that this is the case for the theory of humor embodied in the SSTH/GTVH and in the semi-formal model I am advocating. By semi-formal, I mean that the theory is formal in principle, but none of its implementations can be so, because of constraints on the state-of-the-art components that make it up.[18]

1.3 The Semantic Theory of Humor

As we have ween, the SSTH presupposes and incorporates a full-fledged semantic theory of this type outlined in Raskin (1986).

Raskin (1985) is essentially an application to humor of a semantic theory: presented with a text, the SSTH determines its semantic well-formedness, and then, it proceeds to assess its humorous nature.[19] It presupposes access to the complete semantic network of a language and the usage of the combinatorial rules to establish readings of the sentences of a text, and pass judgements on their "well-formedness." The next sections will explain how a judgement on "funniness" is passed by the SSTH.

1.3.1 Overlapping

During the process of combining scripts, the semantic theory will occasionally encounter stretches of text that are compatible with more than one "reading," i.e., would fit more than one script; for instance, imagine a text describing someone getting up, fixing breakfast, leaving the house, etc. These events could fit the script for GO TO WORK but also for GO ON A FISHING TRIP—hence the stretch of text would be compatible with both scripts.

The "doctor's wife joke" (see below, example 7) will provide a more detailed example. It should be noted that the overlap between the two scripts may be partial or total. If the overlap is total, the text in its entirety is compatible with both scripts; if the overlap is partial, some parts of the text, or some details, will not be compatible with one or the other script.[20]

---

[18] A similar argument can be found in Kintsch 1998.
[19] Once more, the sequential presentation is purely didactic.
[20] This distinction is essentially similar to Guiraud's (1976) coexistence of senses (see Attardo 1994: ch. 3) in puns.

Raskin also introduces the "script-switch" trigger, i.e., the element of the text that causes the passage from the first to the second script actualized in the text. This element is the analog of the "disjunctor" in the Isotopy Disjunction Model IDM (Attardo 1994: ch. 2), although it is not exactly equivalent to it since the script-switch trigger is not opposed to a "connector" element.

1.3.2 Oppositeness

The overlapping of two scripts is not necessarily a cause of humor *per se*. Ambiguous, metaphorical, figurative, allegorical, mythical, allusive and obscure texts present overlapping scripts, but they are not necessarily (if at all) funny. This is because the second necessary and sufficient condition in the SSTH is not fulfilled in these non-humorous texts. The second condition of the SSTH calls for the two scripts that overlap in the text to be "opposed" in a technical sense, to which we presently turn.

Local antonymy

Raskin (1985: 108) introduces the concept of local antonymy with the following definition:

> two linguistic entities whose meanings are opposites only within a particular discourse and solely for the purposes of that discourse.

This definition of local antonymy, is potentially troublesome (Attardo 1997), since it could lead to a vicious circle: if we defined local antonymy based upon the purpose of the discourse (i.e., humor) and then defined humor based on local antonymy, the SSTH would collapse. In Attardo (1997), I presented a pragmatic approach to the locality problem, using the concepts of accessibility and informativeness. While I still believe in the substantial correctness of that approach, I will now develop the other (semantic) approach which I sketched in Attardo (1997: 400).

Mettinger (1994: 161-162) distinguishes between systemic (i.e., lexical) and non-systemic opposites (antonyms). Non-systemic opposites correspond in part to Raskin's local antonyms. Mettinger takes antonymy to involve a "conceptual integrator" i.e., the "basis of comparison" of the two antonyms, or, quoting Coseriu (1975: 36) "what is common to the differences between these terms" [my translation, SA] (Mettinger: 1994: 160-161). The conceptual integrator and the semantic "axis" or "field" mentioned in Attardo (1997) seem to be the same concept. What this boils down to is the fact that *green* is not the antonym of *married* (Attardo 2000: 822): the semantic axis (conceptual integrator) of *married / unmarried* (or *single*) is "having contracted marriage" with a positive or negative valence added on, whereby [+ having contracted marriage] equals *married* and [− having contracted marriage] equals *single*.

Mettinger shows that the conceptual integrator task may be performed by "frames" (161) and "knowledge of the world" (162) which must be common knowledge,

1.3. THE SEMANTIC THEORY OF HUMOR

i.e., assumed available (encyclopedic) or inferrable from context. He hypothesizes the possible existence of a cline of encyclopedic knowledge necessary to establish antonymy, ranging from zero (lexical antonyms) to a maximum (encyclopedic and contextual antonyms).

Of course, the idea of conceptual integrator is not new, and goes back to an even more basic concept, which is that of saliency or emphasis (Raskin 1985: 82), or in yet another terminology, "weights." What this concept describes is the fact that the arrangement of the slot-filler pairs of a script, or the features of a given lexical item, etc. are not flat, but that they are organized hierarchically, not only in the sense that scripts may have other scripts as the filler of one of their slots (see 3.1.3), but also that there is a saliency hierarchy within the material of a script. For example, in the script for DOCTOR (fig. 1.1), intuitively, CURE PATIENTS is more salient than STUDY MEDICINE which is itself more salient than HUMAN.

Scripts come with a default, unmarked foregrounded subset of elements (cf. Langacker 1991: 226ff).[21] The human perceptual-processing system seems to be hard-wired into considering certain types of stimuli more salient than others. Gestalt psychology and more recently cognitive linguistics has pointed out a number of criteria that predetermine saliency/foregrounding. For example, an object attracts more our attention when its contours are closed and when it is an uninterrupted whole. Another principle of perceptual saliency is that an item relatively smaller, and more easily moved around than another element, is more salient, as are moving objects compared to static ones (cf. Ungerer and Schmid 1996: 158-159).

Thus more salient items, which are likely to be figure/trajector, stand out "naturally" from the ground/landmark items. Hence an element of a script is a more normal (unmarked) figure if it is cognitively salient.

As we know, contextual pressure may alter this default; consider the following example:

(6) That's not a thief! He's just a boy.

where the foregrounded (bolded) element switches from "adult **who steals**" to "**adult** who steals."

Attardo *et al.* (forth.) give an account of the oppositeness requirement of the SSTH using precisely this mechanism, in a set-theoretic and graph-theoretic formalism. It would be unnecessary (and perhaps confusing) to repeat the set-theoretic and graph-theoretic treatment, but we can conclude that local antonymy and lexicalized antonymy do not differ semantically, as they both involve a negation along an axis. The difference lies in the fact that the axis is the default (hence, salient) slot-filler pair in lexical antonymy and a different, contextually-forced one, for local antonymy.[22]

---

[21] Cf. also the notion of "culminatore semantico" or semantic apex (Cigada 1969), which anticipated this aspect of cognitive grammar.

[22] The presence of a contextually-forced, non default slot-filler pair in local antonymy holds for at least one of the two script, but not necessarily both.

Levels of Abstraction in Script Opposition

Raskin analyzes a corpus of about 32 jokes (Raskin 1985: 107-110) and finds that the pairs of scripts are all in a relationship of opposition, as required by the theory. Furthermore, the script oppositions fall into three classes: actual vs. non-actual, normal vs. abnormal, and possible vs. impossible. The three classes are all instances of a basic opposition between real and unreal situations in the texts.

These three classes of oppositions are then instantiated in more concrete oppositions. Raskin (1985: 113-114; 127) lists five of the most common oppositions:

good/bad
life/death
obscene/non-obscene
money/no-money
high/low stature

These oppositions are seen as "essential to human life" (Raskin 1985: 113); they certainly are very basic, but the difference in level of abstraction between the three basic types of opposition and the five instantiations should be noted. While it is unlikely that any culture would present a different list of three types of basic opposition, it is perfectly likely that different cultures would show quite a different type of lower-level instantiation. For instance, the opposition "excrement/non-excrement," basic to much humor up to very recently and common in many non-western cultures (see Douglas 1968) is missing from the five oppositions. Chlopicki (1987) presents a list of low-level oppositions that is slightly different from Raskin's (see section 2.1.1).

Recently, the idea of a third level of abstraction in oppositions has emerged (Di Maio 2000): essentially, each humorous text would instantiate a concrete opposition, besides the other two levels, an intermediate one, such as SEX/NO SEX and a very abstract one, corresponding to the three SOs listed by Raskin. In example (7) below, the concrete SO is between LOVER and PATIENT, the intermediate between SEX vs. NO SEX, and the abstract one between ACTUAL and NON-ACTUAL.

Thus, if a text is compatible fully or in part with two scripts, and the two scripts happen to be opposed to each other, then, and only then, will the text be classified as "funny" by the SSTH. Ideally, the SSTH's predictions will match the speakers' and the theory will be confirmed. Alternatively, someone will come up with a text that either fulfills both requirements, and yet is not funny, or that is funny but does not meet either or both of the requirements; in this case the theory will have been falsified. This is a falsificationalist view of the procedure for confirming or disproving a theory. It is a sound, if slightly old-fashioned, procedure. In real life, however, attempts at proving or disproving a theory are more complex, as Kuhn (1962) pointed out.

1.3.3 The Doctor's Wife Joke

The following joke is analyzed in detail by Raskin (1985: 117-127) as a demonstration of the SSTH.

(7) "Is the doctor at home?" the patient asked in his bronchial whisper. "No," the doctor's young and pretty wife whispered in reply. "Come right in."

The first step of the analysis is the listing of all the senses of the words in the text (in other words, of all the scripts activated by the text). The second step is the activation of the combinatorial rules that will combine the various scripts according to compatibility (i.e., they will look for words that evoke the same script) and to syntactic and subcategorization rules, ignored here for simplicity. For example, among the various scripts evoked by the word "is" (from the jokes's first sentence) there is a SPATIAL script; among the scripts evoked by "at" there is also a SPATIAL script. Because the two words have the SPATIAL script in common, the combinatorial rules will choose this script as their preferred reading and continue the analysis. The next logical step, which takes place at the same time as the combination of scripts, as we have seen, is the triggering of inferences. The reader infers that the second line is meant as an answer to the previous question, that the speaker of the first line does not know the answer to the question, and that he/she is interested in knowing the answer to the question. By recursively applying the combinatorial rules and the inferencing mechanisms, an interpretation of the entire text is arrived at.

A semantic reading of the joke can be loosely paraphrased as "Someone who was previously treated for some illness inquires about the presence of a doctor at the doctor's place of residence, with the purpose of being treated for a disease which manifests itself by a whispering voice. The doctor's wife (who is young and pretty) answers (whispering, as the patient) that the doctor is not at home, and invites the inquirer to enter in the house."

The hearer is faced with a puzzle: if the purpose of the patient's inquiry is the desire to be treated for his disease, why is the doctor's wife asking him in anyway, since the doctor is not there and the script for DOCTOR requires physical proximity for examination and treatment of the illness? This situation leads the reader to switch to the NBF (*non-bona-fide*[23]) mode and to start looking for a "competing script" (Raskin 1985: 125), i.e., an alternative interpretation of the story.

The reader will then backtrack and reevaluate the text. The gender of the doctor's wife and her description will be taken into account, as well as the absence of the doctor/husband. This will allow the activation of the LOVER script, which prescribes that an adulterous relationship be acted upon without knowledge of the legitimate spouse. In the light of the LOVER script, the behavior of the doctor's wife becomes meaningful, i.e., she is taking advantage of her husband's absence to have a secret

---

[23] The term *non-bona-fide* refers to those types of discourse which violate Grice's principle of cooperation (Grice 1975, 1989). See Raskin (1985: 100-104), Attardo (1994: ch. 9).

meeting with another man. The text is thus found to be compatible almost entirely with two scripts (DOCTOR, LOVER), and the scripts are opposed on the SEX/NO SEX basis. Hence, it fulfills both requirements of the SSTH and is evaluated as humorous.

1.4 The GTVH

A broadening of the SSTH was presented in Attardo and Raskin (1991). The revised version of the SSTH is called the "General Theory of Verbal Humor" (GTVH).

The revision of the SSTH consisted mostly of broadening its scope. Whereas the SSTH was a "semantic" theory of humor, the GTVH is a linguistic theory "at large"—that is, it includes other areas of linguistics as well, including, most notably, textual linguistics, the theory of narrativity, and pragmatics broadly conceived. These broadenings are achieved by the introduction of five other Knowledge Resources (KR), that must be tapped into when generating a joke, in addition to the script opposition from the SSTH. The KRs are the script opposition (SO), the logical mechanism (LM), the target (TA), the narrative strategy (NS), the language (LA), and the situation (SI). The GTVH also incorporates the idea of "joke similarity" and dedicates a great deal of effort to establishing the concept formally.

The following sections will introduce the six KRs, and then the concept of joke similarity will be discussed in detail. A more complete exposition of the GTVH can be found in Attardo and Raskin (1991; see also Ruch *et al.* 1993).

1.4.1 Language (LA)

This KR contains all the information necessary for the verbalization of a text. It is responsible for the exact wording of the text and for the placement of the functional elements that constitute it.

The concept of paraphrase is essential for understanding the type of variation that this KR accounts for: as any sentence can be recast in a different wording (that is, using synonyms, other syntactic constructions, etc.), any joke can be worded in a (very large) number of ways without changes in its semantic content; for example, a joke like

(8) How many Poles does it take to screw in a light bulb? Five, one to hold the light bulb and four to turn the table. (Freedman and Hoffman 1980)

can be paraphrased as

(9) The number of Pollacks needed to screw in a light bulb? Five — one to hold the bulb and four to turn the table. (Clements 1969: 22)

or in any other way that will preserve the meaning intact.

The above claim applies also to interlingual translation (see Attardo 1994: 29, 95 for a discussion of translation as a heuristic tool in humor). Jokes based on the *signifiant* (puns) are a (marginal) exception. These jokes are commonly referred to as *verbal* (as opposed to *referential*) jokes (see Attardo 1994: ch. 3, for discussion). The exact wording of the punch line of verbal jokes is extremely important because it is necessary for the linguistic element to be ambiguous and to connect the two opposed senses in the text. In this respect, the KR is preselected by SO: the SO determines the exact nature of a specific fragment of the LA KR (i.e., the punch line); note how the rest of the LA of puns is not predetermined.[24] Otherwise, verbal and referential jokes behave identically in respect to this KR.

Another important aspect of the LA KR is that it is responsible for the position of the punch line. The final position of the punch line is essential, both because of the functional organization of the information in the text (see Attardo 1994: ch. 3 and below) and because of the distribution of the implicit information of the text (see Attardo 1994: ch. 9). As will become apparent in the treatment of punch and jab lines (see below, section 5.3), the position of the punch line is quite significant in our analysis.

1.4.2 Narrative Strategy (NS)

The information in the NS KR accounts for the fact that any joke has to be cast in some form of narrative organization, either as a simple narrative, as a dialogue (question and answer), as a (pseudo-)riddle, as an aside in conversation, etc. An issue is whether all jokes are narratives. Attardo and Chabanne (1992) weakly imply a positive answer, but research on this issue is just beginning. However, this claim should not be construed to claim that all humor is narrative. There surely exists dramatic (hence, non-narrative, under certain definitions) humor and obviously there are lots of visual humor (e.g., cartoons) which are not obviously narrative (in the sense that it does not "tell a story," which is not to say that it cannot be paraphrased as one).

It may be argued that the NS is in fact a rephrasing of what is known in literary theory under the name "genre." This claim is rather misleading. Genre theory is a subfield of literary history which classifies (historical manifestations of certain) text-types. Their interest is, at best, tangential to humor research. What the NS KR is trying to capture is rather that any narrative joke will have to be cast in a given type of narrative. Little work has gone towards this KR, probably due to the fact that it seems to consist merely of a taxonomy of NSs.

1.4.3 Target (TA)

The target KR selects who is the "butt" of the joke. The information in the KR contains the names of groups or individuals with (humorous) stereotypes attached to each. Jokes that are not aggressive (i.e., do not ridicule someone or something) have

---

[24] On this aspect of the GTVH, see Lew (2000).

an empty value for this parameter. Alternatively, one can think as this as an optional parameter.

The choice of the groups or individuals that fill the parameter are regulated by the type of stereotype and mythical scripts studied by Zhao (1987, 1988). Davies (1990) provides a good overview of how different groups target different other groups, and has a sociological explanation of their choices.

Some research has been done in this area, which has shown that the original definition of target as a group or individual needs to be broadened by the inclusion of *ideological targets* (Karman 1998), i.e. groups or institutions that do not have a clear consituency, but may nevertheless be made the subject of ridicule (examples are "marriage," "romantic love," "the establishment," etc.). We may speculate that, however vaguely, these ideological targets retain a connection with persons and/or identifiable groups and therefore may be targeted with aggression. It seems that non-human (or at least, humanoid) targets are unlikely, since what would it mean that one targets, say, "trees" with a joke. One cannot be aggressive to a tree (which is not to say that one cannot damage or even destroy a tree, that is a different issue). In short, aggression is a social business.

1.4.4 Situation (SI)

Any joke must be "about something" (changing a light bulb, crossing the road, playing golf, etc.). The situation of a joke can be thought of as the "props" of the joke: the objects, participants, instruments, activities, etc. Any joke must have some situation, although some jokes will rely more on it, while others will almost entirely ignore it. Consider the following:

(10) "Can you write shorthand?"
    "Yes, but it takes me longer."

which presupposes a "writing shorthand" situation, but leaves it almost completely in the background (the only thing that matters is its speed).

Consider now the doctor's wife joke (7) in which a fairly elaborate set-up is created whereby we are told that the wife is at home, the doctor is not there, etc. The doctor's wife joke relies on the situation much more directly than the "stenographer" joke.

Virtually no research has focused on this KR, which seems to consist essentially of a list of things, activities, etc. mentioned in the text. Most significantly, the activation of the relevant scripts provides the relevant props for the joke. In this respect, the SI KR is not unique to jokes at all, in the sense that this is a function shared by all humorous and non-humorous texts.

1.4.5 Logical Mechanism (LM)

The logical mechanism is by far the most problematic parameter. Originally (Attardo and Raskin 1991), it was defined mostly by example, although the connection with the scant literature on "local logic" (Ziv 1984) and "justification" (Aubouin 1948) was pointed out, as was the strong resemblance to Hofstadter and Gabora's (1989) *ur-joke*.

In Ruch *et al.* (1993), LM was the only KR not to behave exactly[25] as predicted by the hypothesis tested in the study, namely that speakers should rate degrees of difference among jokes according to the level in the KR hierarchy (table 1.2) at which the difference occurs. This led Raskin to doubt the significance of the KR (Raskin 1995). Attardo (1997) argues, on the contrary, that the LM embodies the resolution of the incongruity in the incongruity-resolution model, familiar from psychology. A consequence of this claim is that, since resolution is optional in humor (cf. nonsense and absurd humor) it follows that the LM KR would also be optional.

Most recently, work on this KR has yielded a significant analysis of a corpus of *Far Side* cartoons (Paolillo 1998) which results in a list of some 20 different types of LMs. Finally, Attardo *et al.* (forth.) have proposed a formal model of some LMs and claim that, for those LMs that can be modeled using the theory of partially ordered sets and the theory of graphs, there is a general mapping function which introduces a spurious similarity between elements in the scripts involved. This mapping function would then be a very abstract LM, a member of a small set of LMs which underlie all LMs (corresponding to the list of three abstract SOs in the SSTH; cf. section 1.3.2).

The LM parameter presupposes and embodies a "local" logic, i.e., a distorted, playful logic, that does not necessarily hold outside of the world of the joke. Speakers are well aware of the limits of local logic and "go along with it" in the spirit of "willing suspension of disbelief." This issue is strongly connected with the NBF character of the joke. See also the connections with the playful Cratylism of speakers in puns investigated in Attardo (1994: ch. 4).

LMs can range from straightforward juxtapositions, as in the tee-shirt slogan reading:

(11) Gobi Desert Canoe Club

to more complex errors in reasoning, such as false analogies,

(12) A wife is like an umbrella. Sooner or later one takes a cab. (Freud 1905: 93)[26]

or garden path phenomena, as in

---

[25] To a degree; LM is "behaving badly" in relation to the KR immediately before (SI), but works fine in relation to all other KRs.

[26] The wife is the private form of sex as the umbrella is the private form of shelter during transportation, while the prostitute is the public form of sex as the cab is the public form of shelter during transportation.

(13) Madonna does not have it, the Pope has it but doesn't use it, Bush has it short, and Gorbachev long. What is it?
Answer: a last name.

or figure-ground reversals, as in:

(14) How many poles does it take to screw in a light bulb? 5. One to hold the light bulb and four to turn the table he's standing on.
(light bulb: figure; body: ground)

false analogies,

(15) A married man goes to confessional and tells the priest, "I had an affair with a woman - almost." The priest says, "What do you mean, 'almost'?" The man says, "Well, we got undressed and rubbed together, but then I stopped." The priest replies, "Rubbing together is the same as putting it in. You're not to go near that woman again. Now, say five Hail Mary's and put $ 50 in the poor box." The man leaves confessional, goes over and says his prayers, then walks over to the poor box. He pauses for a moment and then starts to leave. The priest, who was watching him, quickly runs over to him and says, "I saw that. You didn't put any money in the poor box!" The man replied, "Well, Father, I rubbed up against it and you said it was the same as putting it in!" (random joke)

and chiastic arrangements:

(16) What's the difference between a Mexican American Princess and a Jewish American Princess? The Mexican American Princess has fake jewelry and real orgasms.

This LM is closely related to false analogy (see above) in that they both share two analogies. But where they are parallel in false proportion (A is to B as C is to D), they cross each other in the chiasmus (A is to B as D is to C). Detailed analyses of the LMs of these examples can be found in Attardo *et al.* (forthcoming). As new analyses of LMs emerge, they will be integrated in the picture that is beginning to emerge.

In table (1.4.5) I reproduce a list of LMs found by Di Maio (2000), in a corpus of over 200 jokes, and expanded in Attardo *et al.* (forthcoming).

1.4.6 The KRs: Script Opposition (SO)

This parameter deals with the script opposition/overlapping requirement presented in the SSTH. It should be noted that the SO is the most abstract (perhaps sharing this degree of abstractness with the LM) of all KRs. Any humorous text will present a SO; the specifics of its narrative organization, its social and historical instantiation, etc. will vary according to the place and time of its production.

1.4. THE GTVH

role-reversals	role exchanges	potency mappings
vacuous reversal	juxtaposition	chiasmus
garden-path	figure-ground reversal	faulty reasoning
almost situations	analogy	self-undermining
inferring consequences	reas. from false prem.	missing link
coincidence	parallelism	implicit parall.
proportion	ignoring the obvious	false analogy
exaggeration	field restriction	cratylism
meta-humor	vicious circle	referential ambiguity

Table 1.1: *List of known LMs*

1.4.7 The Joke, According to the GTVH

From the point of view of the GTVH each joke can be viewed as a 6-tuple, specifying the instantiation of each parameter:

(17) Joke: { LA, SI, NS, TA, SO, LM }

The GTVH presents itself as a mechanism capable of generating an infinite number of jokes by combining the various values that each parameter can take. It should be noted that these values are not binary. The values for the LM and the SO seem to be limited in number (see, respectively, Attardo (1988: 357), and Raskin (1985: 127)), while the possibilities for the SI and LA are much more numerous. Descriptively, to analyze a joke in the GTVH consists of listing the values of the 6 KRs (with the caveat that TA and LM may be empty). As we will see, this technique will be applied to punch lines, where it was originally developed, but also to any humorous instance within the text (jab line).

A highly technical aspect of the GTVH is the issue of the ordering of the KRs. Discussion would be out of place in this context; suffice it to say that various considerations of interdependence and/or independence among the KRs have allowed the determination of the hierarchical organization in table (1.2).

Parameters determine the parameters below themselves and are determined by those above themselves. "Determination" is to be intended as limiting or reducing the options available for the instantiation of the parameter; for example, the choice of the SO DUMB/SMART will reduce the options available to the generation in the choice of the TA (in North-America to Poles, etc.). A complete discussion of the issues surrounding the ordering of the KRs is to be found in Attardo and Raskin (1991).

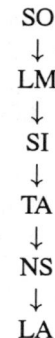

Table 1.2: *Hierarchical Organization of the KRs*

1.5 Outline of the Theory

This section provides an overview of the expansion of the GTVH I suggest: it takes the reader to a whirlwind tour of the approach I will discuss in some detail and introduces most of the significant terms. As such, it is not a complete presentation of the theory.

The theory that I am proposing in this book is grounded in the GTVH. It is, in fact, an extension of the GTVH which broadens its coverage, while not altering most of the tenets of the theory. Specifically, the GTVH is broadened to include (ideally) all humorous texts, of any length. Specifically it is not limited to narrative texts, but also to dramatic and conversational texts, in which there is no narrator (or there isn't one in the text). An example of dramatic humorous text is CBTD, a TV sitcom, while examples of conversational texts, in which there is no narrator, for the good reason that conversations are not "told" but engaged in, are analyzed in ch. (4).

Certainly a large part of the book is taken by narratives (in fact, for a long time, the working title of the book was *humorous narratives*) and indeed, one of the conclusions that emerged early on in the work is that there are no significant differences between narrative and non-narrative texts, from the point of view of humor (except the obvious fact that non-narrative texts may not always exploit metanarrative sources of humor).

Thus, for our purposes, we may safely disregard most of the time the difference between narrative and non-narrative humorous texts. For example, even non-narrative texts develop along a story. But this is not the place for a discussion of the narrative vs. non-narrative status of texts.

Other problems, come from non-linguistic texts which may present very serious

1.5. OUTLINE OF THE THEORY

problems (for example, in order to determine the order in which the elements of the signifier are processed). Finally, there are some types of texts which strain the definition of narrative, in that they seem to lack a well defined, identifiable "story." All these cases may present problems for this extension of the GTVH.

The basic starting point of the theory is that humorous texts divide in two classes: those texts that are structurally similar to jokes (i.e., they end in a punch line) and those which are not. The former can be handled more or less straightforwardly by the GTVH (although they present some interesting issues), the latter, which happen to be much more numerous, can be most profitably analyzed as consisting of two elements: a non-humorous narrative and a humorous component, which occurs along the narrative. This is not an original idea, to be sure, see Attardo (1988: 359).

Traditionally, the humorous ending of a text has been called *punch line*. There is no agreed upon term for a humorous instance that occurs in another position. I introduced (Attardo 1996a) the neologism *jab line* to indicate these non-final punch lines. I also introduced the term *line* as the hyperonym of jab and punch lines. It should be stressed right from the offset that both jab lines and punch lines do not differ semantically, and are amenable to the same GTVH analysis in terms of KRs.

The study of humorous texts reduces then to the location of all lines (jab and punch) along the text *vector* (i.e., its linear presentation). Lines may be related to one another on semantic or formal grounds. The term *strand* indicates generally three or more[27] lines which are related. In a sufficiently large text, there may occur several strands, some of which may exhibit relations with others. Strands of strands are called *stacks* (Wilson 1997).

Finally, when mapping out on a text the position at which the lines occur, one may notice regularities. So far two main configurations have emerged: a sequence of (usually jab) lines concentrated in a small area, called a *comb*, and two (groups of) lines which occur at a considerable distance of one another, called a *bridge*. The reason for the folksy terminology will emerge when the visualization of strands will be presented.

We then move on to the domain of *humorous plots* for which a classification is provided (specifically, plots that end in a punch line, plots that break the narrative frame, and plots that revolve around an event that shows a SO-LM nature), not forgetting that a very common strategy of humorous texts is to have an essentially serious plot, with humor scattered along the vector. Some techniques of humorous disjunction in texts are also examined, beyond the basic jab/punch line placement: diffuse disjunction (where there are many small jabs) and hyperdetermination (where different sources of humor are active at once).

---

[27] There can be exceptions to this rule: hapax-bridges and intertextual lines, see 5.3.7 and 5.3.6, respectively.

1.6 Methodological and metatheoretical issues

To stave off potential misundertandings (particularly easy and aggravating in an interdisciplinary field such as humor research) I will engage in a little methodological and epistemological hairsplitting. The reader uninterested in these niceties may freely resume reading at chapter two.

1.6.1 Competence, not performance

The first point that needs to be considered is that I am proposing a theory of the speakers' *competence* at producing/interpreting longer humorous texts, not a theory of their performance doing so. The distinction between competence and performance was introduced, as is well known, by Chomsky (1965: 4) who modeled it after Saussure's distinction between *langue* and *parole*. There are differences between Saussure's and Chomsky's dichotomies, but for our current purposes we may safely ignore them.

I will thus propose a (partial) theory of the speakers' potential production/interpretation on the basis of their knowledge and skills and not a theory of the actual, concrete interpretation/production of a given text. This is because, just like in the analysis of language, if we look at performance we run the risk of being misled by (possibly random) variation, which may be interesting in and of itself, obviously, but ends up obscuring the system in which we are interested.

The technical term for what I am proposing is *idealization*. In short, I am suggesting that we abstract away from marginal issues to concentrate on those which I take to be central, i.e., the structure of humorous narrative and its contribution to humorous effect. Naturally, how legitimate this move is taken to be depends on one's position towards idealization, to which we turn next.

Idealization

Idealization has had a very controversial history in linguistics. It has been advocated as an indispensable tool of theory building, along the lines of abstraction from friction in the calculation of motion in physics. However, many linguists feel that some forms of idealization effectively strip away significant factors in the object of study. For example, the assumption that a language is a monolithic entity, without variation, common for obvious reasons in formal approaches to grammar, is obviously deleterious where the object of study is variation itself.

What follows from these commonsensical observations, is that the object of study must determine the correct level of idealization. When interested in the structure of a humorous text (mainly, what makes it funny) one can and must abstract away from the reception of said test by any given audience. Their reactions are essentially irrelevant, since what is being investigated is an abstract "ideal" reader's analysis of the text.

1.6. METHODOLOGICAL AND METATHEORETICAL ISSUES

Not a theory of the audience

Thus, perhaps most significantly, I will say virtually nothing about the role of the audience in this book. This is a principled stand, as explained above. However, I would like to stress that I do not mean to imply that it is possible to consider the mechanisms underlying a text without (more or less explicit) reference to its audience. In fact, I believe that the opposite is true, namely that each text encodes in its make an ideal reader ("model reader" Eco 1979) for whom it is written.

This ideal reader is far from being a concrete individual or a group, it is rather the audience postulated by the text. Consider for example that roughly all the information that is explicitly stated in any given text is thereby assumed to be unknown to the model reader, while all the information that is not explicitly stated is assumed to be available to the model reader or retrievable inferentially from what information is provided.[28]

Not a theory of the speaker

More or less symmetrically, I also do not believe it is necessary to provide any detailed discussion of the speaker's role in the text. Note that I am not claiming that there are no circumstances under which such a discussion is essential (deixis leaps to mind). I am merely suggesting that to a significant degree the role of the author in the text, once it has been finished and made available, is marginal. The authorial intent, while significant—in some cases crucial—cannot bind the hermeneutic process. What I am advocating is a "middle of the road" theory of interpretation. One the one hand, speaker intent provides us with a (problematic, but nevertheless available) set of limitations put upon the free range of interpretations imposed on the text. On the other hand, we have the hearer's agenda, intentions, etc. driving another set of interpretations. A compromise between these opposing forces, a middle of the road theory, strikes me as a viable, practical avenue.

My suggestion[29] is that the text itself becomes the foundation of its own interpretation. In other words: if the text has more or less explicit traces leading to a given interpretation, then that interpretation is more likely to be a viable one for the text. Let me exemplify: Borges suggests, in a justly praised short story, that one could read Saint Theresa's *Imitation of Jesus Christ* as if it had been written by De Sade, thus changing the meaning of the text. This is true. However, the text itself would not contain any trace of this interpretation (or at least few). On the other hand, the text will contain numerous, obvious traces of the Catholic faith of its author.

This somewhat abstract discussion is not a purely methodological discussion.

---

[28] There may be exceptions to this broad rule, obviously. They involve marked uses of repetition or violations of Grice's maxim of quantity (1989) for aesthetic effect. Not to mention that the author may "play" with said rule, that is he/she may introduce information that is not already known to the audience to achieve effects of "verisimilitude," for example when depicting a character in a subjective mode.

[29] Which is not at all original, see Eco (1992).

During the process of presenting my own individual analysis of humorous texts to (mostly captive) audiences, it has become extremely clear that different people will not only interpret humor differently, but they will even disagree on the presence of humor altogether. For example, once they caught on to the game of analyzing the text, my students started producing wonderfully complex—and utterly implausible—analyses of jokes and even started seeing jokes where there were, to my mind, none.

Thus two words of caution are necessary. First, we have to be aware of the fact that different audiences may react differently to a text and propose different interpretations of it. When necessary we can use the middle of the road theory of interpretation sketched above to weed out the clearly aberrant readings. Second, what is here presented are fragments of my own, individual, idiolectal analysis. After all, what matters are not the details of the analysis, but its methodology. Consider for example CBTD: it does not really matter if there are n jokes about Ted Baxter's stupidity or really only a few less. What we are attempting is to provide a framework that allows us to understand how the text structures its humorous content.

1.6.2 Semiotics, Text, Narrative

Semiotics of the text

I mentioned at the beginning of the discussion that I intend this approach to be applicable to all texts, in the broad sense used in semiotics, whereby any object is, potentially, a text. I can only refer the reader to the large literature on semiotics for a detailed discussion of these issues. Let me, however, address a potential objection: is any object, in an of itself, potentially humorous? I do not believe that to be the case. In my mind, only objects used as signs qualify as potentially humorous. So a cloud formation resembling Donald Duck, for example, would not be humorous unless perceived by someone as resembling something. In other words, I take humor to exists only within communication, i.e., semiosis. It may well be that I am mistaken on this point. That would only mean that the present approach is applicable only to communicatively based humor. This is of little concern as the examples of non-communicative humor, if they exist at all, are marginal.

Narratology

To a large extent, this entire book is a work in narratology. I do, however, see two major differences between the present work and most narratological work (on which see e.g., Prince 1973, 1987, Bal 1977/1985, Rimmon-Kenan 1983, Toolan 1988).

Focus on Humor This approach is focused on the humorous nature of the text. Narratological work, even when concerned with humorous texts often does not concern itself with their humorous nature (e.g., Fludernik 1996). This approach goes back to Attardo and Chabanne (1992) where we defined a joke (but the definition

1.6. METHODOLOGICAL AND METATHEORETICAL ISSUES

is extensible to all humorous texts) as a text whose perlocutionary goal was to be perceived as funny.[30] I believe that the essence of a humorous text, its *raison d'être* is that of being perceived as funny, and that this is reflected in the text itself.

Rejection of Intuition Narratologists openly acknowledge (e.g., Bal 1977: 9) that large parts of their analyses are performed intuitively. I reject this approach. In the present method of analysis no part of the text is left unanalyzed or given less attention because it is intuitively less significant. On the contrary, all humorous lines are accounted for. Their relative significance may be agreed upon *ex post facto* and is certainly a worthy enterprise, but methodologically it seems to me very important that we approach the text with a blank slate and build the analysis from the morphemic level up. Using computer jargon we could say that I propose a bottom up approach, while traditionally narratology has been top down. Needless to say, I do not subscribe the a radical bottom up approach to parsing, text analysis, etc.

1.6.3 The role of intuition in humor research

It may be objected that my method is just as intuitive as that of traditional literary criticism and that the only difference between the present proposal and the literary analysis discussed above is that we catalog a large number of minute value judgements (i.e., for any unit we have to decide whether it is or is not funny), whereas traditional analyses merely pass a broad, global value judgement.

I believe that this objection is erroneous, on two grounds. The intuitive judgement of whether a given unit is funny or not is qualitatively different from the intuitive judgement of whether any narrative text, or to choose a challenging example, a poem or a series of poems are humorous. While the former question may be answered more or less objectively (there are issues of individual variation, which complicate the issue but do not preclude a methodologically sound solution), the latter is a much more complex question, since the constructs of (say) "humorous poem" or "humorous collection of poems" are undefined. Is a poem otherwise somber, but which contains one jab line, a humorous poem? What if it contains two jab lines? It is clear that while the single individual question can be answered intuitively by the speakers, the complex text-wide question cannot be answered simply, and certainly not intuitively. Incidentally, there is reason to believe that a sophisticated answer to

---

[30]Technically, the definition should be even more complex: a humorous text is a text whose perlocutionary goal is the recognition on the part of its intended audience, which may or may not be the actual audience of the utterance(s) of which the text is composed, of the intention of the speaker or of the hearer of the text to have said text be perceived as funny. Note that the humorous "intention" may be in the eyes of the beholder, so to speak. This is necessary to account for "involuntary" humor. (See Attardo 1992). The actual nature of the hearer's "intention" is problematic and requires further work. It is possible that a weaker requirement may be all that's necessary, i.e., that the humor perceiver's *intention* in the technical sense of Searle (1983), which can be paraphrased as "attending to." This is an issue of surprising complexity, which emerged forcefully during a conversation with Franco Mele.

this question may be possible (in terms of ratios of text to lines, with adjustements for special "focal points", cf. Sala 2000).

The second ground for rejecting the objection above, is that it surreptitiously conflates two different meanings of the word "intuition." Humor theory has shown that subjects may pass an intuitive judgement of whether a given stimulus is funny or not, just as speakers may pass an intuitive judgement of whether a sentence is grammatically well formed, or semantically well formed, etc. at a linguistic level. This is because we take grammaticality and humorousness to be properties of human nature (whether they are innate or emergent is a different issue, which we will not address in this context, or any other, for the foreseable future). On the contrary, poetry, or at least generically codified poetry, is clearly a cultural construct. As such no "intuition" in the grammatical sense may be had by subjects on the matter. All they can have are second hand intuitions (norms) that have been learned through cultural transmission.

We can also address the issue of the status of the analyst's judgments: I claim no privileged status for my judgements. Should other analyses differ, with good reason, I would revise my own. However, I believe that the overall result of my analyses is sound and not likely to be affected by challenges over this or that line in the text. It is possible that different analysts would disagree over their analyses of a given text: should different anlyses lead to different conclusions we would be faced with the fact that a sophisticated text inevitably is open to more than one interpretation. Let us consider a borderline example in terms of complexity: Sexton's *Transformations*.

An analysis may only aspire to being the analysis of one interpretation/reading of the text. Am I advocating a relativistic view of interpretation? On the contrary, I believe that most analyses would corroborate one another (intersubjective verification). However, when one deals with a text as complex as TRAN one has to admit that the text is deliberately being obscure and allusive. However, and this is true also of Wilde's LASC, the size of the text gives one a certain degree of statistical reassurance. It is unlikely that the interpretation of most lines is incorrect: we may get a few wrong, but the overall nature of the text, its strands and stacks, will be substantially correct. Small errors tend to cancel out in large data sets.

Let us return to the idealization issue, discussed above (in section 1.6.1). What the vector/GTVH analyses do is provide an ideal reader's interpretation of the text. Needless to say, we do not have access to ideal readers, so the only possible choice is to idealize from our own idiolectal readings. What matters, however, is that *in principle* we may provide a formal, non-intuitive analysis of the texts and of their humorous components. The fact that the cost of such an analysis is prohibitive, so that no such analysis may be empirically presented, is irrelevant.

Essentially, this is where the fundamental difference between a GTVH analysis and traditional literary criticism lies: the GTVH provides a formal (non-intuitive) basis to ground the analysis (the semantic analysis of the text and of its humorous properties). Thus, we can say that objectively such and such a stretch of text is

1.6. METHODOLOGICAL AND METATHEORETICAL ISSUES 35

humorous, because of such and such factors. Any interpretation of the text starts from this objective hard core of semantic analysis.

A final note: those familiar with the SSTH and the GTVH may perhaps be wondering about the difference in standards between those theories and this proposal. After all the SSTH claims to present the necessary and sufficient conditions for a text to be a joke and that is a far cry from the hedged and more or less defeatist approach just advocated. The difference lies in the different order of magnitude of the uncertainty of interpretation of the text. In a basic joke, we have at most a hundred or so senses, most of which are discarded under contextual pressure. Consider now CBTD, a text running for thirty minutes of television, which incorporates visual and auditory clues, as well as linguistic ones; the sheer number of combinations of senses is impossible to catalog, let alone account for. This fact introduces the uncertainty of interpretation—and hence of analysis—discussed above.

Chapter 2

Literature Review

This chapter deals with the small body of research on humorous narratives, from within linguistics. Because of this deliberate limitation, no attempt is made to address, even in passing, the considerable body of literature on humor within literary studies.

As pointed out in the previous chapter, the SSTH was developed using jokes as material, and it is intended to apply to jokes. Jokes however are only a limited subset of the types of humorous texts. The application of the SSTH to text types other than jokes has been pursued along two approaches (see Attardo 1994: ch. 6). The first approach may be called the "expansionist" approach and is based on the idea of applying the SSTH "as is" to other types of texts. The other approach can be labelled "revisionist" and is based on the idea that the SSTH needs to be revised in order to apply to humorous text types other than jokes. The next two sections will deal with each approach.

2.1 The Expansionist Approach

The expansionist attitude towards the SSTH has been so far the most appealing to scholars. Chlopicki (1987), Gaskill (1988), Kolek (1985, 1989), Dixon (1989), and Marino (1989) can all be linked to this tendency.

The expansionist approach is based on the postulation of an essential deep identity between jokes and other forms of humorous narrative. As seen in the previous chapter, Chlopicki's (1987) analysis of short stories reveals sets of script oppositions that are organized according to pairs (which in part are those proposed by Raskin (1985) and in part are added to handle the new texts, a development explicitly contemplated by Raskin). Dixon (1989) shows how Garrison Keillor's *Lake Woebegone Days* humor can be reduced to one script opposition. Gaskill (1988) analyses early American literary texts in the same way.

The longer texts (short stories) are then reduced to complex cases of jokes. Whereas the joke has one script opposition, short stories have several. To be specific, the oppositions that are found in short stories, given the size of the texts, will tend to be macro-scripts (see above), but this is not a problem for the SSTH, in principle. Practically, there may be problems in handling these "larger" scripts since the idea of script originates within lexical analysis, but it is reasonable to assume that these problems may be solved without important changes to the SSTH. An example of a text that can be handled, within limitations, by the expansionist approach is Poe's TSTF, discussed in Attardo (1994: 255-261)

We turn now to examining Chlopicki's work, by far the most significant controbution within this approach.

2.1.1 Chlopicki

Chlopicki's (1987) basic idea is to take the SSTH as a theory of any humorous text and he shows how the SSTH can handle several Polish humorous short stories.

Chlopicki sees the problem of applying the SSTH to other types of texts as mainly an issue of length. Chlopicki's stand is that his work is an extension of the SSTH, but the broadening of the SSTH is limited to a longer list of basic binary oppositions (cf. section 1.3.2), emphasis on the "shadow opposition," and the introduction of the "dissipated trigger," which are discussed below.

Chlopicki's methodology is as follows. First, all the possible script oppositions in the text are identified. This is an important step, since ordinary jokes usually have only one opposition, or in some cases up to two or three. With short stories, the analyst is faced with many more script oppositions (66, in Chlopicki's first example). Analysis of the short stories reveals some scripts that extend through several sentences and even through the entire text (the "main scripts"). The "shadow oppositions" are the deeper script oppositions, whose scope encompasses the entire text and which are responsible for the overall perception of humor, rather than for the individual surface oppositions (Chlopicki 1987: 19). These scripts are found to overlap with other scripts with which they bear relations of opposition.

This methodology of analysis is powerful and yields insightful generalizations. Chlopicki (1987) shows that the short stories he analyzes can be reduced to a set of binary script oppositions, just as the SSTH predicts. Moreover, the methodology also has heuristic potential: an interesting result that Chlopicki's analysis yields is that the list of basic types of script oppositions will have to be revised (as Raskin (1985) had already suggested) on the basis of the empirical findings of the analyses of texts. This is no small feat in light of the declared universalist approach of the SSTH. The three new oppositions uncovered by Chlopicki are: ABSENCE/PRESENCE, NECESSARY/UNNECESSARY, and MUCH/LITTLE (Chlopicki 1987: 18).

The methodology adopted in Chlopicki (1987) is a paradigmatic textual analysis, i.e., a textual analysis that reduces the plot of a narrative to a set of (often binary)

2.1. THE EXPANSIONIST APPROACH

oppositions (see Attardo 1994: 98), thereby "flattening" it into paradigmatic oppositions. As such, it has its drawbacks. Namely, it obliterates the differences among texts that can all be reduced to the same set of binary oppositions; for example, nobody would claim that a short story is equivalent in every way to a joke, yet, according to Chlopicki's extension of the SSTH, they can both be described in almost the same terms.

In Chlopicki's analysis, the differences between jokes and short stories are marginal. There are some quantitative differences (the number of script oppositions in the text), but otherwise the same mechanisms are at play. The introduction of the dissipated trigger, i.e., "not any single word, but the formulation of the whole phrase or two, or even the whole text of the joke is responsible for causing the script overlap" (Chlopicki 1987: 14) does not introduce any significant difference, since alliterative puns also present "dissipated" disjunctors (cf. Attardo 1994: 139).

Neither does the emphasis on the shadow oppositions, which were already present *in nuce* in Raskin's formulation of the SSTH, where he addresses the possibility of sophisticated jokes involving repeated script oppositions (1985: 133). This fact confirms the substantial identity postulated by Chlopicki between jokes and humorous short stories since they are both analyzed as reduced to oppositions between pairs of (shadow) scripts.

More recently, Chlopicki has developed, the idea of a "character frame" which gathers information from the text and constructs a representation of the character (a repository of information). Since most narratives center on human (or anthropomorphic) characters this approach shows great promise. Details of his more recent work can be found in Chlopicki (2000). Chlopicki also organized two symposia on longer humorous texts, one of which with this writer. A report on the issues debated in the first one can be found in Chlopicki (1997).

2.1.2 Kolek

Kolek (1989) argues that jokes are "a basic narrative unit of comic texts" (132) because they are:

1. "complete in themselves (hence relatively context free)" (Ibid.);

2. "immanently (...) connected with humor" (Ibid.);

3. "the shortest form having all the elements of the narrative and developing a characteristic dynamic sequence of aesthetic effects"

I take it that Kolek by this last remark means that they shown the well known Setup-Incongruity-Resolution sequence (see Attardo 1997). He does not, however, exclude the possibility of humorous effects at lower levels (e.g., word) of textuality.

It is not entirely clear how Kolek's line of reasoning develops: it seems hardly the case that jokes would have to be narrative in order to be the basic narrative unit of a text. After all, a narrative is, at some level, made up of non-narrative units. So one can perfectly well imagine a non-narrative humorous element being part of a (humorous) narrative.

Kolek addresses very briefly the various configurations that jokes may take in longer texts. The following are mentioned:

- single joke incorporated in intact form, basically a joke inserted "as is" in an otherwise serious text

- single joke incorporated in "expanded form," produces "milder comic effects" and creates "sentimental" or "romantic" comedy (133)

- sequences of several jokes integrated by a protagonist or "motif" shared by the jokes

- mixed forms of sequences, e.g., one joke creates the "basis for the tale" and the other jokes are inserted in it.

- "vertical" integration of jokes, e.g., a number of jokes "characterize" a protagonist, who then goes on to being the agent of other jokes.

Also, suggestively if nothing else, he speaks of "joke structures" becoming "intertwined, scattered, superimposed, expanded into processes or contracted as 'points' of parts of narratives" (133). These hints and allusive ideas clearly show that Kolek was also thinking of jokes as constitutive elements of narratives, but also as narratives which can themselves be expanded, filled with other jokes, etc.

Thus it seems fair to conclude that he is systematically confusing two different approaches to jokes-as-building block: jokes as units which can be scattered in the text, according to patterns to be analyzed, or jokes as narratives. Clearly, the two views are not incompatible, and in fact a lot can be said for keeping both approaches under consideration. However, Kolek must be faulted for not addressing the issue of how jokes fare under such alterations as the "expansion" whereby a short form such as a joke is stretched to the size of a novel or short story. It is not enough to say that they produce milder effects: they are structurally different, as we will see.

In conclusion, let me note another interesting aspect of this pioneering work: Kolek notes that "generic-stylistic codes and literary conventions (types of comedy)" (133) are determined by such "properties of comic narratives" as

- frequency/density of joke patterns;

- frequent separation by other matter;

- slow or rapid passages between them;

as well as the "qualities of their points," a remark which I find obscure.

Overall, Kolek's work is highly suggestive and rich in stimulating ideas, but very short on factual proposals. No methodology is given on how to derive even the simplest elements of this proposal, which remains entirely intutive. Kolek (1985) does not deal with any text other than jokes.

2.2 The Revisionist Approach

The revisionist position consists of taking the SSTH as a theory of the text-type "joke" and devising the tools necessary to handle those features that characterize texts other than jokes. The drawbacks of this approach are obvious: the SSTH does not provide any indication as to how these tools should be constructed, and, for that matter, what these tools should consist of or even handle. The positive aspects of the revisionist approach is that the concept of script can be left unchanged because there is no need to broaden its scope to handle new phenomena. Another positive aspect of the revisionist approach is that it is open-ended, and so new tools may be added as the need arises.

This author first presented the revisionist approach in Attardo (1989), but this approach has been the object of little debate until Attardo and Raskin (1991), see below. It should be noted that Raskin (1985) explicitly mentions the possibility of modifications, in the revisionist direction, to the SSTH. Other, more recent, proposals have been presented, which are more detailed and can be analyzed more concretely.

2.2.1 Holcomb

One interesting proposal is that of finding "nodal points" of humor (Holcomb 1992) in the narrative. A nodal point is a "location in the narrative where humor is perceptibly more concentrated than in the immediately surrounding text" (234). Nodal points differ from jokes in that, while the latter are essentially context independent, nodal points are "semantically tied to the entire narrative" (Ibid.)

Holcomb's nodal points are identified and analyzed via analysis in scripts, using Raskin's SSTH (236). In this sense, the nodal point theory is seen as a direct extension of the SSTH. In fact, semantically, nodal points and punch lines do not differ: "a nodal point of humor will contain one or several script oppositions" (Ibid.). The main difference between the SSTH and the nodal point theory (NPT) is that NPT introduces a distinction between "local" and "distant" script oppositions (240-241). No explicit definition is given of the terms, but by their use in context we can gather that Holcomb intends that a local SO is an opposition among scripts that are both present in a given textual stretch, while distant SOs appear to be "tied to other parts of the story" (241). Distant oppositions may be in a relation of "correspondence" with other nodal points, and this fact "semantically connects these nodes to the rest of the narrative." (242)

While Holcomb's ideas are interesting, they are not sufficiently well defined so as to be evaluable. Let us note that the definition of nodal point is based on the perceptible higher level of humorousness of a stretch of text in relation to its context.

The obvious flaw in this definition is that no criteria for "perceptibility," "level of humor," and "location in the narrative" are given. Intuitively, it is clear that Holcomb is correct, in that a punch line is funnier than the rest of the text of a joke, for example. However, in a long text, with a diffuse organization of the humor, the distinction will become increasingly more difficult, until there will not be a clear cutting point. In other words, because the degree of humorousness is a continuum gradient, as Holcomb himself notes, any definition based on levels of humor is vacuous, if not provided with clear cut off points.[1]

The crucial idea of the relations between SOs across the text, and their semantic "connectedness/correspondence" is left unspecified. Again, from the way Holcomb is using the terms, it apears that the idea of connectedness may have to be intended simply as being semantically related scripts, since he argues that scripts activated towards the end of a story "correspond" to opposed scripts activated at the beginning of the story (242).

The concept of local and distant script oppositions is just as ill-defined. No criterion is given to determine the distance of SOs, except that in the text, Holcomb notes that both of the texts he examines in his study start by evoking a number of scripts, which are then used to establish oppositions in the nodal points after having been "held in suspension as the discourse proceeds" (249). Thus it seems logical to assume that distant SOs will span at least several sentences of the text and possibly may span the entire text.

Holcomb's NPT does however anticipate some of the concepts used in this book. Most significantly, the nodal points prefigure the jab lines, especially in their definitions in terms of the SSTH. The connections between nodal points also prefigure strands, with the significant difference, however, that while strands connect (jab and punch) lines, the connections in NPT are between scripts. These connections can then reveal a SO which in turns sets up a nodal point.

2.2.2 Wenzel

Wenzel's (1989) approach falls in a broad narratological and literary framework; however, his analytical tools are very much influenced by linguistic and semiotic theories (e.g. Koch 1989, cf. Vogel 1989, Attardo 1994: 181-182).[2]

Wenzel's approach to the punch line (*pointe*) in jokes sees it as a type of narrative resolution (*dénouement*, the Greeks' "catastrophe") and as the minimal form of the *pointe*. This is taken as a broad literary device, applicable to texts that are not jokes,

---

[1] It should be noted that the theory presented in this book is not based on levels of humor, but is rather a discrete theory, in that it admits only a funny or un-funny evaluation of a line, and does not admit intermediate, fuzzy evaluations of, say, 0.65. I believe this to be a strength of the theory.

[2] On Wenzel's work, see Attardo (1994: 190-192), as well as Mueller (1999) and Hempelmann (2000) which both include detailed discussions of Wenzel's work with long forms. Wenzel's work is given significant attention in Vogel (1989).

2.2. THE REVISIONIST APPROACH

for example detective novels (Wenzel 1989: 12). The obvious point of reference is Jolles (1965), which Wenzel quotes, not without reservations.

Wenzel argues that all "pointed" texts have the same setup/incongruity/resolution arrangement found in jokes (which he describes as a bipartite arrangement; Wenzel 1989: 265). In this respect, Wenzel's analysis is essentially a rewording of the isotopy-disjunction model, with its division into functions. Semantically, Wenzel's definition is similar to, if less specific than, Raskin's SSTH. Wenzel speaks of the "collapse of one frame of meaning" (Wenzel 1988: 124) and further on of two units "which are coordinated and yet *opposed* to each other" (125; my emphasis, SA).

Wenzel introduces an interesting distinction between the breaking of a frame of reference (1989: 33) and the establishment of a frame of reference (1989: 40) as humor-generating devices. The relevance of the distinction lies in the linear order of the procedure: the breaking of a frame of reference (script) presupposes that the part of the text up to the element that breaks the frame had been integrated into a coherent frame, whereas the establishment of a frame of reference, on the contrary, imposes an unexpected coherence on an apparently incoherent set of events/entities. Wenzel acknowledges that both approaches are ultimately subsumed by a broader "frame change" model (Wenzel 1989: 44), but his insistence on the distinction is typical of the narratological emphasis on the development of the action.[3]

It is important to note that Wenzel's definition of *pointe* is weaker than the GTVH's; this important point must be kept in mind when evaluating his contribution to humor theory. Wenzel sees quite well the "radical shift of sense" (1989: 265) brought about by the punch line and speaks (correctly) of the "final punch line revolutionizing the understanding of the whole text" (264). However, his definition of *pointe* does not include the oppositional aspect of the SSTH/GTVH, unlike his definition of joke. For example, in a science fiction short story about lunar colonization by the US Army the "punch line" is that a competing base has been built by the US Navy. While there is indeed a reorganization of the text, from a tale of exploration to a parable about waste of resources, useless rivalry, etc. there is clearly no semantic opposition between the US Army and the US Navy.[4]

Summing up, Wenzel distinguishes two types of texts: jokes, which have a pointe and frame opposition, and pointed narratives, which may or may not have frame opposition. It follows that Wenzel's analysis is largely off the mark, as far as humorous texts go, since he concentrates his analysis on the bipartite (or tripartite, depending on the views) structure of narratives which is typical of narrative texts and not at all

---

[3] Vogel (1989: 157-158) sees a difference in attitude between static models, such as isotopy disjunction (Greimas) or script (Raskin), on the one hand, and Wenzel's dynamic model of frame change, on the other. The issue is probably entirely terminological. Yus (forth.) has applied the same distinction to Relevance theoretic accounts of humor.

[4] A somewhat sophistic objection might be that the two scripts US ARMY and US NAVY are perhaps locally opposite (cf. 1.3.2). The problem for this idea is that nothing in the text leads us to believe that there is a reason why the US Navy could not have been colinizing the moon. Consider the doctor's wife joke (7): either one is there to see the doctor or one is there to have sex with his wife. Both things cannot take place at the same time (barring perverse situations).

unique to jokes or even humorous texts. In Wenzel's terminology, his analysis of *pointierung* (i.e., the property of having a pointe) is limited to the "syntax" of the text, while it should have been broadened to the semantics.

2.2.3 Palmer

Moving outside of more or less strictly defined linguistic research, we find that Palmer, a British film scholar, has made some significant contributions to the theory of long humorous texts. In Attardo (1994: 265) I suggested, in the context of the discussion of register humor, that one may want to distinguish between a non-humorous "narrative core" of a text, whose function is to make the story advance, and the humorous parts of the text. The idea was presented as speculative and extremely tentative. At the time of writing, I was unaware of the work of Palmer (1987) on humor in film and television. Palmer had presented essentially the same idea I had advanced, but in a more elaborate form.

Palmer distinguishes two main cases:

1. "the narrative [...] consist[s] of nothing more than the articulation of jokes together in a joke sequence" (141)

2. "jokes will be linked by something which is not in itself comic, in other words some form of non-comic narrative" (Ibid.) In this latter case, the relationship between jokes and narrative may be as follows:

    (a) "the non-comic narrative is no more than a series of links between jokes" (142)

    (b) "the narrative serves some further purpose" such as character development.

Palmer discusses the work of another film scholar, Terry Lovell, who argues that all comic plots are in fact non-comic plots "turned into the comic mode through the inclusion of comic material" (Palmer 1987: 144). Palmer returned to this topic in Palmer (1994) in which he clarifies his claim even more: "the narrative framework [of comic narrative] (...) is essentially the narrative form of realism" (1994: 117) and "much comedy, no matter how funny, commonly uses a narrative form which is not essentially dissimilar from a realist narrative in general" (113).

Summing up, Palmer, after Lovell, sees humorous narratives as a basic serious plot, disrupted, to a greater or lesser degree, by humorous elements. In fact, Palmer uses the degree of disruption to differentiate among genres and claims that farce and comedy can be distinguished precisely because "comedy is not just mirth creation, it also has serious, important themes; farce is a form where everything is subordinated to laughter production" (1994: 120) or, differently put: "narrative can have a truth value, whereas jokes are devoid of it" (114).

2.2. THE REVISIONIST APPROACH

The claim of the nonexistence of humorous plots is in error. I will deal in some detail with specifically humorous plots below (section 5.5). Despite this drawback, Lovell and Palmer account for some humorous narratives which are produced by the technique outlined by Lovell.[5] Moreover, they account for the fact that the degree of disruption of the "naturalistic/realistic" narrative may vary, thus giving us "realistic" comedies (e.g., Austen's *Emma*) with low degree of disruption of the narrative frame and "crazy" comedy (e.g., *Blazing Saddles*) with an extremely high level of disruption of the narrative.

In Palmer (1988), a further discussion of a theory of humorous narratives is presented, in which Palmer argues for the distinction of competence and performance levels, much along the same lines of section (1.6.1). Palmer also distinguishes two classes of theories of humorous narratives: one that proceeds from traditional literary categories such as "character" and one that proceeds from the structure of the joke. It seems, however, that the theory presented in this book belongs to neither class.

Thus we can say that Lovell and Palmer have made a substantive contribution to the study of long humorous texts by pointing out the possibility of an essentially serious plot turned into a humorous story by the insertion of humorous elements in the text. Indeed, it is possible that this type of humorous long text will turn out to be the most frequent typology of humorous texts.

2.2.4 A digression: Jolles on jokes

An author who has received some attention (Wenzel 1989, Müller 1999) within the domain of long texts, is the Dutch folklorist and literary scholar André Jolles. For him, a simple form is "an occupation of the spirit" (*geistesbeschäftigung*). More concretely, simple forms are a class of texts that do not have an historically determined set of intertextual relationships, as do genres, in the common sense (e.g., the picaresque novel). In other words, they are much more similar to Frye's "modes" (e.g., comedy): thus the simple form "joke" is roughly what contemporary humor research means by "humor" (and Jolles says so quite clearly: "to define the occupation of the spirit from which the joke (*Witz*) originates we use usually the Greek term comic or comical" 1930: 252) Any idea of simplicity in the sense of "made of simple parts" is completely foreign to Jolles.

In fact, Jolles seems to be subscribing to some form of the incongruity theory or perhaps of release theory: "in the form of the joke (...) there always happens a sort of disruptive dissociation, the joke dissolves therefore something that was tied up" (229). Jolles reviews a few categories that can be thus dissociated and concludes interestingly that "in the joke not only language, logic, ethics, or other similar categories may be dissociated, but also (...) the simple forms" themselves (232), thus anticipating the idea of meta-humor.

---

[5]It should be noted that Palmer himself is not uncritical of Lovell's position (Palmer 1987: 145-147), however, this is not the place to go into this amount of detail.

Chapter 3

Semantic Analysis and Humor Analysis

In this chapter, I review the semantic and pragmatic tools necessary to establish the meaning of a given text (either humorous or not) and then propose two (fairly speculative, but not far from current psycholinguistic research) models to account for a) the incremental and dynamic construction of textual meanings, and b) the persistence of traces of the surface structure of the text in hearers. All these elements are necessary to account for long humorous texts. Incidentally, they do not constitute a complete theory of textual processing, which would require a monograph of its own. What I am trying to establish, much more modestly, is that the more or less implicit theory of textual processing assumed by humor theory is not incompatible with what is known about text processing in psycholinguistics and related fields.

3.1 Semantic and Pragmatic Tools

In Attardo (1996), I suggested that a viable model for humorous texts larger than jokes must include a "storage area" to accomodate the various pieces of information that make up the text. In a sense, there isn't much difference between jokes and other texts, since the list of the items that need to be accounted for in the storage area are the same for both classes of texts.

3.1.1 Storage Area

Whatever the shape of the final theory that will account for humorous texts at large there are a few features of this theory which appear to be clear. These aspects, which are largely independent of the humorous aspects of the text, are:

1. the presence of a "storage area" for the information that is being assumed, shared, and developed by the text (be it a conversation between two or more parties or a monological text, such as a novel);

2. the fact that within the larger storage area there are privileged areas in which some or most of the normal (unmarked) features/requisites of the encoding of meaning in the text (both at the literal and inferential meaning levels) are suspended or deliberately violated.[1] To borrow a term from logic, the overall knowledge representation is non-monotonic.

3. the fact that the information stored does not travel in discrete units, but consists of clusters of information (scripts, frames) which in turn come surrounded by a web of associations and links to other clusters of information (cf. 1.1.2);

4. the fact that these clusters of information may consist of scripts nested one inside the other (cf. macroscripts 1.1.2);

5. the fact that the representation of the information in the storage area is not entirely linear, although there are portions of space that are linear and obey all the "Euclidean laws" of semantics (e.g., what happens before time T_0 cannot refer, with a "real" modality, to time $T_{\geq 1}$), or, at least, can refer to non-linear representations of time which are needed to account for the temporal dislocations of the plot (cf. 5.2);

6. the fact that the representation of the information in the storage area admits of multiple strands of information being processed and accessed simultaneously (cf. 5.6.2).

The nature of the storage area is addressed in section (3.2). We turn now to what I take to be the basic elements that will have to be included in a viable model of the storage area.

3.1.2 Contents of the Storage Area

The various components that I am proposing are extracted or inferred from a given text and its context and organized in the storage area. The result of this operation of information gathering, organizing, expanding, and integrating I propose to call the "text world" (TW) of that text. I discuss the TW in section (3.3).

The following are the basic elements that will have to be included in a viable model of the storage area:

1. the propositional content of all the sentences which are uttered in the text,

---

[1] While I will not deal directly with the violation of the Cooperative Principle (Grice 1989) in humor in this context, it is a central issue in humor theory. See Attardo (1993, 1994 ch. 9), for discussion.

3.1. SEMANTIC AND PRAGMATIC TOOLS

2. their presuppositions,

3. all pragmatic presuppositions,

4. all "accomodations" triggered by the text,

5. modal judgments as to the actuality, possibility and reliability of the information,

6. all non-trivial inferences derivable from the above sets of semantic objects.

I readily admit that this is a large body of information, but it is clear that well-known pragmatic principles (such as Grice's cooperative principle) prevent it from being infinite and/or indefinite. In other words, we are handling a finite, and potentially well defined set of semantic "objects." Their combinations give rise to the meaning of the text. This meaning is taken to be compositional.[2]

In what follows I will characterize the type of information that I believe needs to be accounted for in that specific storage area and I will briefly review the techniques used to determine what belongs in each area, when some are available.

Propositional content

I take this to be the "literal meaning" of the utterances. It should be noted that metaphorical expressions of the kind studied by Lakoff and Johnson (1981) fall under the rubric of literal meaning. So if one of the utterances of a text is "John fixed the leg of the table" or "Mary camped at the foot of the hills" I take it that the speaker does not recognize the frozen metaphor and treats it as an idiom, i.e., as a more or less unanalyzable whole.

I am of course well aware of the claims that pragmatic factors compenetrate the semantic base of the text (e.g., Carston 1988) but for our purposes this fact is irrelevant. In fact, this position is probably expandable outside of humorous texts: regardless of the use of pragmatic factors in determining it, it remains the case that there exists a basic "literal" meaning of a given sentence/text, which is then used for pragmatic inferencing. For discussion, see Attardo (in preparation b).

The literal meaning of a sentence is largely determined by the lexical items that occur within it (and by their arrangement, a.k.a., syntax). We take the lexical meaning of lexemes (and phrasemes) to be defined by a clusters of links across a semantic web, commonly known as scripts or frames (cf. section 1.1.2, above). Given the significance of this concept, scripts are summed up again separately in section (3.1.3).

The propositional content of the text corresponds to what Kintsch (1998) calls "textbase." The textbase is generated, within Kintsch's construction-integration model, by the bottom-up activation of all the senses of the words, while the selection of the

---
[2]I have referred to a much more limited, but similar, concept as "presuppositional basis" (Attardo 1993) in the context of the communicative function of jokes.

incompatible meanings is done subsequently. This parallels closely the combinatorial explosion described in (1.2.1).

Presuppositions

The literature on presuppositions is quite large. A well-regarded compendium can be found in Levinson (1983). A traditional test for presupposition is "constancy under negation" i.e., the fact that any given sentence's presuppositions are the same as the negation of the sentence's. Thus for

(18) The cat went outside.

and

(19) The cat did not go outside.

we can deduce the following presuppositions:

(20) $\exists$ cat, $\exists$ outside, the cat could go outside

The negation test is not without its problems (see Karttunen 1973, Levinson 1983: 185) but it does capture well the basic concept behind presupposition, namely that they embody the "background assumptions" (Levinson 1983: 180) of the sentence.

Inferences

Inferences are propositions that "follow" from their premises. "Following" is a technical term, denoting the fact that if

(21) $p \supset q$ (proposition p implies q)

then if p is true, q is also necessarily true.
   For example, if I say

(22) If it rains, I'll go to the movies

and, upon checking, it is found that it is raining, logically I am committed to going to the movies.
   Inferences are interesting, in this context, because they are often used to lead the hearer (in the technical sense defined above) to draw conclusions which are important for the understanding of the text. For example, in the context of the previous example, suppose that the text has established (22). Now, the next thing we read is

(23) It started raining.

we can safely infer that

(24) I am going to the movies.

3.1. SEMANTIC AND PRAGMATIC TOOLS

When we define "inference" as a logically necessary relationship the number of inferences activated by a given sentence is fairly limited. However, if we define "inference" more broadly, to include for instance implicatures (in the Gricean sense; cf. Grice 1989) then we find that inferences are no longer logically necessary, but become to a greater or lesser degree a matter of probability. Relevance Theory (Sperber and Wilson 1986), for example, is such a system which admits strongly and weakly backed implicatures. If we admit probabilistic inferences there arises the problem of constraining the inferential tree.

For example, given utterance (25)

(25) Mary won a Nobel prize

we can infer that Mary exists and that Nobel prizes exist (presuppositions). However, we open the door to an infinite set of inferences, such as "Someone else did not win the prize," "a Nobel prize is a good thing (at least in the eyes of the speaker)," etc. Progressively, as we move away from the literal meaning of the sentence and introduce encyclopedic information, we may infer fairly remote and increasingly less secure inferences such as "Mary is very intelligent," "Mary works a lot," and "Mary is a well-regarded scholar," all of which I am sure the unjustly passed over, non-Nobel-prize-winning colleagues of Nobel prize winners will gladly testify are not necessarily true at all.

Fortunately, such pragmatic principles as Grice's Cooperative Principle and Sperber and Wilson's Relevance Principle are readily available to provide us with heuristics capable of reducing the number of inferences by limiting them to those relevant to the situation. Thus, if (25) is uttered as an answer to the question

(26) Is Mary smart?

the inference that Mary studies a lot is discarded as irrelevant.

An interesting type of inference is the generation of macropropositions (Kintsch 1998: 177), i.e., activation of macroscripts. It is indeed the case that, when there are no explicit textual markers, such as titles or headings, the integration of the low-level scripts into higher-level ones is done inferentially.

Pragmatic presuppositions

The concept of "pragmatic presupposition" is far from being clear (see Gazdar 1979: 104-105 and Caffi 1994 for a review of various definitions). It is however sufficiently clear that pragmatic presuppositions are related to the concepts of "common ground" and "mutual knowledge." A good starting point is the following definition given in Levinson (1983: 205): "An utterance A pragmatically presupposes a proposition B iff A is appropriate only if B is mutually known by participants." Levinson notes (Ibid.) that mutual knowledge is too strong a requirement and that mere consistency with the common ground is necessary (1983: 209; cf. also Gazdar 1979: 106-107).

We can define very roughly mutual knowledge as the amount of information that speaker and hearer share. Crucially, this involves also knowledge about what knowlege the other party possesses. Mutual knowledge has been the center of some fairly heated discussion (see Smith 1982 for a collection of essays). Essentially, the discussion revolves around the issue of whether mutual knowledge involves an infinite regression (which would make it psychologically and logically unwieldy). Consider for example the following situation:

(27) I know A
You know that I know A
I know that you know that I know A
You know that I know that you know that I know A
etc.

Sperber and Wilson (1986) have suggested to replace mutual knowledge with the notion of mutual manifestness, a weaker notion which they claim does not share the same problems that mutual knowledge has. This claim has itself been challenged (Talbot 1994).

Clark (1996: 92-100) presents a very thorough discussion of mutual knowledge/common ground. Clark notes that common ground can be defined in three different ways: only one involves infinite regression, while the other two involve self-reference. The arguments against mutual knowledge attack primarily infinite regression and hence a definition of common ground based on self-reference is immune to those criticisms. Clark notes that self-reference is itself "suspect" in many logical circles (primarily because it leads to the kind of paradoxes that Russels theory of types resolved). However, he also points out that in recent logical approaches (e.g., situation semantics) self-reference is no longer a problem (Clark 1996: 100). Under Clark's self-referential definition, common ground is defined as follows:

p is common ground for members of community C if and only if:

1. every member of C has information that basis b holds;

2. b indicates to every member of C that every member of C has information that b holds;

3. b indicates to the members of C that p. (Clark 1996: 94)

Using this definition of common ground we can now return to the definition of pragmatic presupposition and conclude that an utterance A pragmatically presupposes proposition b, if A's appropriateness is dependent on b being part of the common ground for the participants to the interaction. As we will see below, if b is not part of the common ground it is added to it.

Finally, let us note that Caffi (1994: 3322) provides a very interesting list of differences between pragmatic presuppositions and implicatures which can be used as heuristics for classification.

3.1. SEMANTIC AND PRAGMATIC TOOLS

Accomodations

It has been pointed out that if we introduce some previously unknown fact or some fact that is not part of what has been previously assumed as common ground, we simply change the common ground to accomodate the new knowledge. Thus if one walks in late at a meeting and utters

(28) I am sorry to be late, my daughter came down with the flu

assuming that the fact that he/she has a daugther was unknown to his/her audience, the hearers restructure their common ground to incorporate this fact. This has been called "accomodation" (Lewis 1979). On accomodation see also Thomason (1990), and Seuren (1986, 1994); an essentially similar concept is called "bridging" (Clark 1977).

From this perspective, we can now refine the definition of sentence-level incongruity[3] (under the cover of "local antonymy"; cf. section 1.3.2) as what happens when an utterance directly states, presupposes, implies, implicates, or pragmatically presupposes a proposition which is incompatible with a proposition which is already part of the common ground. Let us note in passing that there's an open issue: namely a redefinition of "local antonymy" such that it accomodates all the semantic constructs above.

Modal evaluations

Modality (or mood) is the part of grammar that deals with the "way" (modus) in which the main predicate of a sentence is presented. In English, modality covers such distinctions as actual vs. potential (Mary wins/Mary may win), possibility vs. necessity (You may eat/You must eat), intention vs. necessity (I will go/I have to go), etc.

There are two (related) reasons to want modal information pertaining to the above mentioned categories: 1) several of them (presuppositions, primarily) have been shown to be sensitive to modality, and 2) it is essential for the constituting of the TW to know which parts of a given sentence are actual and which parts are merely possible or perhaps appropriate or necessary (cf. section 3.3).

3.1.3 Scripts

As is well known the SSTH, as the name states, is based on script-theory. "Script" is taken as a neutral term among the various proposals (e.g., frame, schema, daemon, etc.) and thus does not have exactly the common meaning of the term AI. A script is defined as a complex of information associated with a lexical item. Thus the

---

[3]"Sentence level," since antonymy may be lexical, and since we are defining incongruity in terms of antonymy, it would be possible to think of lexical incongruity. Of course, when we speak of presuppositions, implicatures, accomodations, etc. we generally consider sentences/utterances, not words.

canonical example in Raskin (1985) is the script for DOCTOR, while in Schank and Abelson it is for GOING TO THE RESTAURANT. In this context, we will continue to use the term "script" as a neutral choice, equivalent to "frame." (See section 1.1.2.)

Types of scripts

Let us recapitulate, Raskin (1985) introduces, but does not exploit to their fullest potential, the notions of complex script and macroscript. As we will see, these could potentially be very helpful in our task.

The difference between scripts (frames), complex scripts, and macroscripts is primarily one of level: a script is the simplex form; a macroscript is a group of scripts organized chronologically (what some authors would call a script, as opposed to a frame or schema); a complex script is a script made of other scripts but without chronological organization. The RESTAURANT script in Schank and Abelson (1977) would be an example of macroscript while a complex script would be WAR. For example, if a text activates the script WAR the actants slots are likely to be filled with scripts such as ARMY or BATTALION rather than individuals (such as Mary or Bob). Naturally, the presence of such "subscripts" makes it legitimate to activate such individualizing scripts as COMMANDER IN CHIEF or GENERAL. The hierarchical organization of scripts (and other such constructs) is a common assumption, cf. Mandler (1984: 15) and references therein.

Earlier (1.1.2) we introduced a distinction between

- lexical scripts, activated by having their lexematic handle instantiated (occurring) in the text; and

- inferential scripts, which instead can be activated inferentially

Recall also that structurally scripts and inferential scripts are not different, i.e., they encode the same types of information.

3.2 How is information added to the storage area?

We enter here an area of script theory that has not been the object of much attention, within the humor research community. Essentially, I wish to suggest that the storage area is a dynamic construct,[4] which is changed by the information it is exposed to.

---

[4]This is not a novel idea: Feldman (1975) and Collins *et al.* (1978) posit such a dynamic model. An interesting issue, brought up by Bower *et al.* (1979: 216) is whether a dynamic model is more compatible with a static script model (as is the one they present) or with a simple "network of concept" (as the one used in the text). They conclude that the latter seems better suited to the dynamic revision model they propose. The dynamic aspect of scripts is now more or less taken for granted, cf. the following quote:

> schemas came to be thought of, not as fixed structures to be pulled from memory on demand, but as recipes for generating organizational structrues in a particular task context (Kintsch 1998: 37)

3.2. HOW IS INFORMATION ADDED TO THE STORAGE AREA? 55

As a sort of null hypothesis, we can start with the idea that the storage area is an empty sentential script, which is filled by the lexical and inferential scripts activated by the text. As soon as the text activates a script, it is uploaded in the storage area and connected via links to the other scripts already stored there. Thus, for example, the sentence

(29) Mary kicked the ball to Paul

would activate lexical scripts for MARY and PAUL, which would include the feature [± female] as well as [+ human] (which of course inherits the default fillers for the partonomic components of a human body, i.e., arms, legs, a head, etc.). The lexeme *kick* would activate the script KICK with the AGENT slot filled by *Mary* and the goal slot filled by *Paul*. The patient (undergoer) slot would be filled by BALL. The sentence would also probably activate an inferential script SOCCER which would partonomically allow the inference of the presence of a goal, etc.

Simplifying a lot, and with the convention that dots will represent parts of scripts that can be filled out by the reader, the inferential script may look something along the lines of:

```
(SOCCER ...
    (agent (MARY, PAUL))
    (partonyms ... kick ...))
(KICK
    (agent (MARY ....
                (partonyms ... foot ...)))
    (goal (PAUL))
    (undergoer (BALL))
    (instrument (FOOT))
    (time x))
```

Note that SOCCER is activated only in the grounds of the partonym KICK and the compatibility of the human agents with the agents required by SOCCER. The activation is, needless to say, probabilistic: it may turn out to be faulty. Furthermore, we infer that the kicking was done with one of Mary's feet, since we know that Mary is a human and humans have feet, or, to put it differently, the script MARY inherits the partonyms of its hyperonym HUMAN.

None of the inferential material need be actually activated, but it would remain available if needed. For example, if the continuation of sentence (29) were

(30) but hurt her foot.

this would obviously activate the FOOT script.

Let us assume that the next sentence is something along the lines of

(31) Later they went for drinks.

we would then close the first script, making sure that is it time-stamped (say, time = 0), and open a second script, carrying over the actants (the anaphor "they"), but changing the location (from a soccer field to a pub), etc. Ulterior scripts would be activated, lexically and inferentially, until, for example, a COURTSHIP script would be activated, because perhaps Mary and Paul after performing several entertainment scripts (play soccer, have drinks, ...) together would eventually decide to get engaged to one another.

At a macro level, every text can be summed up (with ruinous aesthetic effects, needless to say) in a more or less stereotypical situation/script (e.g., *Romeo and Juliet* = love story that ends tragically; *The Stranger* = murder of an Arab; *Moby Dick* = unsuccessful whale hunt; etc.). There seems to be no reason that this reduction to a basic script should not be possible outside of literary texts. In fact, something very similar explicitly underlies Schank and Abelson's (1977) model: they distinguish between a high level "knowledge structure" and a low level conceptual dependency, itself further subdivided in a fine and a macroscopic level (160-161). Mechanisms, unfortunately left vague, collapse scripts into macroscripts, at the knowledge structure level (150-153).

Incidentally, this is very similar to Van Dijk's (1980) concept of *macrostructure*, but with significant differences. Van Dijk sees macrostructures as the result of the operations of macrorules, listed below:

1. Deletion/Selection: Given a sequence of propositions, delete each proposition that is not an interpretation conditon (e.g., a presupposition) for another proposition in the sequence.

2. Generalization: Given a sequence of propositions, substitute the sequence by a proposition that is entailed by each of the propositions of the sequence.

3. Construction: Given a sequence of propositions, replace it by a proposition that is entailed by the joint set of propositions of the sequence. (Van Dijk and Kintsch 1983)

Essentially, the difference is that the Van Dijk/Kintsch model (see also Kintsch 1998: 66-67) is destructive, while the approach I am using is not. What I mean is that in the Van Dijk/Kintsch approach the macroproposition generated by any of the macrorules replaces the propositions it used as input (the verbs in the definition above are explicit: "delete," "substitute," "replace") whereas in my model the macroscript has the constituent scripts as fillers within it. I should emphasize that the are probably a majority of situations in which this is irrelevant, as for simplicity constituent scripts are often just listed by their lexematic handle and therefore unexpanded. However, in principle, the necessity in humorous texts to target specific phonological strings (in puns), or sections of the text (in bridges), require the retrievability of the original wording of the text(base).

In this sense, the model of text processing that I am outlining, consists in activating sequentially scripts, until the main script of a text is determined, and then the entire text is interpreted as an instance of that script, filled with the actual details of the text instantiating the script. I don't think that this approach differs that much from the macrostructure approach, in that both macrostructures and macroscripts are generated as part of the process of making sense of a text.

There is considerable evidence for the fact that this approach has psychological reality. The evidence for the macrostructure approach is summarized in Kintsch (1998), and Van Dijk and Kintsch (1983). Bower *et al.* (1979) reach the conclusion that scripts are organized hierarchically, as a " 'tree' of events with several levels of subordinate actions" (186) and furthermore that "any sequence of subordinate actions within a given [event] can be summarized by the superordinate action."

3.3 The Text World

Lexical script activations establish what Kintsch (1998) calls the textbase of a given text, i.e., its propositional information, from which a situation model is developed. The situation model includes inferential script activation and various inferential bridgings and accomodations, as well as personal information that the speaker may have, etc.

Thus the situation model is the fullest representation (which is still propositional, in Kintsch's theory) of the overall meaning of the text, including the inferences, abductions, interpolations, and plain misunderstandings and pure guesses of the reader/hearer. When the reader/hearer of a text has created a situation model, he/she also creates in parallel, and strictly in relation with the situation model, what I will call a *text world (mental) representation* (TWR) along the lines of mental spaces (Fauconnier 1985) and mental models (Johnson-Laird 1983). It should be noted, along the lines of Ronen's (1994) argument, that the uses of the concept of "possible world" in narratology is quite distinct from the use of the same concept in philosophy, where it originated. I take a "world" to be a set of presuppositions defined by a set of propositions, along the lines of Eco (1979). On text worlds, see also Emmott (1997: 56-59) and references therein.

Let us consider Fauconnier's definition of mental spaces, in the following linked quotations:

> Linguistic expressions will typically establish new spaces, elements within them, and relations holding between the elements. I shall call space builders expressions that may establish a new space or refer back to one already introduce in the discourse (1985: 17)

> Spaces can be introduced explicitly by space builders or implicitly on pragmatic grounds (e.g., fiction, theater, free indirect style, or (more simply) cases when changes of time or belief is not formally marked (1985: 161)

Mental spaces are aptly named: they are entirely mental, i.e., they are detached and independent from the text that has helped establish them, and they are not necessarily tied to reality (i.e., they include fictional and even counterfactual thoughts; cf. also Fauconnier 1997). Fauconnier points out the similarities between mental spaces and frames (in the Goffman sense of the term, as in a "play frame").

Johnson-Laird defines similarly the meaning of mental model (of a syllogism):

> a mental representation based on the meaning of the premises—that is, a model of the state of affairs that they [syllogims premises] describe" (Johnson-Laird 1986: 34)

Other types of mental models include spatial, temporal, cynematic, and dynamic models (Johnson-Laird 1983).

Along the lines of these definitions, a TWR of text t is a mental representation, not (necessarily) propositional,[5] of the state of affairs that holds within the text. The TWR is significant in the discussion of humorous texts, because the realistic illusion whereby you have to be coherent to your world is obviously based not on the "real" world but on the TWR of text t. I will not address the issue of the type of representation used in TWRs.

3.4 Surface structure recall

An interesting issue, brought up by the concept of *bridge*, introduced earlier, is the degree to which hearers (or readers) retain a memory of the actual text they have heard/read. We know, from psycholinguistics, that memory of the surface structure of a text fades quickly.

For example, Sachs (1967, 1974) found that recall of the surface structure of sentences faded after only twenty seconds of reading. However, there is also evidence that surface structure is not necessarily impossible to retain:

> Although it is generally true that meaning is retained better than surface memory (...) long-term retention of surface form is by no means rare (...). Indeed, surface form is retained best when the way something is expressed is pragmatically significant and thus relevant to the situation model. It matters a great deal whether a partner in a discourse has said something politely or aggressively, and in these situations the wording is quite well remembered (...). Outside of a social context, however, in laboratory studies of memory for sentences, memory is in general propositional, and surface features are typically reconstructed (...). (Ericsson and Kintsch 1995)

---

[5]According to Johnson-Laird, definitely not propositional. It is plausible that non-propositional types of representations would be used in TWR. On "mental images" and the likes, cf. Shepard 1980, Paivio 1986, and Kosslyn 1980, 1983, 1996.

In fact, Bower *et al.* (1979) found that their subjects "dispaly[ed] considerable 'surface memory', at least at a 20-min retention interval" (192) as evinced by the fact that they reproduced two to three times more scripts they had actually read than those they had inferred. Their model allows for the annotation of scripts with a record of whether they have been lexically activated (cf. also Mandler 1984: 110). Kintsch (1998: 177) states also that "the surface structure of [literary texts] plays a much bigger role in determining comprehension and memory than for non-literary texts."

These experimental data, allow us to propose a speculative solution to the bridge problem. This problem, which emerged forcefully during the 1996 symposium in Holland (Chlopicki 1997), can be stated fairly simply: if readers lose track of the surface structure of the text after a relatively short time span, how is it possible that they will recognize a bridge (i.e., two related jab or punch lines occurring at a considerable distance from one another) when the relation between the two lines is formal (i.e., related to surface structure)? The example that triggered the discussion, reads as follows:

(32) "I'm an analyst, not a magician." (...)
"I'm a magician, not an analyst." (Allen 1975 (1989): 42, 53)

The ellipsis marks the deletion of ten pages of text. We recognize the common chiasmus arrangement of the terms (see 1.4.5), but the problem is that it will take any reader longer than 20 seconds (Sachs' figure for surface information decay) to read 10 pages of text. Therefore, we would expect the readers to have forgotten the surface structure of the relevant jab line by the time they encounter its mate.

Yet, readers recognize these structures and appreciate their humor (in fact this is a common technique in stand up comedy, see 4.1.1). The speculative solution to this problem that I wish to propose is that

- jab lines and especially punch lines are semantically and pragmatically marked in the text, i.e., they attract attention to themselves;
- humorous texts may position the jab lines strategically, in locations that will favor retention, and
- punch lines are by definition located in a prominent (final) position.

Therefore, if all of the above is true, it would follow that, by putting lines in a prominent location, humorists maximize the natural likelihood of verbatim retention of the humorous lines, which derives from their semantic markedness.

3.5 Summing up

From the preceding discussion, we have ended up with a fairly complex process leading to the construction and representation of the textual world (or mental space of the text) which has to have two significant features:

- it must be psychologically real(istic), and
- it must be computationally tractable, i.e., formal(izable)

These features follow from the necessity of accounting for some phenomena, such as the "bridge" effect, which take into account the actual processing of the texts, and the preferability, on methodological grounds, of a formal (or at least formalizable) framework, respectively.

From a more traditional linguistic outlook, it may be worthwhile to emphasize once more that the SSTH, and the GTVH after it, reject the old tripartite arrangement (syntax, semantics, pragmatics) except as a pedagogical tool. All available psycholinguistic evidence shows that all three levels of processing take place simultaneously, online, so to speak. Thus, it is only to simplify the exposition that we've looked at the semantic construction of the literal meaning of the text, followed by the calculation of its implicatures. As we've seen, in reality the two processes take place simultaneously, and influence one another. In other words, the SSTH/GTVH are not semantic theories, somehow detached from pragmatics, but are semantico-pragmatic theories, which encompass all effects of meaning.

Chapter 4

Beyond the Joke

As we saw in the previous chapters, current research on humor in linguistics has developed primarily and with few exceptions on a specific text-type, the joke. In Attardo and Chabanne (1992), a number of reasons were given for the prominence of jokes in the linguistics of humor. Jokes are typically short, easy to collect, and simple (i.e., they tend to have only one source of humor). While those reasons remain valid, it is clear that longer texts, while they share significant aspects with jokes, also have idiosyncratic aspects.

As is often the case, the distinction between jokes, on the one hand, and "longer texts," on the other, is far from being clear cut. We will therefore consider a number of phenomena that "bridge" the gap between short and long humorous texts, in the belief that doing so will make the analysis of large texts easier to approach.

We will start with canned jokes as they occur in context, first in stand-up routines and then in a joke telling context, moving on to free conversation. We then move to joke cycles, a macro-text which consists of hundreds of jokes. Furthermore, this chapter sets the stage, so to speak, for the following ones by exploring and defining some concepts, such as "intertextuality," that play a significant part in the development of a broad theory of humorous texts.

In the following section, we turn to sequences of jokes.

4.1 Narrative vs. Conversation

We may find, at least pre-theoretically, a major difference between narrative (or canned) jokes and conversational jokes (see for fuller discussion Attardo 1994: 298-319). The following are the distinguishing features of canned and conversational jokes:

- Narrative/Canned jokes are typically told by a narrator who often prefaces the joke with an announcement of the humorous nature of the forthcoming turn and who holds the floor through the telling and releases it for the reaction turn of the audience.

- Narrative/Canned jokes are "rehearsed" i.e., they have been heard or created by the narrator *before* the telling.

- Narrative/Canned jokes are generally detached from the context in which they are told.

Conversely, conversational jokes have the following features:

- Conversational jokes are told as a regular turn in conversation, without prefacing.

- They are created by the teller "on the fly" and are strongly context-dependent.

The idea of a categorical distinction between canned/narrative and conversational jokes has been abandoned with the introduction of the concept of "recycling" which shows that canned jokes are adapted to the context in which they are told, often to a great extent (Zajdman 1991), thus making it virtually impossible to determine whether a joke is really conversational or if it is a clever recycling of a canned one. In fact, it has been claimed that canned jokes originate from conversational jokes which have undergone a process of decontextualization (Oring 1999).

Rarely do jokes occur in isolation. We review the most common situations in which canned jokes are clustered: stand-up routines, joke telling contests, and conversations. It should be noted that we start with a highly artificial, scripted genre and move progressively towards less structured contexts, paralleling in this the distinction bewteen canned and conversational jokes. Since canned jokes have been the prototypical type of humor analyzed in humor theory, we are also progressively moving away from the focus of traditional humor research.

4.1.1 Stand-up routines

The prototypical locale for canned jokes is perhaps the stand-up routine. Far from being improvised, a stand-up routine is a highly rehearsed, planned text, which consists in (a sometimes large) part of canned jokes. While it is tempting to see stand-up comedy as a zero degree of connectiveness of jokes, this view would be simplistic in the extreme. We will examine stand-up routines using Rutter (1997), which focuses on this genre.

Canned jokes might be strung together with little or no concern for their connections, although stand-up comedians and other performers tend to introduce transitions and across-jokes links as well as try to group jokes thematically, connect jokes to biographical information regarding the performers (Rutter 1997: 150), or contextualize the performers' act to the specific locale and audience of the show (174). In

4.1. NARRATIVE VS. CONVERSATION

fact, Rutter shows that stand-up peformances use the same rhetorical arrangements of materials (e.g., lists, announcements, etc.) as other forms of podium communication (e.g., political speeches) (221). Stand-up performers use also comedy-specic devices, such as the establishment of recurring jab lines (which Rutter calls "re-incorporations") (226) to establish cohesive links in the performance.

Moreover, Rutter shows convincingly that the openings and closings of comedic routines are structured. See for example, the following quote:

> the openings of stand-up routines are, unlike the act that follows them, consistently non-humorous, they do not contain jokes and rarely even contain humour or witticisms. Performers do not start their act by going into the first of their canned jokes, instead they go through a series of turns in which the audience begins to be drawn into the performance narrative. This non-comic opening sequence may be viewed as a parallel to the opening of telephone conversations in which the initial turns have an apparently perfunctory nature bearing very little connection to the topic(s) of the later conversation. (Rutter 1997: 143)

Another author that has pointed out the contextual nature of stand-up routines is Greenbaum (1999), who points out that stand-up comedians "must be prepared to adapt their discourse to the needs of the audience" (1999: 40) and that they use a "dialogic" style (1999: 34, 38; i.e., they interact with the audience).

Therefore we may conclude that stand-up routines, while largely made of canned jokes, are not simply a sequence of unrelated texts, but that these routines

1. have a certain degree of structure, with structured beginnings and endings;
2. there are cohesive links within some of the jokes (either short range or long range, i.e., comb-like or bridge-like structures); and
3. there are contextual links with the settings of the utterance of the routine.

A side issue: are stand-up routines counterxamples of the IR theories?

Let us note, in passing, that Rutter's (1997) otherwise excellent work is hampered by his misunderstanding of the scope of Incongruity-Resolution (IR) theories of humor (most specifically of the SSTH/GTVH kind). IR theories have traditionally been *exemplified* with canned jokes, but they are in principle applicable to conversational jokes as well. Thus claims such as the following:

> performances without several instances of audience laughter before the first canned joke is delivered are conspicuously rare. As such it becomes impossible, as joke theory does, to see the first joke (or any of the act's subsequent ones) as isolated from the whole ongoing interactional process which differentiate the telling of jokes from the performance which is stand-up. (Rutter 1997: 187)

are clearly in error: any occurrence of humor (jab line) in the performer's text would be seen as a joke (although not as a canned joke).

Or the claim that the following repeated joke (from a Woody Allen routine) is a problematic case:

(33) 14 WA: And there's a law in New York State against driving
15 with a conscious moose on your fender - Tuesdays,
16 Thursdays and Saturdays.
(...)
49 WA: So I'm driving along with two Jewish people[1] on my fender.
50 And there's a law in New York State
51 Aud: ((Laughter))
52 WA: Tuesdays, Thursdays and especially Saturday.
53 Aud: ((Laughter))

In any form of analysis based on traditional humour theory the audience laughter of lines 51 and 53 is difficult to fully explain. For example one approach may suggest that the idea of bylaws prohibiting the carrying of people on cars on specific days raises laughter because of the incongruity of the image. However, this text based analysis is limited. It cannot explain the relationship of line 49-52 to the rest of the quoted passage or suggest why the phrase is reused by Allen and why this technique marks the joke as in anyway different from its use in lines 14-16. (Rutter 1997: 227)

while, in fact, this is a "bridge" jab line configuration (see 3.4). Interestingly, another example of bridge by Woody Allen has figured prominently in the discussion on the theory of longer humorous texts (see Chlopicki 1997: 342-343).

Rutter claims (passim) that the materials he is examining present a serious challenge to IR theories. While in a sense he is right, and the present work aims at filling these theoretical gaps, he takes the phenomena he is describing to be counterexamples of the IR approach, which is obviously in error, as the present work demonstrates.[2]

---

[1] A couple dressed up as a moose, which the narrator has mistaken for the original moose. SA.

[2] While generally an excellent contribution, at times, however, Rutter does encur in the occasional blunder, as when he claims that the use of suprasegmentals "cannot be understood" by any joke theory (including a linguistic one). The literature on the use of suprasegmental clues of irony is reviewed in Attardo (2000c), for example.

4.1.2 Joke telling contests

In conversations, speakers will at times engage in joke telling "contests" i.e., speakers will compete informally[3] on who can tell the best joke, or who remembers the most. A variant of the joke telling contest is what Chiaro (1992) has called the joke capping contest.

Joke contests

Several examples of joke telling contests are recorded in Chiaro (1992: 105ff). The following example has the advantage of being shorter than others:

(34) A. Mummy, Mummy, there's a man at the door with a bill! Don't worry chuck, it's probably only a duck with a hat on! (1)

B. . . .(unclear speech) . . . the one about licking the bowl? . . . Mummy, Mummy, can I lick the bowl? (2)

C. No darling, pull the chain like other children.

A. Yes. Mummy, Mummy, can I play with Grandad? No, you've dug him up three times already this week. (3)

B. Mummy, Mummy, what's a vampire? Shut up and eat your soup before it clots! (4)

C. . . . (unclear speech) . . . have to go to France? Shut up and keep swimming! (5)

D. Mummy, Mummy, I don't like Daddy! Leave him on the side of your plate and eat your vegetables. (6)

E. Mummy, Mummy, does the au pair girl come apart? No darling, why do you ask? Because Daddy says he's just screwed the arse off her! (7) . . . How do you make a cat go 'woof'? (8)

A. Dunno. How do you make a cat go 'woof'?

E. Douse it in paraffin, chuck it on the fire and it goes 'woooof'!

A. How do you make a a dog go 'Miaow'? (9)

C. What's red and sticky and lies in a pram? (10)

A. That's horrible!

C. A baby with a razor blade.

A. How do you make a dog go 'Miaow'?

E. Dunno. How do you make a dog go 'Miaow'?

---

[3]Theer exist more or less formal joke telling contests in which tellers are judged and win prizes. We ignore this kind of activity in this context.

A. Tie its tail to the back of Concorde and it goes 'Miaaaaow'.

E. How do you make a cat drink?

A. A cat drink?

E. Yeah.

A. Dunno. How do you make a cat drink?

E. Put it in a liquidizer.

From this example, we can see how the speakers select a topic (which may also be a genre) and then compete on who can produce the most or better joke on the subject. Note that these contests are of course informal and may be entirely undeclared: it is sufficient that after the telling of one joke, another speaker say something along the lines of "that reminds me of another joke" to create the conditions for a potential joke telling contest. Whether it is received as such by the other speakers will depend on a number of idiosyncratic factors, such as whether the speakers perceive the remark as a challenge, their desire to uphold it, etc.

Joke capping

Joke capping was first described in humor research literature by Chiaro (1992).[4] Joke capping is a sequence of jokes each of which uses the previous text as the setup of the SIR sequence (the sequence of Setup-Incongruity-Resolution, see Attardo 1998). Interestingly, the capping turn and the capped turn may belong to different speakers.

Consider again the example (34), and particularly the sequence of jokes following (1): each preceding joke (and the sequence thereof) provides the context for the speakers' interaction, so that they can dispense entirely with introductory materials. It is of particular interest that the speakers actively compete for the floor, and in fact in one case (10) the speaker C interrupts the adjacency pair "riddle/answer" to force his/her riddle in the conversation.

In its most extreme form, of which (34) is a good example, when the conversation becomes a joke capping contest, joking takes over entirely the conversation and the latter becomes entirely focalized on the participants telling jokes. As Chiaro noted already (1992: 109), however, the jokes remain clustered either thematically or formally.

4.1.3 Conversation

Finally, we turn to jokes occurring in general, unstructured conversation. It is obvious that a humorous conversation is not the same as a sequence of jokes (cf. Norrick 1993b). Speakers tend to tell jokes that are related thematically with the serious context and with one another (Chiaro 1992: 105; Norrick 1993b: 126).

---

[4]For a critical evaluation of this work, see Attardo (1993b).

4.1. NARRATIVE VS. CONVERSATION

Nor is it the case that conversational humor is an inherently solitary activity. Speakers can spontaneously engage in coordinated forms of joking, such as duetting humor, cf. C. E. Davies (1984). C.E. Davies considers three "styles" of joint joking, which she describes as "a group activity" drawing on the resources of two or more people who construct a "joking footing" (after Goffman 1981).

Let us quote a short example, to see how the speakers jointly construct the joking footing. The speakers are two faculty members who meet in the faculty lounge and are arguing about who should pay for the coffee:

(35) 1 Ed: I'll pay for it.
     2 Joyce: No, I already got it.
     3 Ed: You shouldn't pay for my coffee.
     4 Joyce: Oh, that's OK... you're worth every penny.
     5 Ed: (laughs) I see your opinion of me has gone up.
     6 Joyce: Not really. I'm coming back later to take
              15 cents out again.
     7 Both: (laugh)

Note how Joyce's quip on line 4, is met by laughter, and followed by another (self-deprecating) joke (on line 5) by Ed, which is met by Joyce's playful one-upping of the deprecation (on line 6), which results in joint laughter. Note also how Joyce introduces a theme (Ed is worth a cup of coffee, say 25 cents) which Ed takes up (25 cents is higher than some previous, fictitious, evaluation of his worth) and that Joyce finally caps (Ed is wrong, her evaluation is still 10 cents—or possibly has gone down to 10 cents—as Joyce is only pretending to pay 25 cents for the coffee and will later retrieve some of the money). More specifically the notion of joking "theme" can be made more explicit: in this case the common theme is a given SO: VALUE/NO VALUE, instantiated in the HUMAN BEING/CUP OF COFFEE equation.

It should be noted that SO is not the only similarity possible. The following fragment of conversation was recorded over lunch among co-workers. Speaker A was explaining how he dislikes some forms of modern art.

(36) 1 A: When someone paints a white canvas, I don't un-
            derstand it.
     2 B: Leave Mahlevich alone!
     (...)
     3 A: Take Picasso...
     4 C: (interrupts) Leave Picasso alone!

Here speaker C uses the same exaggerated aggressive reaction used by speaker B, matching B's choice of idiom ("leave X alone!") thus marking a cohesive connection between the two turns, which were separated by several intervening turns. In this case, the similarity is based on LA.

Joint joking is inherently related to "humor support" i.e., a set of strategies used by hearers to support (encourage, reward) speakers who use humor. Humor support has been the object of extensive work by Hay (2000; see also Hay forthcoming). She lists, besides contributing other humor, which is the joint joking strategy we have just examined, the following:

- laughter
- echoing the humor (i.e., repeating the humorous segment)
- offering sympathy
- contradicting self-deprecating humor
- using overlap or other strategies to show heightened involvement

Hay points out that certain forms of humor (ironical, for example) do not require support, nor does supportive humor itself (i.e., if A offers a joke in support of B's joking, B or C need not support A's humor).

We can conclude that joint joking and humor support (by providing other humor, or repeating it) will tend to produce joke clustering in naturally occurring conversation.

Joke Similarity

As we have seen, speakers cluster jokes by thematic or topical similarity. In this context, the GTVH seems to offer great promise. The GTVH specifically introduces a metric for "joke similarity," which essentially captures how similar or dissimilar two given jokes are based on the six KRs. The theory has been confirmed to a great extent by empirical studies (Ruch *et al.* 1993). Based on that metric, it seems that it should be possible to determine a ranking of the degree of similarity of jokes.

However, undue optimism would be naive. First, we can foresee serious problems in the application of the GTVH to this problem: to begin with, despite its claims at generality, the GTVH was developed on the basis of canned jokes and its application to conversational humor is less than straightforward, as this book shows. Moreover, it is not entirely clear what the psychological reality of the various KRs is. The experimental studies mentioned above (Ruch *et al.* 1993) established that five out of six KRs produced ratings of similarity/dissimilarity as predicted by the GTVH, with the partial exception of the LM, as we saw in (1.4.5). It is not clear whether the abstract nature of the LM is responsible for the incorrect prediction of the GTVH. Similar factors may affect a rating of "thematic affinity."

If it is possible to extrapolate from folk-taxonomies of jokes, the classificatory schemata of folk-taxonomists are limited to three levels: SI, TA, and NS. The most common is TA grouping: thus we have lawyer jokes, blonde jokes, Clinton jokes, Polish jokes, Italian jokes, etc. There are SI groupings, such as light bulb jokes, bar jokes, computer jokes, and also, but more or less marginally, NS groupings: knock-knock jokes, "What do you get when you cross an X and a Y?" jokes, limericks, etc. There seem to be no examples of jokes classified by SO or (worse) LM by non-specialists. The obvious explanation being that these levels are too abstract to be accessible to non-trained taxonomists. Conversely, one does not find joke taxonomies using LA, because presumably this is too obvious a criterion, which moreover would not distinguish interesting classes of jokes.

In conclusion, let me add an observation concerning the reason why speakers would choose to cluster thematically similar jokes together. After all, since they are engaging in a violation of the Cooperative Principle (Grice 1989), why aren't speakers violating the maxim of relevance as well, by choosing unrelated jokes?[5] My suggestion is that speakers use thematic similarity to gain a certain degree of "justification" or "local logic" (Ziv 1984) for their jokes (i.e., of resolution of the incongruity, cf. Forabosco 1992: 59, Attardo 1997). By being topically relevant, jokes "have a point" which topically irrelevant ones lack. The issue clearly deserves further discussion, see Attardo (in preparation b) and Nelms *et al.* (2000) on the Least Disruption Principle, which presents a broad pragmatic theory which encompasses this issue.

4.2 Joke cycles

We turn now, appropriately enough since we are building up from them, with the consideration of jokes, but no longer seen in isolation or compared to other jokes individually (as the concept of joke similarity in the GTVH implies) but as part of large clusters of mutually related texts. The main purposes of this section are to present the notion of joke cycle, and to sketch the relationships among the texts involved in a joke cycle.

4.2.1 Definition of Joke Cycle

The notion of joke cycle originates in folklore studies. At a basic (and intuitive) level a joke cycle is a set of jokes that are related. The prevalent relationship seems to be that of thematic links between the jokes, often mirrored in the folk taxonomies of jokes reviewed in section (4.1.3) above. While the subject matter of the jokes is clearly important, the GTVH has argued that this is not the only link among the jokes, and moreover that it is not the most important link among the jokes.

The Jokes in Relation to other Text-Types

Jokes have some peculiar features that they share with a few other types of texts. To begin with they are widely circulated, whereas the vast majority of texts is either produced for one one one exchanges (letters, or conversations, etc.) or for small

---

[5]Note that there are two levels of cooperation (or lack thereof): one within the jokes and the second in the larger conversation/narrative, where the thematic affinity principle holds.

audiences (small groups, etc.). Canned jokes (conversational jokes do not give rise to cycles) are clearly meant for a vast and generalized audience. In this, they are similar to novels and other works produced for mass consumption.

In their circulation, trace of the original author is almost always lost, even if several jokes circulate with spurious attributions. In this respect jokes are the same as urban legends, folk songs, fairy tales, etc. Most significantly, jokes circulate in numberless variants, i.e., the same joke is presented in different wordings, etc.

4.2.2 A little history

The "original" light bulb joke runs as follows:

(37) How many Polacks does it take to screw in a light bulb? Five—one to hold the bulb and four to turn the ceiling (chair). (Dundes 1987: 143)

Clements (1973: 22) reports 28 versions of this joke in the Indiana University Folklore Archives, prior to 1969. By 1978-79 the light bulb joke cycle "had swept the country" (Dundes 1987: 144). The collections of light bulb jokes currently available add up to more than a thousand of variants, targeting hundreds of groups and individuals (e.g., Guntheroth 1990 and Marcush 1996).

Thus, from the available historical evidence, it appears that light bulb jokes originated as an ethnic slur, in the "canonical" form shown above (37), where the implied insult is stupidity. Soon a large number of jokes emerged where the charge of stupidity, essential in the original "light bulb joke," had been dropped, and instead the way in which given groups performed the action of "light bulb screwing" was used to point out the peculiarities of the targeted group (Kerman 1980).

4.2.3 Two generations of jokes

These "second generation" jokes (*para-jokes*) are based on an implicit intertextual[6] reference (defined below) to the original light bulb joke, since otherwise the frame "joke" would not be established, and the texts would simply be absurd. It should be noted that the absurdity of the text when the intertextual reference is missed can be read as humorous, thus complicating the analyst's task. It is however clear, at least theoretically, that the hearer would be laughing at a different joke if he/she does not understand the intertextual reference (see below).

A "third generation" of jokes emerged in which the teller fails to deliver a light bulb joke, and in fact delivers a joke based on the fact that the hearer was expecting a joke and does not receive one. Or, to put it in Lefort's words: "the incongruity is that there is no incongruity in this [...] type of joke" (1992: 154). This is known as a second degree joke, or meta-joke[7].

---

[6] On intertextuality in humor, see Norrick (1989).

[7] Cf. Attardo (1988: 359-361), Lefort (1992: 153-154, 1999); a definitive treatment of metahumor is in preparation, Attardo (forthcoming a).

4.2. JOKE CYCLES

A definition of intertextuality

I should begin this attempt at a definition of intertextuality by noting that the concept is fairly controversial, and there is disagreement on the boundaries of the phenomenon. In any case, a reasonable definition could be the following:

> a text (T_i) will be said to have an intertextual relation to another text (T_j) when the processing of T_i would be incomplete without a reference to T_j.

The nature of this "incompleteness" is essentially open, but it may involve reference to any of the elements that constitute a text (its meaning, its formal organization, such as word choice, syntactic structure, the circumstances of its production, etc.). The most common forms of intertextuality are the quotation, in which T_i includes a fragment of T_j in its body, the paraphrase, in which T_i states the same contents of T_j (or a fragment thereof) in different surface structure,[8] and the parody, in which, while reference is made to the formal organization of T_j, T_i more or less subtly pokes fun at T_j by changing the contents of the text. [9]

Reconstructing the Joke Frame

The basic problem of the intertextual relationships of joke cycles is to determine that the joke frame has been activated, or in other words, that a given text is, say, a light bulb joke (henceforth, LBJ [10]) or a sorority joke. To do so we will examine two jokes.

(38) "How many Californians does it take to screw in a light bulb?" "Ten. One to screw it in and nine others to share the experience."

Compare the text above (where the joke frame is established) with the following one where it is not:

(39) *"How many Californians does it take to make toast?" "Ten. One to make it in and nine others to share the experience."[11]

(39) fails to activate any known script for a genre of jokes, and hence the hearer is faced with the problem of deciding whether (39) is a joke or not, whereas (38) successfully activates the intertextual script for LBJ and hence the hearer is certain that the text is a joke.

---

[8] Using the GTVH's terminology, with a different LA KR.

[9] It should be noted that originally, as is apparent in the etymology of the word *parody* (para-odon) no element of ridiculing was present in the idea of parody, and in fact some literary devices can be seen as non-ridiculing parodies (for example, Joyce's mapping of *Ulysses* on the *Odyssey*).

[10] I apologize for the presidential acronym, but it is unlikely that any confusion will result from the coincidence.

[11] I indicate with * the pragmatic infelicity of the text.

Naturally, given a sufficiently intelligent hearer, he/she will be able to process (39) and identify a script opposition between the triviality of the activity of making toast and the fact that one would want to invite nine people over to witness the event. If the hearer has available the humorous script that Californians are especially gregarious, then he/she will be able to decode the allusion to the script, and will draw the required inferences (Californians are acting according to stereotype) and draw some humorous pleasure from the facts.

In fact, even someone who has never heard a LBJ, and is faced with (38) may successfully decode the text, identifying the script opposition. However, he/she will be missing the intertextual reference to why the teller is specifically choosing light bulb changing and not, say, making toast or washing one's teeth. In other words, even assuming that the hearer successfully processes (39) as a joke, he/she will appreciate it as an isolated joke, whereas (38) will be appreciated as an instance of the LBJ genre. Incidentally, let me point out that this is not an entirely hypothetical discussion. One of my students claimed to have never heard the "original" LBJ, and yet was able to appreciate a LBJ similar to (38).

This last consideration opens the way to a question: what is the status of the primacy of the "original" LBJ? Clearly, no actual psychological primacy is likely to be the case, as the above anecdote shows. It may be that the case recorded is not unique and perhaps many speakers who are familiar with many LBJs have never heard the "original" LBJ. Historical primacy seems to be confirmed by the available folkloric sources. But from a linguistic point of view, and from the point of view of intertextuality, it is not obvious where the primacy lies.

Clearly, from the speaker's point of view, it is impossible to produce a LBJ without having ever been exposed to either the original LBJ or some examples of the second generation of LBJs. Chances of randomly recreating the combination of KRs that make up a LBJ are negligible. Thus, we can safely assume that LBJs assume previous knowledge of the joke frame on the part of the speaker. From the hearer's point of view, on the other hand, as we have seen, no previous knowledge is required, but that does not exclude knowledge of the LBJ frame, which is achieved inferentially. In other words, the hearer may well have been unaware of the existence of LBJs, but after hearing one he/she becomes aware of the existence of one such joke, which works in this case as an isolated joke, and not as a joke instantiation participating in a joke cycle.

The hearer must recognize that the joke is a light bulb joke, and not another type of joke. This is very important, because the light bulb joke carries a set of connotations (see above). The GTVH can be of help in the explication of this aspect of the process. Let us begin by giving an informal GTVH analysis of the canonical light bulb joke, summed up in table (4.1). The SO is SMART/DUMB which can be abstracted into the high-level SO NORMAL/ABNORMAL. This joke has been used as the canonical example of the LM "figure/ground reversal," so there's little doubt about that. The SI is obviously that of "light bulb changing," and the targeted group

4.2. JOKE CYCLES

are obviously Poles. The NS is a very common formula, the "question and answer," while the LA units are the various morphemes used in the sentences of the text, its synatx, etc.

- SCRIPT OPPOSITION: "normal/abnormal; smart/dumb"
- LOGICAL MECHANISM: "figure/ground reversal"
- SITUATION: "changing a light bulb"
- TARGET: "Poles"
- NARRATIVE STRATEGY: "question and answer"
- LANGUAGE: "How", "many," etc.

Table 4.1: *The Canonical LBJ in the GTVH*

Recall that jokes differing by higher level KRs, are perceived as more different than jokes differing in lower level KRs (see Ruch et al. 1993) in the hierarchical organization of the GTVH, already presented in table (1.2), also reproduced for the reader's convenience in table (4.2).

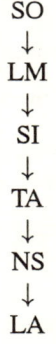

Table 4.2: *Hierarchical Organization of the KRs (= Table 1.2).*

The light bulb joke cycle is identified by SI and NS:

- SI: screwing in a light bulb (with a few variants: such as, changing a light bulb)

- NS: Question and Answer.

All the other KRs may vary.

The following are intertextual clues to the light bulb joke frame:

- LA: the wording of the question is essentially set. The reply to the question is also fairly set "[number]. [number] to [action] and [number] to [action]."

- NS: the organization of the text is a question and answer.

- SI: all light bulb jokes involve screwing in a light bulb.

Inferential processing

Given this information, we are now in the position to outline a schematic summary of the inferential processing for a second generation joke (para-joke):

1. Process the text "How many..."

2. Identify "light bulb joke" frame; LA, NS, SI (= intertext). Among the inferences activated by the intertextual acknowledgement of the light bulb joke frame are:

    - TA will behave stereotypically;
    - TA will approach SI in an abnormal way (this is required to get a SO);
    - the number of TA persons required by SI will be greater than one, or will involve some ulterior specification (e.g., their roles).
    - TA is not Poles and the stereotype will not be stupidity (or not necessarily).

3. Process answer (second part of the text);

4. Identify "stereotypical" trait of the TA in the behavior described;

5. Confirm internalized script about TA in unexpected manner;

6. Perceive humor.

4.2. JOKE CYCLES

- SCRIPT OPPOSITION: normal/abnormal; not limited to smart/dumb
- LOGICAL MECHANISM: may vary, but connected to stereotypical trait in TA
- SITUATION: screwing in a light bulb
- TARGET: free variation
- NARRATIVE STRATEGY: Question and Answer
- LANGUAGE: free variation

Table 4.3: *Para-Jokes in the GTVH*

Inferential Processing of Meta-jokes

The previous discussion is based on the second generation of LBJs, roughly definable as parodies of the original LBJ. With the third generation of jokes the situation is different. Again, speakers must be aware of the existence of the LBJ frame, but in this case hearers must be aware of it too, otherwise the joke is impossible to understand.

The inferential processing for a third generation joke (meta)will look like something along the following lines:

1. Process text "How many..."
2. Identify "light bulb joke" frame (LA, NS, SI). Trigger the same inferences as second-generation joke;
3. Process answer (second part of the text);
4. Fail to locate expected development of the frame;
5. Reinterpret situation as intentional violation of the LBJ narrative frame;
6. Identify "stereotypical" trait of the TA in the way the violation is presented;
7. Perceive humor.

Addendum: LBJs examples

The following examples have been collected from Internet postings, and are used as examples of the intertextual mechanisms present in the light bulb joke cycle. The

- SCRIPT OPPOSITION: LBJ/no LBJ
- LOGICAL MECHANISM: may vary, but connected to stereotypical trait in TA
- SITUATION: free variation
- TARGET[indexTA: free variation
- NARRATIVE STRATEGY: breech of the LBJ narrative frame, typically, but not necessarily, by introducing the first half of the adjacency pair question/answer
- LANGUAGE: free variation

Table 4.4: *Meta-Jokes in the GTVH*

author does not share, endorse, or condone any of the stereotypes portrayed in the texts.

The following abbreviations are used:

- Meta = meta-jokes;
- Para = intertextual parodies;
- NFB = narrative frame breach.

where NFB stands for the breach of expectation set up by the production of the beginning of a sequence that sets up a given narrative (e.g., an adjacency pair "request-denial" introducing a joke).

1. How many Feminists does it take to screw in a light bulb?
    (a) That's not funny!!! [Meta; NFB; cf. 2]
    (b) Two. One to change the bulb and one to write about how it feels. [Para]
    (c) Three. One to screw it in and two to talk about the sexual implications. [Para]
    (d) Four. One to change it, and three to write about how the bulb is exploiting the socket. [Para]
    (e) Three. One to change the bulb, and two to secretly wish they were the socket. [Para]
    (f) Two. One to screw in the light bulb and one to kick the balls off any man trying to help the first one. [Para]
2. How many Radcliffe girls does it take to screw in a light bulb?
    It's "Women", and it's not funny! [Meta; NFB; cf. 1a]

4.2. JOKE CYCLES

3. How many lawyers does it take to screw in a light bulb?
    (a) How many can you afford? [Meta; NFB; cf. 4]
    (b) Fifty four. Eight to argue, one to get a continuance, one to object, one to demur, two to research precedents, one to dictate a letter, one to stipulate, five to turn in their time cards, one to depose, one to write interrogatories, two to settle, one to order a secretary to change the bulb, and twenty-eight to bill for professional services. [Para]
    (c) You won't find a lawyer who can screw in a light bulb. Now, if you're looking for a lawyer to screw a light bulb ... [Meta, LA is pertinent (pun)]
4. How many accountants does it take to screw in a light bulb?
   What kind of answer did you have in mind?[Meta; NFB; cf. 3a]
5. How many jerks who ask stupid questions does it take to change a light bulb?
   Change it to what? [Meta; NFB]
6. How many hackers does it take to screw in a light bulb?
   Huh? You mean it's dark in here? [Meta; NFB]
7. Do you know how many musicians it takes to screw in a light bulb?
   No, big daddy, but hum a few bars and I'll fake it. [Meta, LA is pertinent (pun)]
8. How many New Yorkers does it take to screw in a light bulb?
    (a) None of your damn business![Meta; NFB; cf. 10]
    (b) Five. One to change the bulb and four to protect him from muggers. [Para]
    (c) 201. One to put it in and 200 to watch it happen without trying to stop it. [Para]
    (d) "Fifty." "50?" "Yeah, 50; it's in the contract." [Para]
9. How many New Jersey residents does it take to change a light bulb?
    (a) Leave us alone – we take enough s**t as it is. [Meta; NFB]
    (b) Three. One to change the light bulb, one to be a witness, and the third to shoot the witness. [Para]
10. How many Teamsters does it take to screw in a light bulb?
    TWELVE!! YA GOT A PROBLEM WITH THAT??[Meta; NFB; cf. 8a]
11. How many surrealists does it take to screw in a light bulb?
    (a) Two. One to hold the giraffe, and the other to fill the bathtub with brightly colored machine tools. [Para]
    (b) Fish! [Meta; NFB]
12. How many thought police does it take to screw in a light bulb?
    None. There never *was* any light bulb. [Meta; NFB]
13. How many board meetings does it take to get a light bulb changed?
    "This topic was resumed from last week's discussion, but is incomplete pending resolution of some action items. It will be continued next week. Meanwhile..." [Meta; NFB]
14. One.
    How many psychics does it take to screw in a light bulb? [Meta; NFB, Q& A frame for "light bulb joke" violated]

15. How many amnesiacs does it take to change a light bulb?
    Uhh, I forget. [Meta; NFB]

16. How many Engineers does it take to screw in a light bulb? One. [Meta; frame for "light bulb joke" violated; cf. 17]

17. How many dull people does it take to change a light bulb?
    One.[Meta; frame for "light bulb joke" violated; cf. 16]

4.2.4 Recapitulation

From the discussion on joke cycles we can define a joke cycle as a macro text consisting of a set of jokes connected by three types of intertextual links:

1. similarities in any of the KRs (with the proviso that only TA, SI, NS links are psychologically realistic)

2. intertextual links (parajokes)

3. a special subclass of intertextual links which subverts the expectations of the genre (metajokes).

As formulated, the SSTH could handle some of these relationships, with the use of allusive material (Raskin 1985: 46, 136-139), since intertextuality is merely allusion to other texts; however, I believe that the treatment of joke cycles we have just reviewed has several aspects to recommend it over one built exclusively within the SSTH's purview, and primarily that of explicitness.

4.3 Conclusion

This chapter was dedicated to the proposition that the distinction between jokes and "longer humorous texts" is not a clear cut phenomenon and that there are plenty of intermediate structures. We have addressed several aspects of humorous phenomena which go beyond canned/situational jokes in one aspect or another, without straying too far from that genre. We are now ready to move on to the discussion of longer texts proper.

Chapter 5

A Theory of Humorous Texts

This chapter develops more systematically the theory outlined in section (1.5).

5.1 Method of analysis

The method of analysis consists in locating, via standard semantic analysis (as in the SSTH or the GTVH), all the humorous elements (a.k.a., lines) of a text. These are then mapped on a vector, which represents the linear nature of the text itself (i.e., the fact that it components occur in a given linear order, be it at the level of phonemes or morphemes and sentences). Finally, relationships between lines are highlighted and those lines which show similarities are grouped in strands and stacks.

The vector is segmented in its constituent narratives[1] (see section 5.2 below) and their hierarchical status is established. The position of the various humorous elements of the text in relation to the narratives on the vector is then determined and on this basis we distinguish, along the lines of Attardo (1998), two types of humorous events in narratives: jab and punch lines.

The configurations of lines and the nature of the strands and/or stacks can be then analyzed to reveal aspects of the humorous element of the text (and in some cases, of the text itself).

5.2 Narratives

Before setting out on the detailed discussion of the method of analysis it is best to go beyond the intuitive meaning of narrative and provide some theoretical definition of

---

[1] We will ignore, for the time being, the issues posed by non-narrative texts. The problem of segmentation exists in non-narrative texts as well. In fact, non-narrative (e.g., dramatic, under certain definitions.) texts behave surprisingly like narrative texts in many respects, e.g., they may introduce embedded narratives (told by a character), etc.

the term. Let us begin by trying to make more explicit the definition of "narrative" which can be taken to be

1. a text;

2. relating a story; we distinguish, following the Russian formalists between the "actual" events and the order of their presentation; the original terms are *fabula* and *szuzjet*, we choose the easier pair fabula/plot.

3. told by a narrator; we distinguish, following many (but by no means all) narratologists, between two levels of narrators: an actual narrator (explicit or implicit) and an implied narrator (necessarily implicit). Neither is the actual author. The narrator is a character in the story, which may or may not explicitly "say" anything. Its presence is axiomatically necessary for a text to be a narrative (it has to be *narrated*). The implied narrator is much more elusive and some (e.g., Toolan 1988: 78) have taken this as a sign of uselessness of the notion. On the contrary, research in humor, shows that the postulation of a second level of narrator who is "making fun" of the first level narrator is necessary (LASC, HRCI, TRAN)

4. with realistic illusion; i.e., the TW of the narrative must not contain events or presuppose anything that is not compatible with either the representation the speaker and the hearer have of the world they live in (realism) or must be consistent with a possible world assumed by the text as "reality." Thus, if I assume that there exists an individual named Sherlock Holmes, who lives on 221b Baker Street, then, as long as the narrator sticks to events compatible with the above, the realistic illusion is maintained. See also section 3.3.

5. Finally, narratives are recursive, i.e., any character in a narrative (who is able to do so in the TW) may initiate another narrative embedded in it.

Micro- and Macro-narratives

A very useful concept in narratology and hence in the analysis of humorous texts is that of "minimal[2] story or narrative." I have thus introduced the concept of "micronarrative." A micronarrative is the simplest possible narrative, in the sense that it consists of one action/event. An event is a "change of state" (Chatman 1978: 44). An event may be brought about by an agent or by other forces (e.g., nature). Events may or may not be significant from the point of view of the fabula. (Ibid.)

A macronarrative is defined as any combination of micronarratives. It is tempting, but misleading (see below) to consider all jokes as instances of micronarratives.

---

[2]Cf. Bremond (1973), Prince (1973) "minimal story," Labov (1972) "minimal narrative."

5.2. NARRATIVES

From the (pre-)definition of jab and punch line (cf. 5.3 for a full discussion), it follows that identifying the various narratives potentially present within a text becomes a central issue. The key to that problems lies in the *segmentation* of the text itself.

Segmentation

The issue can be framed as follows: if the defining feature of a punch line is that it occurs at the end of the narrative,[3] then identifying the end of a narrative is a preliminary condition for determining which of a pool of candidates for punch line qualifies as such. Now, whereas identifying the end of a short simplex narrative is trivial, larger narratives are obviously composed of numerous simpler narratives, arranged in a vector. In turn these simpler narratives may be analyzed as being composed of shorter simpler narratives, and so on, until one reaches the level of the simplex narrative again. Deciding when one narrative ends and the other(s) begins is however far from trivial.

From the analysis of CBTD, first and other texts afterwards, some, among the many possible, empirical techniques for the segmentation of the text vector emerged:

- explicit metatextual authorial cues (e.g., "end of act one," "Chapter 2," "Volume III," etc.)

- changes in setting

- exits (or entries) of major character

It should be noted that one cannot adopt a different strategy, namely finding narrative boundaries based on the presence of punch lines, since the difference between punch and jab lines is defined in terms of positions within the narrative.

Narratives (micro and macro), narratives of level$_n$, metanarratives

Furthermore, there presents itself the issue of multiple levels of embedding of narratives. As we saw, a character in a text may initiate a narrative within the narrative. More confusingly, any narrative may suddenly be revealed to have been uttered by an heretofore undisclosed narrator.

In order to handle this jumble of narratives, I introduce the concept of "level" of a narrative. Each narrative is said to occur at a given level$_n$. Narratives introduced *as narratives* within the (macro)narrative are said to occur at level$_{n-1}$, while narratives within which the narrative of level$_n$ is introduced as a narrative are said to occur at level$_{n+1}$. Any narrative occurring at level$_{m>n}$ is said to be a metanarrative in relation to the narrative in level$_n$.

---

[3] As stated before, I will not distinguish between narrative and non-narrative texts. The latter are segmented into episodes, or events. The issues remain the same.

We can now redefine[4] in terms of levels the concept of macronarrative, as follows: a macronarrative is a framing narrative which may incorporate at least one narrative of level$_{n-1}$. The macronarrative of level$_0$ is called the (main) storyline. It is usually the level at which the text begins and ends.

An example may clarify things. Within CBTD we may identify the main storyline (Chuckles dies, etc.) but there are other narratives introduced within the text. For example, one character delivers an impromptu speech.[5] The clearly "set aside" nature of the speech qualifies it for the narrative of level$_{-1}$ status. Within the speech the speaker quotes another character's (Chuckle) song. The song qualifies as level$_{-2}$ status.

A similarly complex situation arose from the analysis of Sexton's collection of poems (TRAN): the narrating voice of each poem was naturally taken to be the level$_0$ narrative, this however led us to attribute the framing prologue to level$_{+1}$ and the dedication to an imposing level$_{+2}$.

The same happens in Wilde's LASC and Allais' HRCI: the narrator says things that are so clearly not shared by the author that it becomes necessary to postulate an implied "metanarrator" who is "making fun of" (distancing him/herself from) the narrator, thus operating at level$_{+2}$.

Finally, let us introduce the concept of *excursus narrative* which is a narrative$_n$ which occurs within a narrative of the same level$_n$ but is not germane to the broader narrative (i.e., it does not develop the narrative). This is what is commonly known as "digression." An example can be found in HRCI, cf. section (7.5).

5.3 Lines and their Configurations

This section deals with the opposition between jab and punch lines and the various ways in which their configurations affect the texts.

5.3.1 Jab lines

The concept of *jab line* was introduced in Attardo (1996a,b) to distinguish between punch lines, which have been found (Attardo *et al.* 1994; Oring 1989) to occur virtually exclusively in a final position in jokes, from a type of humorous trigger which occurs in the body of a text. Jab lines differ from punch lines in that they may occur in any other position in the text. Semantically speaking they are identical objects. Their only difference lies in the textual position in which they occur and in their textual function.

Jab lines are humorous elements fully integrated in the narrative in which they appear (i.e., they do not disrupt the flow of the narrative, because they either are

---

[4]This definition is not opposed to the first definition in terms of complex narrative, it is rather complementary to it.

[5]See section (5.4.5) below for more detail.

5.3. LINES AND THEIR CONFIGURATIONS

indispensable to the development of the "plot" or of the text, or they are not antagonistic to it). The malfunction of Persky's machine which prevents Kugelmass from sending Emma Bovary back into her novel is humorous in and of itself but it is also the ultimate cause of Kugelmass' undoing (KUGE).[6] Hence it is an example of indispensable jab line. Another such example is Lord Savile, who takes the cheiromantist's reading so seriously as to commit murder because of it (LASC).

Naturally, not all jab lines are narrative elements. In the case of register humor, the presence of several markers of, say, a highly formal register in the context of a trivial situation, or of a situation which is usually associated with informal registers, will work as jab lines, since obviously they do not interrupt the narrative flow. These markers (for an analyzed example, from CAND , see 6.2.5) are non-essential non-antagonistic jab lines.

5.3.2 Punch lines

There is a vast literature on punch lines (see Attardo 1994) which deals primarily with their semantic nature (e.g., Raskin 1985). However, in this context, we will not concern ourselves with the semantic nature of punch lines, but rather focus on their textual function.

From a textual point of view, punch lines act as disrupting elements. The isotopy-disjunction model (Attardo *et al.* 1994, Attardo 1994: ch. 2) well represents this aspects of the punch line: while the setup part of the text establishes a given script, the occurrence of a disjunctor (punch line) forces the reader to switch to a second script. From this basic structural fact, comes the disruptive nature of punch lines: by forcing the hearer/reader to backtrack and reinterpret the text, or by forcing him/her to produce a new and incompatible (locally opposite) interpretation of the text, the punch line cannot be integrated in the narrative it disrupts (which is the one that has set up the first script). In essence, the very concept of incongruity tells us that the second script is non-congruous with the first one, and hence that the punch line, which brings the second, non-congruous script about, cannot be congruous with the script set up by/in the narrative.

5.3.3 Strands

A strand was defined in Attardo (1996) as a (non-necessarily contiguous) sequence of (punch or jab) lines formally or thematically linked. It should be noted that strands may be established textually or inter-textually. In the case of textually established strands, three or more instances of related lines occur in a given text. Intertextual strands may also connect lines that occur in different texts.

---

[6]Woody Allen (Allen Stewart Konigsberg, b. 1935) is a world-famous director, humorous writer and performer. Some discussion of KUGE's humor can be found in Chlopicki (1997); see also Champion (1992).

Let us clarify the requirement that at least three instances of a line occur before a strand is determined to have occurred. The repetition of three is a well known pattern in jokes (cf. Attardo 1994: 304) since it is the lowest number of occurrence of a given item that establishes a series. Note how two occurrences could be a coincidence. With three occurrences this possibility diminishes greatly. Hence the requirement that a strand involve the occurrence of at least three related lines. As we saw, however, there are two exceptions to this rule: hapax-bridges (5.3.7) and intertextual jokes (below).

Substrands

Within strands we occasionally distinguish sub-strands, i.e., a subset of the lines that constitute a strand which share some combination of features which is not common to the strand at large. Consider the following example of strand, consisting of seven lines, with the following features (ordered vertically under each line):

1	2	3	4	5	6	7
a	a	a		a	a	a
b	b	b	b	b	b	b
c	c	c	c	c	c	c
d	d				d	d
e	e		e			e

Given this distribution, we have a strand based on features b and c common to lines 1-7. However, we also have a substrand $a - d - e$ common to lines 1, 2, and 7.

Examples of substrands can be found in LASC (with the peculiar "everyday objects turned into bombs" substrand cf. chapter 8, note 254), and HRCI (the "phallic" substrand within the "sexual exuberance" strand, cf. section 7.5.1).

Central Strands and Peripheral Strands

A *central* strand is a strand that is central to a given text (in a broad sense, including for example all the episodes of a sitcom). The notion of "centrality" is necessarily fuzzy but we may define it as one or more strands which tend to occur throughout a significant (say, greater than 75% of the text) part of the text. Our cases studies have found two instances of central strands: two script oppositions in TRAN and several in LASC: for example Lord Arthur Savile is the target of 89 out of 253 punch/jab lines. A second TA strand for lady Windermere (23 occurrences) occurs throught the text.

Because of the definition of central strand as a statistically significant degree of occurrence, it follows that a shortish text cannot be really said to have central strands, as most strands would qualify. Conversely, a peripheral strand is a strand which occurs only in one (or few) instance(s) in the text. For example, within LASC we find

5.3. LINES AND THEIR CONFIGURATIONS

several peripheral strands such as the "stereotypical grumbling" strand which occurs seven times in the text (17, 89, 201, 214, 221, 222, and 223), the "liberty strand" and the "fixation with clothing strand" which occur only in a letter by Jane (an embedded narrative). Similarly, a peripheral strand of jab lines that target the Dean of Chichester occurs only six times, the first five within Jane's letter, and the last one, in the wedding scene. This is a general pattern in LASC: minor characters may have a strand that sees them as targets associated with them. This limits the occurrence of that strand to their presence in the text: thus there are fourteen occurrences of jabs that target Lady Clementina, most of which cluster in the episode of Lord Savile's visit to her. Similarly, Herr Winckelkopf has eleven jabs targeting him, concentrated in Lord Savile's visit to him.

Chlopicki (1987) introduced the idea of "shadow opposition" i.e., an opposition between scripts underlying an entire text. The idea of ranking strands as more or less central comes from the idea of shadow opposition, although it departs from it in several ways. For example, the present proposal deals with strands (humorous, by definition, and not limited to SOs), whereas Chlopicki's shadow oppositions are script oppositions, exclusively.

5.3.4 Repetition

It becomes necessary to address the issue of repetition. Repetition has not attracted a lot of attention in the literature on jokes, although there are some examples of uses of repetition within canned jokes, reviewed by Norrick (1993a):

- the 1, 2, 3 formula (Norrick 1993a: 386-387 "repetition with variation")

- repetition routines used by children to embarrass the speaker (Norrick 1993a: 385-386)

- knock-knock jokes (Norrick 1993a: 388)

- intertextuality (Norrick 1993a: 389; 1989)

- alliteration (Attardo 1994: 139)

Repetition in spontaneous conversational joking is also documented where it primarily takes the form of the mention of a previous speaker's words (e.g., for ironical or punning purposes; cf. Norrick 1993a for discussion and examples). However, the presence of repetition *inside* the jokes should not lead us to forget that it has been repeatedly noted that the repetition of jokes diminishes their humorous effect. See Attardo (1994: 289-290) on the connection between the implicit aspects of text and surprise in jokes.

Conversely, repetition is very significant in longer texts, for example, repetition is a well known feature of comedy: "repetition may be the single most important mechanism in comedy" (Charney 1978: 82) (and a big headache for theories based on surprise, naturally). Consider for instance the catch phrases of many sitcoms, or the repetitions of narrative motifs in Feydeau's comedy, or the repetition of phallic images in Allais (Attardo 1997b; cf. 7.5). Repetition can be accompanied by slight variation, thus introducing an element of novelty as well as the pleasure of virtuoso variation. For example, Wilde introduces in LASC the central strand "murder as duty" with fifteen istances of jab lines in a small stretch of text of 372 words and manages to introduce nine different variants of the basic SO MURDER/DUTY (these are listed in note 104 of ch. 8).

It seems that pure repetition of a given unit can establish a strand. "Strand" was defined above as a bundle of punch and/or jab lines. "Unit" should here be construed broadly as ranging from semantic features to broad motifs and even to large cultural scripts.

It should be noted that there is no need to differentiate between the "normal" repetition of semantic features found across the board in language (e.g., agreement, anaphora, subcategorization, cohesion, etc.) and repetition for humorous purposes: both are repetition of features and/or larger linguistic units, with the only difference that repetition for humorous purposes repeats units that are (or have been at some point of the text) involved in a jab line (or, less frequently, a punch line).[7]

5.3.5 Stacks

Stacks are groups of strands that are thematically or formally related. They can be thought of as strands of strands occurring in different macronarratives (which can be seen as belonging together on internal or external causes, e.g., authorship, thematic similarity, chronological vicinity, etc.) Thus far they have been postulated (Wilson 1997) to account for obvious correlations between strands within different humorous commercials and further exemplified in Attardo (1998).

Wilson (1997) analyzes the popular ESPN commercials aired in 1996. More than 40 commercials are analyzed and three stacks are postulated to account for the similarities among strands. These are short narratives, slightly more complex than jokes. The idea of a level above the strand implies that we consider a given corpus of texts (the forty plus commercials in Wilson 1997, for example) as one higher level text. I take the (fairly common) stand that a set of texts having some obvious common features (e.g., having been authored by the same individual, having the same principal characters, etc.) make up a single large "text." For example, the complete episodes of *Seinfeld* or all the *Jeeves* stories by Wodehouse make up a single very large text.

---

[7]So, in this specific sense, a treatment of strands in terms of isotopies (cf. Attardo 1994 for a review and critique of this concept) is ruled out, unless one were willing to alter the definition of isotopy, by making it selective, i.e., capable of discriminating whether, for example, the word *genius* is used in a strand, or not, cf. LASC jabs 11 and 108 where, while the word genius does indeed occur (thus guaranteeing the activation of the script GENIUS), no strand is instantiated because the SO is different and because the three lines requirement for strand activation is not met.

5.3. LINES AND THEIR CONFIGURATIONS

Let us consider an example: in the sitcom *Cheers*, Norm, a popular patron of the eponymous bar, utters a witty repartee to the bartender's greeting upon each of his entrances in the bar. These have been called by fans "Normisms." Suppose that in a given episode Norm utters two or three Normisms. This constitutes a strand (identity of utterer, similar topic—Norm's desire and love for beer—etc.). We can then look at the corpus of all *Cheers* episodes and collect all strands of Normisms, occurring in the various episodes. This set of strands constitutes a stack. Note that this picture is slightly complicated by intertextual jokes (see below), which allow the occurrence of one-instance strands.

5.3.6 Intertextual jokes

Intertextual jokes rely on allusions that go outside of the text being considered and involve references to other texts. An example of intertextual joke will be found in CBTD, section 7.1, line XI. Allusion, parody, and other forms such as travesty are all well known comedic formulae relying on intertextuality (see section 4.2.3).

Besides explicit reliance on contextual information, intertextual jokes are not different semantically or otherwise from non-intertextual jokes. The mechanisms involved are essentially the same. Intertextuality *per se* is not humorous at all, witness citation, the quintessential intertextual mechanism.

As mentioned above, the occurrence of intertextual humor allows one to create strands which consist of only one instance of a line. This is so because the other instances are "virtually" present in virtue of the intertextual allusion.

5.3.7 Bridges and Combs

We introduce a distinction within the category of strand. The lines of a strand may occur in significant spatial patterns. So far, two such patterns have been described: bridges and combs. Others may emerge with further research.

In and of themselves bridges and combs do not matter much. What matters is that there are patterns that we see repeated: in some cases lines will occur very close to one another; this reinforces the humor by repetition. In other cases, lines that are obviously related occur very far apart, where they clearly cannot be recalled by short term memory. This is the intuition that the distinction bridge/comb tries to cover.

Combs

We can thus define a comb as a type of strand which shows the occurrence of more than 3 lines (jab or punch) within a narrow space. The exact definition of what counts as "narrow" space is an empirical matter, although I venture to speculate that this is an inherently fuzzy category. Operatively, we can venture a rough estimate of less than 10 % of the overall length of the text.

At this point in the research, there are virtually no data available on cross-text comparisons of placements of combs and/or bridges in text. Combs, by their very nature, tend to create areas of the text where there is a concentration of humor.

Bridges

A bridge is a type of strand in which two groups of lines (most commonly jab lines) occur at a considerable distance from one another. An hapax-bridge is a bridge which consists of two lines which are otherwise unrelated to any other line (are not part of a strand). Hapax-bridges violate the rule which requires strands to consist of three or more elements, probably dues to their high saliency in the text.

Bridges, by their nature, tend to conform to the "bathtub" placement (see below, section 5.4.5) of lines in humorous texts, as discussed in Attardo (1998). Combs, on the contrary, do not, as by definition they consist of closely occurring repeated lines. No data are available about cross-text comparison of bridge placement.

5.4 A typology of line position

The following sections will attempt a preliminary taxonomy of line positions in a humorous text. I would like particularly to stress the preliminary nature of the taxonomy because it seems clear that as more texts are analyzed more configurations will emerge. The primary purpose of the present list is therefore more to exemplify the variety of combinations than to be in any way exhaustive.

5.4.1 No line

It may be useful to start this discussion by briefly recalling that serious, non-humorous narratives are taken by narratologists (e.g., Bremond 1973; Bal 1985: 19-23) to have the following structure:

1. setup
2. disruption of the equilibrium
3. restoration of the equilibrium

It is important to note that this structure is taken to underlie any narrative, including serious ones. This is significant because early research (Morin 1966; see Attardo 1994: 82-90 for discussion and references) in the narrative structure of jokes mistook this feature of all micronarratives for a significant feature of *humorous* narratives, as we recalled above.

The functions of serious text in an otherwise humorous text can be numerous:

- set up for jokes

5.4. A TYPOLOGY OF LINE POSITION

- development of the narrative

- serious relief

The function of the set up of jokes is quite significant: in order to have incongruity one has to have some background of expectations to violate. The set up fulfills this requirement. The development of the narrative may, in fact, be achieved through humorous means as well, so we are not dealing with a necessary and sufficient condition. Rather, it is a common tendency in humorous narratives to develop the narrative via serious indications of events, etc. and "add" the humorous events to this fundamentally serious storyline. For example, a typical Wodehouse novel may be given a totally unfunny summary. That corresponds to the amount of serious narrative development in the text.

Finally, we turn to the most interesting type of serious text in a humorous narrative, which I have dubbed *serious relief*. By serious relief (obviously calqued on "comic relief") I mean any stretch of text in an otherwise line-rich context that contains few or no jab lines. Segments of serious relief are often used for "morals" or to develop "depth" in the characters of the show. A prime example of serious relief can be found in a *Murphy Brown* episode, immediately following the dispute between former Vice-President Dan Quayle and the fictional character Murphy Brown.[8] At the end of the episode in which Murphy Brown dealt with being attacked by the VP for being a single mother, her character delivers a speech about diversity of family types which is devoid of any humorous effects and is in fact a deliberate serious response to the attack launched by Quayle.

Serious relief, without moral or character development purposes (and therefore perhaps suspicious), occurs in LASC at the end of ch. II, after jab 87, for a span of 638 words, and then at the beginning of ch. III, for another 362 words, for a total span of 1000 words (the figure is surely a coincidence).

5.4.2 Final punch line

A text may consist of a non-humorous narrative development which is closed by a punch line. In a sense, we can conceive as the typical joke-book jokes as representing this class of texts.

At this point it will be useful to introduce a way to notate these combinations. For the reader's convenience, the following table (5.4.2) sums up the notation conventions introduced in representing the vector of the text.

Schematically, therefore, a non-humorous narrative concluded by a punch line may be represented as:

$$[\mapsto - P \to]$$

---

[8] I will leave to post-modern theorists the fun of analyzing the issues involved in having a "real" political figure debate a fictional one.

-	non-humorous text (of any length)
→	end of narrative + material occurring after a punch line
J	jab line
P	punch line
[...]	beginning and end markers of a narrative
...	any occurrence of - and J
↦	the beginning of the text

The symbol "-" may be annotated with the duration in seconds of the performance, or the number of lines or words spanned, or other useful measurements.

Table 5.1: *Text Vector Notation*

We will refer to simple narratives concluded by a punch line as jokes. By simple we mean here both that a) there are no jab lines in the narrative, and b) their text consists of a simplex micronarrative. It should be noted that this definition is more restrictive than the normal, non-technical sense of the word joke, which incorporates texts which display jab lines (usually called elaborate or complex jokes) and texts that are slightly more complex than a micronarrative, for example because they consist of two micronarratives chained together. A possible conceptualization of this type of text is that the text is an extended joke, since the structure is similar to the basic joke, with the exception that the introduction is stretched out.

5.4.3 Episodic

A main storyline links several (independent) smaller narratives. Each of the narratives (including the main storyline) may include jab lines and/or end in a punch line. Examples of this kind of texts include picaresque novels, framed collections of stories (*1001 Nights, Decameron, Canterbury Tales*), etc. Peacham's MDMT is an example of episodic text analyzed in section (7.3). Consider now an illustrative example:

$$\mapsto ... [\mapsto \text{-P} \rightarrow] \text{-} [\mapsto \text{-J-J-P} \rightarrow] \rightarrow$$

In this case we see an hypothetical text consisting of a main storyline which links two narratives, one which is a joke, and the second which incorporates of two jab lines and ends in a punch line. Note that I am omitting the outermost square brackets for simplicity.

5.4.4 Mere sequence of jab lines with final punch line

This is more of a tendency that texts may have, rather than an actual type of text. It would consist of a narrativeless text which would consist only of a sequence of jokes. The jokes would be loosely strung together on formal or content basis, without any continuity from beginning to end of the chain. The last joke in the chain would be "promoted" to punch line status by its position. Some primitive stand up comedian act may have this structure (or lack thereof).

5.4.5 Bathtub placement

In psycholinguistics, the "bathtub effect" is the colorful term used to indicate that the beginning and the end of a word or sentence have a naturally salient status. We similarly label "bathtub placement" instances of embedded narratives or punch lines placed at the beginning or the end of a macronarrative.

Naturally, a punch line outside of an embedded narrative cannot subsist, which leaves us with three possibilities.

Initial position

$$\mapsto [\mapsto \text{-}P \to]\text{-}...\to$$

This consists of a joke that opens a narrative. It is current practice to have sitcoms on television be opened by "teasers": short humorous bits which may or may not be connected with the rest of the action.

Final position

$$\mapsto ...\text{-}P\to$$

Similarly, it is common practice to close sitcoms with a small joke, called the "tag," which often does not continue the action developed in the story, but acts rather as a comment on or as a parody of the story. In some cases, the producers include "bloopers," i.e., errors collected during taping which have been edited out of the show itself. An example of tag in a narrative context can be found in Allen's KUGE, i.e., Kugelmass' fate being chased by a Spanish irregular verb...

Pseudo-final position

The only difference between a final position and a pseudo-final position, is that the punch line occurs within the level_0 narrative in a final punch line, whereas it occurs within a $\text{level}_{<0}$ narrative in a pseudofinal punch line.

A good example of this technique occurs at the end of the first act of CBTD. The death of Chuckles has just been announced and Ted Baxter is ad libbing a tribute.

The speech is fairly long (about 200 words), with only one turn by one speaker (Ted), and it is clearly set apart from the rest of the text, so it is easy to classify it a micronarrative embedded within the storyline. The speech ends on a punch line (followed by an identifying tag, see Attardo et al. (1994)), which coincides with the end of the act (and hence of a non-debatable segmentation point). In a sense, we could say that the storyline (level$_0$ narrative) is "stealing" the embedded narrative's punch line.

$$\mapsto ... [\mapsto ... \text{-}P \rightarrow] \rightarrow$$

5.5 Humorous Plots

Last but not least, we finally come to the complex relationship between plot and humor. It may be useful to recall that narratology distinguishes the plot from the *fabula*. The *fabula* are the events narrated in the text in their chronological order, the *plot* are the events in the order they are presented in the text. Flashbacks, for example, present events that happened before a time T_0, *after* T_0. For our purposes, we seldom need to distinguish between the two (but see below).

An important point from our current perspective is that the development of the plot is stored in the storage area and is then accessible as a topic of humorous manipulation (metanarrative disruption functions only in the presence of an established script for a given genre/narrative mode). Significantly, the fabula is also constructed, on the basis of the plot and stored separately, as both have to be accessible.

A way to address the issue of the differences between jokes and other narratives would be to try to capture the difference between humor that belongs to the plot of the story and humor that is external to the plot. We will begin by considering those forms of plot that are humorous in and of themselves, incidentally, contra the claim that there are no such forms (2.2.3). We will review narratives that are structurally similar to jokes, metanarrative plots, plots with humorous fabulae, and finally serious fabulae (i.e., the absence of a humorous plot).

5.5.1 Narratives Structurally Similar to Jokes

I have referred to the first kind of text being analyzed (Attardo 1996a) as narratives that are structurally analogous to a joke (i.e., end in a punch line). The literature on humor has emphasized the importance of the punch line. However, not until recently (Oring 1989, 1992; Attardo et al. 1994) have there been claims that the position and nature of the punch line structurally determined the type of humorous text. Roughly, Oring's point is that a joke must end on a punch line. This theoretical claim has been confirmed by an empirical study (Attardo et al. 1994).[9]

---

[9]This should not be taken to mean that the final position of the punch line is the necessary and sufficient condition for a joke text to be such; the claim is the much weaker one that the final position of the

5.5. HUMOROUS PLOTS

Thus, if the defining characteristic of a text as a joke, is the position of the punch line,[10] it seems a viable hypothesis that there will be humorous texts not commonly classified as jokes that are nevertheless structurally homologous to a joke (i.e., they end in a punch line). An example would be a micronarrative within a macronarrative. We discussed this in further detail in (5.3).

The complementary claim is obviously that there will be a class of humorous texts that are structurally dissimilar from jokes, i.e., that do not end in a punch line.

An example is the short story *Feuille d'Album* by Katherine Mansfield[11] in which a painfully shy young artist falls in love with a young woman and in despair for an excuse to meet her, follows her while she's shopping. As she is about to return home, he runs up to her:

> Finally, she stopped on the landing, and took the key out of her purse. As she put it into the door he ran up and faced her.
>
> Blushing more crimson than ever, but looking at her severely he said, almost angrily: "Excuse me, Mademoiselle, you dropped this."
>
> And he handed her an egg. (227-228)

Note how the Mansfield story literally ends on the punch line. In this sense, it can be seen as an extremely elaborate joke with an overlong setup phase (ignoring Mansfield's artistry, of course).

Similalrly, Poe's TSTF (analyzed in Attardo 1994: 255-262) is a long setup which ends in the buffoonery and slapstick farce of the tarred-and-feathered guards subduing the lunatic asylum inmates who had taken over the asylum, while a band plays "Yankee Doodle" thus suggesting that the entire story is a parable of the democratic process in the US during Poe's time. We will ignore in this context the satirical, anti-American aspects of TSTF (see Attardo 1994: 261 and Van Doren Stern 1945: xxxv[12]). Instead, we will focus on the structure of the story. One of the main reasons to claim that TSTF was structurally similar to a joke (Attardo 1994: 255) was the "systematic witholding of information" within the text. A different way of putting this fairly obscure remark would be that the fabula and the plot must differ in specific

---

punch line discriminates among a class of humorous texts which share other features (e.g., brevity, Setup Incongruity Resolution arrangement, etc.).

[10] It should be noted that here "punch line" is taken as a technical term, i.e., in GTVH's terms, as consisting of a SO, LM, etc. unlike, for example, Wenzel's use of *pointe* which is more general.

[11] *Feuille d'Album* by Katherine Mansfield (1888-1923), from: *Bliss, and Other Stories* by Katherine Mansfield. New York: Alfred A. Knopf, 1920. pp. 218-227.

[12] This also explains the curious title, and the names "Tarr" and "Fethers." Evidently Poe's perception of this typically American custom was that it was somewhat barbaric, and hence his choice to characterize the behavior of insane people who have arrive by cunning and deception to a ruling position. In this sense Poe is comparing the ruling class of his time to a group of lunatics on the loose. Needless to say, Poe is also satirizing the treatment of insanity at his time, as well as Dickens (cf. Fisher 1973, and references therein). Even further, Poe is satirizing himself: Fisher (1973: 49; 1977: 138-142) argues convincingly that the introduction of the tale is rich in parallelisms with Poe's own *The Fall of the House of Usher*, to the point of "self-parody."

ways such that the surprising aspects of the "punch line" are not given away before the occurrence thereof (i.e., the end of the text).

In this sense, there is a class of texts which is similarly structured: the plot must accommodate the presence of a punch line at the end of the text (cf. *Feuille d'Album*). The nature of the difference between plot and fabula lies essentially in cancellation of either a) clues to the presence of a second macroscript which will be revealed to have been overlapping throughout (large parts of) the text, or b) clues to the presence of a resolution such that two opposed and otherwise non-overlapping macroscripts are in fact (at least partially) overlapping (cf. Wenzel's arrangement, section 2.2.2).

These examples show that there is a class of plots that share the structural features of jokes (i.e., they end on a punch line, in the technical sense we have seen).

5.5.2 Metanarrative Plots

There exists another class of plots that, while they may not match the structure of a joke as the examples above, involve such manipulations of the narrative conventions as to shatter them entirely. Consider for example, the ending of *Blazing Saddles*[13] in which the characters jump off the screen and ride off into "reality" (actually merely a $level_{n+1}$ narrative). Woody Allen's *Purple Rose of Cairo*[14], Maurizio Nichetti's *Ladri di saponette (The Icicle Thief)* [15] and many other movies brilliantly play with these crossings between $level_0$ and $level_1$ narratives. Nor is this technique a postmodern development or limited to the cinematic medium; let is suffice to quote possibly the greatest such virtuoso, Laurence Sterne, *Tristram Shandy*'s author (1759-67).

In all of these plots, let us call them *metanarrative plots*, the conventions of the narrative mode are violated for the purpose of humor to the point that the narrative development (plot/fabula) is hijacked by the humorous goal of the text. A significant issue is of course that this diversion of textual resources breaks the naturalistic/realistic convention of realist narrative, as Palmer noted (see section 2.2.3). We now consider two examples of metanarrative plots.

Spaceballs

One of my favorite examples of this narrative disruption is the superb self-referential scene in which the characters in *Spaceballs*[16] rent a video tape of *Spaceballs* and fast-forward through it up to the point in the plot in which the characters in *Spaceballs* rent a video tape of *Spaceballs* and then are astonished when, looking at the screen, they see themselves looking at the screen. The ensuing dialogue is worth quoting in full.

---

[13] Written and directed by Mel Brooks (1974).
[14] Written and directed by Woody Allen (1985).
[15] Written by Mauro Monti, directed by Maurizio Nichetti (1989).
[16] Written, directed, and produced by Mel Brooks (1987)

5.5. HUMOROUS PLOTS

SANDURZ Pardon me, sir. I have an idea. Corporal, get me the video cassette of Spaceballs-the Movie.

CORPORAL Yes, sir.

(...)

SANDURZ Try here. Stop.

The movie stops at the exact same thing that is actually happening now. HELMET looks at the camera, then he turns back to the monitor. SANDURZ looks at the camera when HELMET looks back at the monitor, then he looks back at the monitor. HELMET looks at the camera when SANDURZ looks back at the monitor. When HELMET turns back, he waves his hand. He turns back to the camera.

HELMET What the hell am I looking at? When does this happen in the movie?

SANDURZ Now. You're looking at now, sir. Everything that happens now, is happening now.

HELMET What happened to then?

SANDURZ We passed then.

HELMET When?

SANDURZ Just now. We're at now, now.

HELMET Go back to then.

SANDURZ When?

HELMET Now.

SANDURZ Now?

HELMET Now.

SANDURZ I can't.

HELMET Why?

SANDURZ We missed it.

HELMET When?

SANDURZ Just now.

HELMET When will then be now?

Un drame bien parisien

Another example, analyzed in detail in Eco (1979: 194-218), albeit not from a humorous point of view, is Alphonse Allais' story *Un drame bien parisien* which ends on the total destruction of the narrative conventions (the characters described at the end are not those in the story). Eco argues that the story is essentially "impossible" (i.e., that there exists no coherent reading thereof) and that it ends up being a metaphor for the act of reading itself.

> The (implicit) lesson of *Drame* is in fact coherently contradictory: Allais wants to tell us that not only *Drame* but any text is made of two components: the information provided by the author and that added by

the Model Reader, the latter being determined and oriented by the former. To prove this metatextual theorem Allais pushes the reader with informations that contradict the fabula, forcing him/her to cooperate in erecting a story that does not stay up by itself. The failure of *Drame* as fabula is the victory of *Drame* as meta-text. (Eco 1979: 196-197)

A different interpretation is provided by Corblin (1995). Corblin begins by summarizing Lacan's reading of the story, which boils down to taking the explicit statement in the text that the two characters are not who the readers (and the characters in the story) think they are, as metaphorical, i.e., that under the empire of desire the two characters are *someone else*. (1995: 216-218)

Corblin presents another interesting, if far fetched, analysis which claims to provide a possible reading of the story, by postulating that the two main characters coincidentally hit upon the same idea of exposing each other's jealousy by sending to one another an anonymous letter, claiming that they will be attending a masqued dance. Interestingly, he argues that the aesthetic pleasure of the text arises from the "illusion that parallel representations, necessarily disjoint, may coexist" (225) a definition reminiscent of the GTVH.

Metanarrative Disruption

Metanarative comments are passages of a narrative in which the narrator comments on, or otherwise interrupts, the flow of the narrative to speak about the narrative or its characters. Generally, metanarrative comments are fairly subtle, and consist of the choice of an adjective or a given verb (as in Manzoni's immortal line from the *Promessi sposi* "La sventurata rispose" which sums up in three words a life of sin[17]). In some instances, they may be quite obvious, as when the narrator addresses the audience directly. However, we are interested here in metanarrative disruption, i.e., cases in which the narrator's comments effectively "sabotage" the narrative. For example, the narrator in Wilde who says: "It was one of Lady Windermere's best nights" (LASC 12) when the cotext makes it clear that it is a pathetically bad party. Consider now the following passage, from T. L. Peacock's[18] Nightmare Abbey (NIAB):

(40) At the house of Mr Hilary, Scythrop first saw the beautiful Miss Emily Girouette. He fell in love; *which is nothing new*. He was favourably received; *which is nothing strange*. Mr Glowry and Mr Girouette had a meeting on the occasion, and quarrelled about the terms of the bargain; *which is neither new nor strange*. The lovers were torn asunder, weeping and vowing everlasting constancy; and, in three weeks after this tragical event, the lady was led a smiling

---

[17] The passage is taken from the description of the nun of Monza, who is seduced by a noble, who addresses her first through a window. The text means "The wretched one answered."

[18] On Peacock and his humor, see section 6.1.2.

5.5. HUMOROUS PLOTS

bride to the altar, by the Honourable Mr Lackwit; *which is neither strange nor new* (NIAB 41, my italics, SA).

This passage has little structural importance in the remaining text of NIAB (it occurs at the beginning of the first chapter), and in fact constitutes a digression. It is a remarkable example of Peacock's complex humorous constructions. The names of Miss Girouette (=weathercok) and Mr Lackwit (=lack wit) are the standard Peacock jokes (on Peacock's *penchant* for onomastic jokes, see section (6.1.2) note 4). What is more relevant is that in a few sentences Peacock provides the plot of a typical Romantic love story. The ending is of course completely against the conventions of the Romantic novel, and Peacock is playing with them. Consider also that Peacock qualifies the wedding arrangements of "bargain." However, the most interesting sources of humor are the numerous italicised authorial comments that follow every sentence in the passage. In his comments Peacock insists that none of the events he is relating is either new or strange, and hence interesting. It is a very sophisticated ironical touch for an author to claim that his subject matter is not worth telling. This kind of self-deprecating humor is not isolated in NIAB. For instance, it is found in the following passage:

(41) Mrs Hilary hinted to Marionetta, that propriety, and delicacy, and decorum, and dignity, &c. &c. &c.[1], would require them to leave the Abbey immediately (NIAB 55).

note 1: We are not masters of the whole vocabulary. See any novel by any literary lady (NIAB 263).

Peacock refuses to provide the reader with the list of social reasons that would require leaving Nightmare Abbey, on the pretence that the reader can "look it up" in any novel by a female author. This attitude of irreverence towards the medium of the novel is further evidenced in Peacock's refusal to use his name on the front cover of his novel. In a (probably) parodic imitation of Scott, *Headlong Hall* appeared anonymously, and all of Peacock's following novels were attributed to "the author of *Headlong Hall.*"

5.5.3 Plots with Humorous Fabulae

Finally, there is a class of texts that, while respecting the narrative illusion and not ending in a punch line, can be nevertheless considered a "humorous fabula." Wilde's LASC is a case in point, in which the central narrative complication (cf. jab 90)[19] the fabula revolves around is itself humorous (in this case the "murder as duty" strand).

---

[19]The "central narrative complication" is the most significant episode in the text. It would be the event that cannot be deleted in any macrostructure, or the basic source of oppositions in a Greimasian analysis. In this context we do not attempt a formal definition, as too little is known about this subject matter.

Another example is Eugène Labiche's[20] *Un chapeau de paille d'italie* in which the horse of a man on his way to his marriage eats the straw hat of a lady having an extramarital affair. In order to avoid a scandal the man has to find a replacement for the Italian straw hat. In the end, the only such hat available turns out to be precisely the one eaten by the horse.

Summing up, a plot with humorous fabula is one in which the central complication involves a humorous SO, but does not (necessarily) end in a punch line and does not (necessarily) breach the narrative illusion.

5.5.4 Plots with Serious Fabulae

The consideration of humorous plots should not lead us to the error of perspective of believing that a majority of humorous narratives have humorous plots/fabulae. In fact, the opposite is probably true: for most humorous narratives, the humor is, so to speak, superimposed on an essentially serious fabula. An excellent example is Umberto Eco's *Il nome della rosa* (ROSE), further discussed below.

5.5.5 Humorous disruption and realistic illusion

Summing up, the relationships between plot and humor are more complex than Palmer (and Lovell) claim: there is a continuum ranging from narratives that are entirely functional to the humorous event (and thus are essentially structurally similar to a joke) to narratives that are essentially serious but have some degree of humor within them, passing by narratives that are disrupted by humor to a varying degree.

Disruption of the fabula will necessarily involve an interplay with the realistic illusion of narrative. Realistic narrative is a fairly constrained genre in which the realistic illusion (see above) is respected.

It should be noted that the idea of disruption of the realistic narrative as the constituent element of humorous narrative is put under serious doubt by the observation that self-referential devices (which totally disrupt realistic narrative) have been used in tragic theater (e.g., Pirandello's *Six Characters in Search of an Author*) without comic effects. Therefore, it follows that narrative disruption is not *eo ipso* humorous. In any event, even script opposition is not necessarily humorous. It becomes so only if it is accompanied by the other requirements of the SSTH. Thus the fact that narrative disruption by itself does not cause humor should not come as a surprise. Narrative disruption is perceived as funny when it causes the opposition of two (macro)scripts.

---

[20]Labiche (1815-88) was a prolific author of light comedy, among which is *An Italian Straw Hat* (1851), the source of the film of the same title by René Clair (1927).

5.6 Humorous Techniques

We can now sum up our discussion of plot-level humorous techniques, before broadening it up to other techniques that involve large parts of texts. As we have seen, plots may be serious or humorous. The following schema sums up the previous discussion, and introduces some of the themes to be dealt with in what follows.

- serious
    - without jab lines (not funny)
    - with jab lines
- humorous
    - ending on a punch line
    - having a humorous central narrative complication
    - using metanarrative disruption
    - using coincidences
    - hyperdetermined humor
    - using diffuse disjunction (see ch. 6)

5.6.1 Coincidences

Within essentially serious plots, besides the occurrence of jab lines and the breaking of narrative frames, a very significant source of humor in narratives are coincidences. These can be defined as a statistically highly improbable event taking place in circumstances that do not explain away the statistical unlikelyhood. Turning around the corner and running into a long-lost friend is a coincidence, doing so at your high-school reunion is not.

Coincidences are among the most typical disruptive elements of the narrative frame (Palmer 1994: 113). Coincidences or other highly improbable events, would be avoided in naturalistic narrative, but are normal fare for humorous narrative. Palmer (1987: 115-140) presents an analysis of *Fawlty Towers* focusing on the highly improbable "bad luck" of Basil Fawlty, the neurotic owner of the hotel who seems always to be having the worst day of his life.

Consider the following example, which strikes me as paradigmatic:

(42) [Basil] turns the bathroom light switch, which is just outside the door [...] [Raylene, an attractive guest] mov[es]to the wall by the bathroom door [...]. Without looking, [Basil] reaches out of the bathroom for the switch. His hand engages Raylene's left boob. He tries to switch it on, sense something is wrong, and feels it. Raylene looks down in disbelief just as Sybil [Basil's wife] enters the room. (Cleese and Booth 1988: 202-203)

It is already highly improbable that the attractive guest would choose to position herself exactly in the only position of the wall where Basil would be looking for the switch, but that Basil's wife would walk in exactly at the moment he is feeling her breast is totally improbable. Presumably the information available in the storage area and the known encyclopedic information about the likelihood of events (not to mention their social consequences) interact to mark the above violation of naturalistic narrative conventions as humorous.

This approach to the interpretation of humorous texts which has access to the narrative development of the text as it is processed has the advantage of accounting for metahumor, which can be easily explained as a play on the expectations built by the inclusion in the storage area of the opening sequence of a known humorous sequence/narrative, which are then deliberately thwarted.

5.6.2 Hyperdetermined

We can define hyperdetermined humor as the presence of more than one active source of humor at the same time, or as the simultaneous activity of a given source of humor in different contexts. So as to be able to refer to these two kinds of hyperdetermination let us label the presence of several active sources of humor *textual hyperdetermination*, while we will use the label of *punctual hyperdetermination* for the case in which one source of humor works at different "levels."

Consider the following example of textual hyperdetermination: in HRCI by Allais (7.5), we find satirical references to writers of the time and the text is structured as a parody of the themes of exotism which they were fond of (strand 1), but we also find a theme of sexual exuberance (reinforced by a number of phallic references; strand 2). These strands, which by and large constitute the plot (which interestingly starts on the first theme and ends on the second), are interrupted repeatedly by onomastic and topographical puns (strand 3) and authorial asides (strand 4). In one case, a punning "gag" hijacks the narrative for a large part of the text (about one third) and the self-contained narrative excursus is in fact built to justify a pun. It is interesting to note that this excursus has largely the structure of a joke (punch line at the end).

The other type of hyperdetermined humor (punctual) includes cases in which a joke is active at different levels simultaneously. Thus, for example, in the Candide example (6.2.5) we find the register humor discussed above (level 1) but the text is also simultaneously an attack on Leibniz (whose terminology it parodies; level 2) and a sexually titillating description (level 3), as well as a somewhat misogynistic innuendo (level 4), and possibly a satirical critique of current sexual mores (level 5).

Let us note that the SSTH and the GTVH cannot elegantly handle this type of hyperdetermined humor, since they are programmed to identify a unique humorous trigger, and terminate the analysis. With sophisticated and complex texts such as Voltaire's CAND, cf. example (58), the hearer cannot simply assume that all the remainder of the text will be funny and that the humor has been ascertained once and for all. Let me point out that, in a sense, the basic intuition behind GTVH and SSTH remains valid: all these themes and their various jab and punch lines can be handled individually by the idea of script opposition and overlap and are ultimately examples of incongruity and resolution. What is lacking in humor theory is a sense of how to handle more than one humorous line at the same time, or the same line functioning in more than one "dimension" at the same time.

Furthermore, although the components of the humorous text, opposite and overlapping scripts, are present, it is impossible to pinpoint a unique element causing the passage from the first to the second script (i.e., a disjunctor or script-switch trigger). It may be assumed that the accumulation of allusions (i.e., weak links to other scripts) would end up triggering the actualization of the second script.

The punctual hyperdetermination issue can be handled easily when it is assumed that a jab/punch line can belong to several strands at once. Since the definition of strand makes it clear that the defining feature of strands is the semantic or formal similarity of their components, it follows that a line l_1 which is similar in one aspect (feature f_a) to another line l_2, may be similar in f_b to l_3, and f_c to l_4, etc. Thus l_1 would belong simultaneously to strands a, b, and c. Textual hyperdetermination is handled implicitly by the idea of having a storage area that reads input from the text and builds strands and other textual representations. Crucially, several such textual representations (possible worlds, inferential chains, etc.) can be open at the same time; therefore, the model will have to be able to handle simultaneous multiple strand construction. Further discussion of hyperdetermined humor will be found in section 6.1.2.

5.7 General Considerations

In this section, we briefly look at the incremental nature of the theory in which each theoretical entity is built by units at lower levels. Consider the following chart which presents an overview of the discussion.

joke	narrative	text	intertext
GTVH	Vector	Strands	Stacks
punch/jab line	CBTD	HRCI/TRAN/LASC	TRAN/LASC

On the upper row we have different levels of textuality, ordered from smaller to larger units. On the second row we have the aspects of humor theory that have been introduced to allow for their analysis. The bottom row lists some examples used in the text.

It should be noted that the theoretical elements to the right presuppose and incorporate the analyses to their left. Thus, the vector analysis of a narrative presupposes necessarily an analysis of its jab and punch lines by the GTVH. An analysis of stacks, presupposes an analysis of the strands built in the text, etc. Thus the approach we are proposing is incremental. This is important, as it is the foundation for our claim of non-intuitiveness (objectivity) of the analysis: each increasingly complex level of analysis is justified on the basis of the immediately preceding level and the bottom level, that of the individual line, is justified via formal semantic analysis (see section 1.6.3).

Chapter 6

Diffuse Disjunction

This chapter deals with humorous techniques that do not have clear punch lines, but rather are based on the occurrence of small jab lines throughout the text (or stretches of the text). Essentially, we will deal with register humor and with irony, the two clear examples of such humor. Register humor will be investigated mainly in some examples from T. L. Peacock, and a blend of register and ironical humor using a passage from Voltaire's *Candide* .

6.0.1 Discrete or diffuse disjunctors

Jokes have discrete, unique, clearly identifiable[1] disjunctors, while other forms of humor may have diffuse disjunctors (i.e., markers). A diffuse disjunctor is any type of disjunctor which does not occur alone in a humorous (micro)narrative, insofar as it is unable to trigger the script-switch by its mere presence. Register humor and irony are good examples of diffuse disjunctors since the incompatibility/inappropriateness between the context and some elements of the utterance is the sole necessary and sufficient marker of humorous or ironical intention. See below for discussion of irony and register humor.

The idea of a diffuse element in humor is central to Chlopicki's work on humorous short stories (1987). A diffuse trigger (or "dissipated" in Chlopicki's terminology) is "not any single word, but the formulation of the whole phrase or two, or even the whole text of the joke [which] is responsible for causing the script overlap" (Chlopicki 1987: 14). See also section 2.1.1.

The issue at hand is the relationship between diffuse disjunctors and punch lines. Punch lines are equivalent to disjunctors[2] (Attardo 1994: 87) which are equivalent to script switch triggers (cf. Attardo 1994: 82). From Chlopicki's definition above

---
[1] The technique is spelled out in Hockett 1973 and applied in Attardo *et al.* 1994.
[2] The disjunctor is the item that cause the passage from the first to the second script, see section 1.3.1.

we gather that a dissipated trigger is however *not* in fact a disjunctor or trigger in the sense of the SSTH, but rather a connector, i.e., the textual element that makes the copresence (overlap) of two scripts possible. In puns, this is quite often simply an ambiguous element (cf. Attardo 1994: 134-135). Narratives do not necessarily have ambiguous elements, so it becomes harder to see how a dissipated trigger/connector should work.

In sum, diffuse disjunctors remain to be accounted for. While a contribution to the solution of this problem was given by introducing the concept of "jab line" (5.3.1) and by considering diffuse disjunctors as a type of jab line, much remains to be done. This chapter attempts to advance our understanding of diffuse disjunction by considering two typical examples: register humor and humorous irony.

6.1 Register humor

In what follows we will not try to define register (see Attardo 1994: ch. 7 for discussion). We will assume that register is a linguistic variety defined by subject matter, social situations (of the speakers), and discursive functions (of the exchange). Essentially, for our purposes we can think of register as a set of links between linguistic features (particularly, lexical items and collocations, i.e., the likelihood that two items may co-occur) and connotations (of various kinds, but primarily of the formal/informal kind). An attempt at a script-based theory of register and connotation can be found in Attardo (1994: ch. 7).

6.1.1 Literature Review

Bally (1909) had already noted the possibility of register humor; see Attardo (1994: 233-235). Fishman (1972) identified register humor, and its cause, i.e., incongruent elements in a situation. Holmes (1973: 5-6) also has some examples. They all stop short, however, of providing a theory of register humor, and their accounts are largely anecdotal.

Haiman (1990: 199-202) has examined the use of register clashes as indicators of the "sarcastic" nature of the text in some detail, and with much finesse. Much of the considerations that apply to sarcasm seem to be valid for humor as well.

Alexander (1984: 58-62; 1997: 190-191) presents several examples of register humor and identifies the phenomenon clearly. Alexander notes that some cases of humor originate in the "comical confusion" of two registers. A technique to generate register-based humor "is that of selecting a lexeme or phraseological unit from a different style level than the context would predict" (Alexander 1984: 60). To illustrate the notion of register humor consider, as an example, this short passage by Woody Allen, quoted in Alexander (1984: 60):

(43) He was creating an Ethics, based on his theory that "good and just behavior is not only more moral but could be done by phone." Also, he was halfway

6.1. REGISTER HUMOR

> through a new study of semantics, proving (as he so violently insisted) that sentence structure is innate but that whining is acquired. (Woody Allen *Remembering Needleman* In *Side Effects*. New York: Ballantine. 1981.)

Alexander comments:

> Allen builds up expectations of a particular level of style and even of field of discourse – *Ethics* (with a large E) and *good and just behavior* – only to deflate them by introducing *done by phone*. Similarly he introduces incongruity in following up *new study of semantics* and *phrase structure* with *whining* (Alexander 1984: 60)

Alexander's analysis is correct, but largely impressionistic; for example, it may be noted that the technical terms that select the register *linguistics* ("semantics," "phrase structure") are used exclusively for their connotation (see below), i.e., because they connote "linguistics talk" independently of their meaning (phrase structure is not part of semantics). As a matter of fact, the reader is not supposed to have access to the sophisticated knowledge of what phrase structure is to understand the joke. A vague association with "linguistics" or even just with "academic talk" is sufficient. These aspects of the problem are left unexplored, as are the specific mechanisms by which "evocation" of a register is achieved.

Alexander (and Attardo 1994, for that matter) seems to be conflating two slightly different phenomena, namely register clash *in absentia* and *in praesentia*. The "selection of a lexeme (...) from a different style level than the context would predict" operates on one register which appears in the text and refers to another that does *not* appear in the text. Conversely, the cooccurrence in the cotext of "phrase structure" and "whining" oppose two registers that are present in the text at the same time.

The following section develops a treatment of register humor in some selected passages from two novels NIAB and HEHA (1815) by Thomas Love Peacock[3]. Our

---

[3] Thomas Love Peacock was born in 1785 at Weymouth. He left school at thirteen, but apparently continued to educate himself on his own. His first volume of verse was published in 1806. In 1812, when Peacock had already published three volumes of verse, he met Shelley. They became friends and Peacock was introduced to the group of people who had gathered around Shelley (among these J. F. Newton, who appears in *Nightmare Abbey*). In 1814, Shelley's elopement strained his friendship with Peacock, who sided with Shelley's wife, Harriet. Peacock and Shelley reconciled, and in the following years they collaborated extensively. During that time, Peacock wrote his first two novels: *Headlong Hall* (1816) and *Melincourt* (1817) which show a clear Shelleian influence. Slightly after Peacock published his last long poem *Rhododaphne* (1818). In 1818, the Shelleys went to Italy, and Peacock wrote *Nightmare Abbey*. In 1819, Peacock began to work for the East India Company, where he worked for the next 35 years. His career was not only long but successful. As a result he acquired financial independence, and married soon thereafter. During his career he continued to publish minor poetry and some novels, including *Crotchet Castle* (1831). After his retirement in 1856 he wrote his *Memoirs of Percy Bysse Shelley* (1858-1862) and another novel *Gryll Grange* (1861). He died in 1866. Setting aside Peacock's poetry and critical writings, his production amounts to seven novels, ranging from 1815 (*Headlong Hall*) to 1861, the year of the volume publication of *Gryll Grange*. On Peacock see: Burns (1985), Butler (1979), Dawson (1968, 1970), Madden (1967), Mulvihill (1987), Sage (1976).

purpose is to exemplify how texts acievehumorous effects using register. A further example of diffuse disjunction can be found in LASC, note 72.

6.1.2 Register Humor in T. L. Peacock

Consider this example, from *Nightmare Abbey* (NIAB) which occurs in a discussion between Scythrop[4] and his father, the latter having announced his decision to marry his son to a lady of his choice. Scythrop has refused, on the grounds of "liberty of action, which is the co-natal prerogative of every rational being" (NIAB 55).

(44) 'Liberty of action, sir? there is no such thing a liberty of action. We are all slaves and puppets of a blind and unpathetic necessity.'

>'Very true sir; but liberty of action, between individuals, consists in their being differently influenced, or modified, by the same universal necessity; so that the results are unconsentaneous, and their respective necessitated volitions clash and fly off in a tangent.'

>'Your logic is good, sir: but you are aware, too, that one individual may be the medium of adhibiting to another a mode or form of necessity, which may have more or less influence in the production of consentaneity; and, therefore, sir, if you do not comply with my wishes in this instance (you have had your way in every thing else), I shall be under the necessity of disinheriting you, though I shall do it with tears in my eyes.' Having said these words, he vanished suddenly, in the dread of Scythrop's logic. (NIAB 55)

In this passage, the author manages to present a quarrel between father and son in terms of a metaphysical debate on necessity. Scythrop begins by claiming "liberty of action" as an excuse not to comply with his father's request. The father's reply is not that liberty of action has little to do with a paternal order, but instead he refuses to admit that free will exists. Schythorp grants the destruction of his previous excuse, but only to find another, in the fact that, although necessitated, and hence not free, the modes of the necessitation are different, and hence unpredictable, which is the same as claiming that in fact there is liberty of action (although theoretically there might not be). Mr Glowry, Scythrop's father, replies again by granting the opponent's point, only to proceed to empty it of any content by a series of apparent logical passages. His (pseudo-)argument proceeds as follows: an individual can be the instrument of necessity; if Scythrop will not marry the lady of his choice his father will disinherit him, his father will be in the necessity of doing so. By repeating

---

[4]Peacock is very fond of of the humorous use of names, often involving sophisticated ethymological jokes; thus Scythrop comes from the Greek $\sigma\kappa\upsilon\vartheta\rho\omega\pi\sigma\varsigma$ "of sad or gloomy countenance" (NIAB 261n), or more simply, like in "Toobad" (= too+bad), or "Cypress" a character who is closely associated with cemeteries. Peacock's novels, and in particular NIAB, can be read as *romans à clef*, each character satirizing a specific public figure. Thus the character of Mr. Flosky (the Kantian) satirizes Coleridge, Scythrop is a satire of Shelley, Mr. Toobad (the manichean Millenarian) of J. F. Newton who was a member of Shelley's circle, Mr. Cypress of Byron, etc. (cf. Mills 1969: 136).

6.1. REGISTER HUMOR

the word "necessity," in the two senses of "metaphysical necessity" and "social obligation" Peacock uses the register typical of a metaphysical discussion to describe a father-son argument. The register/subject matter mismatch is the marker of the script oppositeness. The SO itself is between the subject matter typically associated with the metaphysical register and the register typically associated with quarrels (low, familiar). Schematizing we have:

metaphysics	high/formal
quarrel	low/familiar

and hence the SO METAPHYSICS/QUARRELL, expressed at the register level by the formal/familiar opposition. The opposition between philosophy and a much less prestigious activity (sexual intercourse, in this case) will be found also in the extract from *Candide*, see section 6.2.5.

Let us consider now a passage from HEHA. It is an excellent example of physical comedy, but in this context it is particularly interesting how the humorous material is presented by Peacock. The passage consists of the description of Mr. Escot's entrance in the room where breakfast is being eaten, carrying a human skull since he is planning to lecture on phrenology.

(45) Several of the ladies shrieked at the sight of the skull; and Miss Tenorina, starting up in great haste and terror, caused the subversion of a cup of chocolate, which a servant was handing to the Reverend Doctor Gaster, into the nape of the neck of Sir Patrick O'Prism. Sir Patrick, rising impetuously, *to clap an extinguisher*, as he expressed himself, *on the farthing rushlight of the rascal's life*, pushed over the chair of Marmaduke Milestone, Esquire, who, catching for support at the first thing that came in his way, which happened unluckily to be the corner of the table-cloth, drew it instantaneously with him to the floor, involving plates, cups and saucers, in one promiscuous ruin ... Mr. Escot was a little surprised at the scene of confusion which signalised his entrance (HEHA 56).

As usual, the main problem with the analysis of complex passages such as (45) is that a fine-grained tool such as semantic analysis produces a combinatorial and inferential "explosion" (see 1.2.1); therefore, in order to keep the analysis within manageable limits, only a few informal comments will be provided. It remains that, in principle, a complete analysis could be performed.

The quoted passage consists of three sentences. The second one is 70 words long, a figure sensibly larger than the average sentence. The effect produced by such a long sentence may be impressionistically described as "accumulation." This effect is further reinforced by the presence of several embedded parenthetical sentences, which in turn have embedded parentheticals inside them. The overall effect is that of accumulation and confusion, which skillfully matches the events described in the text. The final sentence works in part as a "punch line," i.e., closes the scene with a sudden outburst of humor (in this case, an example of understatement).

Beyond these stylistic considerations, it should be noted that there is an incongruity of register between the trivial events described (dropping a cup, falling) and the "formal" style of the presentation. Consider the following lexical choices: "subversion" for "fall over," "rising impetuously" for "spring up," and "promiscuous ruin" for "general fall." It may be argued that the substitutions proposed here are not semantically neutral and that they add or subtract meaning to the paraphrases, but the precision of the paraphrase is not the issue. What matters here is that the reader will recognize the lexical instances above as instantiating a "latinate," "flowery," "formal" style, while the subject matter is, as pointed out above, trivial. If the labels "high" and "low" are attached respectively to the register and the subject matter, a typical opposition is established. It should be noted that the opposition is between registers and not between lexical scripts. This is a significant broadening of the SSTH, in keeping with the discussion in Attardo (1994: ch. 7).

To show the procedure by which the instantiation of the "formal" register is achieved formally, one would have to show that the lexical items highlighted above all are linked with long-distance links to scripts such as LATINATE, HIGH-BROW, etc., which in turn would activate a register-script FORMAL. The length and syntactic complexity of the sentences in the passage would also be taken into account to determine the register. The next step would then be the activation of the synonyms and near-synonym scripts, and their long-distance links to situational and general knowledge scripts that would reveal that the most common, typical, unmarked expression of the topic at hand is achieved through a "familiar" register.

An interesting aspect of (45) is the authorial digression which comments metalinguistically upon the way the characters are expressing themselves. Sir Patrick intends *"to clap an extinguisher, as he expressed himself, on the farthing rushlight of the rascal's life,"* Peacock's emphasis on the character's way to express himself is indicative that this is a relevant issue. Indeed, the flowery expression quoted may be paraphrased as "kill." This redundant and deliberately obscure way to word a simple thought violates several of Grice's maxims (quantity, manner, perhaps quality, but, interestingly, not relevance) and is in fact a good example of "formal" register. Needless to say, "to kill" is usually expressed in this context (being scalded by hot chocolate) with much more succinct and colloquial expressions. Peacock is showcasing another example of register-based humor, to which he attracts the reader's attention.

Consider another example of authorial digression

(46) Mr. Escot passed a sleepless night, the ordinary effect of love, according to some amatory poets, who seem to have composed their whining ditties for the benevolent purpose of bestowing on others that gentle slumber of which they so pathetically lament the privation (HEHA 51).

6.1. REGISTER HUMOR

which pokes fun at poets, accusing them of putting people to sleep. Consider in (46) the use of expressions such as "gentle slumber," "benevolent purpose," "bestow" "pathetically" which all connote gentleness and caring, with the expression "whining ditties" characterizing the works of the poets. "Whining" connotes "annoying, disturbing." While "to bestow gentle slumber" is definitely a "formal" register, "to whine" is familiar and informal; moreover, to say that someone's verses put people to sleep is, again, a familiar expression, here expressed in formal register.

Next, consider the following example:

(47) the rage and impetuosity of the Squire continued fermenting to the highest degree of exasperation, which he signified, from time to time, by converting some newly unpacked article, such as a book, a bottle, a ham, or a fiddle into a missile against the head of some unfortunate servant... (HEHA 6)

in which the use of a periphrasis for "throw" ("convert into a missile") and the use of adjectives such as "unfortunate" and verbs such as "ferment" and "signify" impose repeated switches from formal to informal registers, and clash with the subject matter of the text (throwing objects at someone else's head).

As pointed out above, these cases of "register" humor are mostly created by authorial intrusions and/or comments, since they involve an evaluation and a skillfully controlled contrast between the expected style and the stylistic choice made in the text.

An important point that should be made is that neither the "plot" of HEHA nor the passages analyzed are particularly funny, beyond their wording. There is nothing inherently funny in someone throwing things at servants. The position of the humor in these texts is radically different from texts structurally similar to jokes, such as the short story by Poe, discussed in Attardo (1994: 255-262), see section (5.5.1). In Poe's text, as in jokes, the *raison d'être* of the story is to build a humorous climax; in Peacock's passages, the story moves on without much concern for its humorous aspects. Consider the fact that in Poe's story the text actually ends shortly after the "punch line" has been reached. Peacock's passage occurs at the beginning of the text. The first type is narratively an elaborate joke, while the second is a narrative text to which humorous elements have been applied, but to which there is a non-humorous narrative core, see section 5.5.

Hyperdetermination in Peacock

We turn to to the analysis of a short passage from Peacock's NIAB which combines the register humor we have been discussing with slapstick comedy and satire. Humor of action is considered one of the most basic kinds of humor; the man slipping on the banana peel is often given as an example of the simplest form of comic. Some examples of slapstick comedy are to be found in Peacock, and their function is usually that of providing a counterpoint to the long abstract debates. Consider the following passage:

(48) She (Marionetta) disengaged herself suddenly from Scythrop, sprang through the door of the tower, and fled with precipitation along the corridors. Scythrop pursued her, crying, 'Stop, stop, Marionetta - my life, my love!' and was gaining rapidly on her flight, when, at an ill-omed corner, where two corridors ended in an angle, at the head of the staircase, he came into sudden and violent contact with Mr Toobad, and they both plunged together to the foot of the stairs, like two billiard-balls into one pocket. (NIAB 52)

All the typical resources of slapstick comedy are here used, e.g., the comparison to objects (the billiard-balls), a fall down the stairs, two characters bumping into each other. Moreover the passage is narratively extremely sophisticated, with three parenthetics delaying the occurrence of the humorous fall ("at an ill-omed corner, where two corridors ended in an angle, at the head of the stair"), and the now familiar humorous stylistic underpinning by the use of elevated diction in the description of the accident ("came into sudden and violent contact").

However brilliant the comedic interlude, its funniness is not the only reason for the passage to be found humorous by the reader. The reason for Marionetta's flight is that Schythrop has just proposed her to "open a vein in the other's arm, mix our blood in a bowl, and drink it a a sacrament of love" (NIAB 52). Marionetta, relates Peacock, "had not so strong a stomach" and "turned sick at the proposition." While the contemporary reader might agree with Marionetta, Peacock's contemporaries probably also saw the allusion to the novel *Horrid Mysteries* published in 1796, in a translation from the German author Grosse. Thus, an element of satire is intertwined in the farcical behavior of the characters. In effect, shortly after the quoted passage, Scythrop and Mr. Toobad exchange a few comments on their fall, which are another occasion for Peacock to satirize the pessimistic attitudes of Toobad.

The general point about hyperdetermination that bears repeating here is that there are several sources of humor active at the same time: register humor, farcical humor, satire on the characters, and parody. The overall effect is rich humor, which it would be impossible to ascribe uniquely to any of the above sources alone.

In conclusion, we have seen that an opposition between a register's associations and the subject matter of the text may trigger a humorous incongruity, as well as the coprenence of incongruous registers in the same stretch of text. Furthermore, we have seen how register humor may be only one of several sources of humor active at the same time in the text

6.2 Irony

We continue the examination of diffuse humorous modes by examining irony. The discussion is organized as follows: we start out by distinguishing between recognition and interpretation of irony and we deal with both aspects. We then move on to examine irony markers. We follow up by examining the reasons, both social and

6.2. IRONY

rhetorical, for using irony and finish by considering briefly the mode factivity aspect of irony tied to the residual violation of the maxim of manner in the use of irony.

I will present a model of irony,[5] which is Gricean at the core, but includes several significant departures from Grice's own model. Grice's treatment of irony as an implicature can be found in Grice (1975, 1979, 1989); a good discussion is in Cosenza (1997).

Let us start with the following points:

- the ironic meaning is arrived at inferentially and more or less independently from the literal meaning of the utterance, hence

- irony is entirely a pragmatic phenomenon

The reconstruction of the ironists's intended meaning is supposed to be based on a set of shared presuppositions: the hearer[6] knows that the speaker cannot mean p, the proposition conveyed by his/her utterance u, and the speaker knows that the hearer knows that, and therefore the speaker can count on the fact that the hearer will not stop at the speaker's literal meaning of p, but rather look for a more suitable meaning among the infinite set of other meanings which may have been implicated by the speaker with u.

Furthermore, the inferential path of the hearer's reconstruction of what the speaker my have meant is guided by Grice's CP, which leads us to two further points:

- the interpretation of the ironical meaning depends crucially on the active guidance of the CP, ergo

- the CP needs to be immediately restored into functionality after having been violated. The principle that embodies this point is called the "principle of least disruption" (cf. section 6.2.1).

In the following sections we will look at the processes whereby the ironical meaning is arrived at and at the least disruption principle, before turning to the discussion of the theory of irony presented in Attardo (2000).

Since we saw that irony is a completely pragmatic phenomenon, with no semantic correlates, it follows that it is entirely dependent on context, including but not limited to, the speaker's intentions and goals. The ironical meaning needs to be inferred, it is never "said" (in Grice's sense), i.e., found in the text itself.

The fact that irony does not necessarily implicate the opposite or the converse of the literal meaning is important. Schaffer (1982: 15) sums up the situation brilliantly:

---

[5] A review of the literature on irony can be found in Attardo (2000). A treatment of the reasons for being ironical can be found in Attardo (2000c)

[6] I keep the pragmatic terminology, of speaker and hearer, with the memento that no speech-centrism need to be read in the terminological choice: speaker stands for writer, signer, etc.

Recognition of irony rarely comes from the words themselves [...], but rather from cues in the conversational context or nonverbal communication of the speaker. The ironic implicatures resulting from such cues *merely point to the possibility that the speaker's meaning may be other than that of the literal content of the utterance*; other conversational implicatures and semantic considerations can then supply an alternative interpretation. [my emphasis, SA]

This point is quite important and bears restating: there are two distinct phenomena at work: 1) the determination that a (part of) a text is ironical (the recognition of irony),[7] and 2) the determination of the intended meaning of the irony (the interpretation of the value of the irony).

We turn first to the determination of the value of the irony and will return to the recognition of irony in a subsequent section (6.2.2).

6.2.1 Principle of least disruption

Let us assume that the hearer has recognized an inappropriate utterance. In order to understand the inferential path that allows the hearer to determine the value of the irony (its import, a.k.a., the ironical meaning), we need first to discuss an extension of Grice's CP.

Let us start with the observation of the fact that Grice's CP, overridden when an ironic utterance is first encountered, since the hearer notes the violation of at least one maxim[8] becomes fully operational again once the first step of rejecting the literal meaning has been taken: for example in:

(49) S: "What nice weather." (Context: it is raining.)

H will assume that the utterance is relevant to the condition of the weather, and not to, say, the location of one's cat.

I have explained this fact by postulating a least disruption principle (LDP; Attardo 2000; forthcoming). The LDP's specific wording is as follows:

> Super-maxim: Minimize your violation of the CP;
>
> - limit your violation of the CP to the smallest possible conversational unit (one utterance, one conversational turn, one speech exchange);
> - try to link the entire CP-violating unit to the rest of the interaction, for example by finding a certain appropriateness to the CP-violating unit;

---

[7] Note that the "recognition" of the irony may be somewhat of a misnomer, since it does not mean that H necessarily labels the utterance as ironical, but merely the recognition of the inappropriateness of the utterance.

[8] Actually, as will appear below, this is strictly not true, since the violation of a maxim not contemplated by Grice may occur, but as a beginning this wording will do.

6.2. IRONY

- limit your violation of the CP to smallest possible distance from its requirements;
- lie in the direction of your audience's expectations.

In other words the LDP warns the speaker to limit his/her violation of the CP to the least amount necessary.

Thus, in example (49) above, the hearer, upon noticing the disruption of the CP does not withdraw from the conversation (which would be a safe move since his/her interlocutor has just given manifest proof of being untrustworthy) but assumes that the violation of the CP is the smallest possible and, therefore, that the violation must somehow refer to the context, and be meaningful. Let us note that in principle, one might say

(50) What nice weather.

with an ironical tone while it is raining, and upon the hearer's interpretation of utterance (50) as ironical say something along the lines of

(51) I was just kidding, as a matter of fact I love rain.

In other words, here the speaker would be deceiving the hearer about his/her intention to be ironical. There is no *a priori* reason for limiting the violation of the CP to the smallest possible context, except for the desire of the speakers to facilitate communication even when a violation is present or necessary. This means that there is another, broader communicative principle, that tolerates violations as long as they are kept as limited as possible. This issue is further developed in Attardo (2000; forthcoming) and by Nelms et al. (2000).[9]

Irony differs, in this respect, from other implicatures. In simple flouting implicatures the violation of a maxim is reduced to a flout when an inferential path (i.e., the implicature) to reduce the violation to a flout is found (i.e., the violation is done for a communicative purpose that is CP-compliant). The ironical flout remains in abeyance of the CP since irony violates the maxim of manner which recommends to

---

[9] An interesting issue, brought to my attention by Rachel Giora, is the problem of how the principle of least disruption can be reconciled with entire texts, such as *A Modest Proposal*, which violate the CP. At one level, the issue is fairly simple: by advocating a practice the author finds abhorrent (cannibalism), he draws attention on the conditions of the Irish poor (via relevance); thus the text behaves acording to the second part of the principle of least disruption. However, it remains that the text as a whole violates the CP in that it seems to fly in the face of the first requirement of the principle of least disruption. I have come to believe that the issue should be seen in terms of the realistic illusion. Given a premise, the author can freely elaborate on it, a good example is in LASC and involves the murder-as-duty premise: once killing someone is a duty, then homicide is praiseworthy, and so on. Once Swift has set up a world (cf. section 3.3) in which eating children is acceptable, the issue of how to cook them is perfectly coherent. I refer to this phenomenon as "mode factivity," i.e., the fact that irony sets up a mental space (cf. Fauconnier 1985, 1997, section 3.3, and below) which the speaker and the hearer may choose to inhabit (temporarily). Thus a long ironical text is a text that starts from an ironical premise. It is obvious that further work is needed here.

"avoid obscurity" and to "avoid ambiguity". It is clear that an ironical statement is both more obscure and more ambiguous than the direct expression of one's beliefs.[10]

In fact, the common observation that the speaker could always have stated directly his/her ironical meaning has not been taken to its logical consequences. From it, follows the fact that irony remains a violation of the CP *after* the implicatures have been worked out (i.e., the ironical meaning has been arrived at). Consider that if the speaker could have stated non-ironically his/her intended meaning, it follows that he/she is using some way of expressing it that is different than those that he/she should have chosen to be CP compliant. Hence, the speaker is in abeyance of the CP.

Grice himself realized that his original account left a significant gap in the description of irony, namely, that irony points to an evaluative aspect of S's intention (or intended meaning). Grice remarked that irony was problematic in a straightforward implicational framework because "irony is intimately connected with the expression of a feeling, attitude, or evaluation" (1989: 53). On the basis of the principle stated above, it is now easy to see how the expression of a speaker's attitude towards the ironical referent would fit the descriptive framework, since the ironical utterance would be interpreted as referring, cooperatively, to some element of the context, towards which a feeling, attitude, or evaluation is held.

It is necessary, however, to further specify the cooperative nature of the inferential process that determines the value of the irony. I am here suggesting that two factors direct the inferential processing of the value of the irony:

1. the maxim of relevance

2. the antiphrastic/antonymic assumption of irony (cf. Giora 1995, 1997, 1999, Giora et al. 1998).

In other words, after having recognized (a part of) a text as ironical, the hearer assumes that the maxim of relevance holds and that the relevance of the irony lies in the direction of an antiphrastic meaning (i.e., in the direction of the opposite of what the speaker is saying) with a special emphasis on S's value judgments. Berrendonner (1981: 183) argues that an utterance can be used ironically only if its has an "argumentative value" (*valeur argumentative*), i.e., it can be seen as part of an axiological and/or teleological system from which it acquires its value. In other words, someone is trying to do something with the utterance, such as convince someone or argue for something; see also Braester (1992: 84-85).

6.2.2 A contextual-appropriateness theory of irony

Irony Recognition

As mentioned above, the interpretation of irony should not be confused with its recognition. In fact, that the two steps in the processing of irony are distinct can

---
[10] Irony may also be longer (less brief) than direct statements.

6.2. IRONY

be shown with a simple example. Consider the following situation:

(52) Two linguistics professors run into each other on campus. Prof. A says: "Oh, B, did you know that linguists are the last people you should consult about language?"

Assume that B has not read the campus paper in which another professor's (C) words to that effect have been printed. Then, B will presumably be aware that A is ironical, since the utterance in (52) is clearly absurd and hence inappropriate as A's utterance. However, B will not be able to reconstruct A's intended ironical meaning, and namely that A's opinion of C is negative (or some such point). Thus, B will recognize (52) as ironical, or at least inappropriate, while being unable to understand its ironical import.

We need now to define inappropriateness. We have seen that irony is non-cooperative at first reading. In what respect does irony violate CP at that first moment? This is an interesting issue, since every ironical utterance seems to be literally false and/or not appropriate to its context. Let us consider a few examples, starting with the standard Gricean violation of quality. If one says

(53) I love children so

while, in fact, disliking them, clearly, one is technically lying, but one's tone of voice or other signals[11] may make it clear that one is deliberately and conspicuously violating the maxim of quality, and signaling to the hearer(s). Then one is not "really" lying (since one wants to be "outguessed") but rather being ironical. This type of example can be readily explained as an implicature. Let us turn now to examples that would be problematic for a strightforward Gricean model.

Katz and Fodor's (1963: 481) famous example of inappropriateness[12]

(54) This is the happiest night of my life [uttered during the middle of the day]

is neither true or false (hence, it does not violate quality), when pronounced in daylight, but it is inappropriate, i.e., it violates the rules that determine the deictic anchoring of discourse in reality.

In the appropriate context, (54) could also be ironical (if for instance pronounced in the early morning by a speaker well known for his/her late-rising habit). Or consider the following situation:

(55) Two farmers in a drought-stricken area are talking and farmer A says: "Don't you just love a nice spring rain?"

---

[11] Including, most notably, a clash between the utterance and its context, cf. below.
[12] The notion of appropriateness explored in the text differs significantly from the one used incidentally in de Beaugrande and Dressler (1981) where it is only a stylistic element.

While probably literally true (farmer A and B may like spring rains) and not (necessarily) a mention or an echo of another utterance, the utterance is contextually inappropriate because it is not raining.

The earlier example (49) uttered while it is raining, clearly belongs to the inappropriateness category of irony as well, but unlike (54), it also involves a literal non-truth. In other words, appropriateness and several other conditions and maxims can be violated in an ironic utterance, just as the violation of more than one maxim at a time in a joke is a common phenomenon (see Attardo 1993, and references therein).

What examples (49), (54), and (55) have in common is that they would fail to be identified as ironical by a Gricean account of irony (they fail to violate a maxim); however, they all entail an inappropriate utterance given the context in which they occur. Violation of a maxim, needless to say, creates an inappropriate utterance. Therefore, all examples of irony accounted for by implicature can be accounted for as inappropriate utterances as well. Consider again (53) above: if one does not like children, then it is inappropriate to say that one does.

It is possible to extrapolate from these observations and define as ironical an utterance that, while maintaining relevance,[13] explicitly or implicitly violates the conditions for contextual appropriateness, either deictically or more broadly in terms of the knowledge by the participants of the opinions and belief systems of the speakers (see Searle 1979: 113 for a brief mention of an account of irony in terms of inappropriateness).

Since we are drawing an inference on the basis of a rule not included in the CP, this introduces an interesting exception to it: "be contextually appropriate" (which is not the same as being relevant, for discussion, see Attardo 2000). Thus, this is an extension to Grice's CP. The pragmatic aspects of this estension are dealt with in Attardo (forthcoming b).

The following is the operational definition of appropriateness given in Attardo (2000): an utterance u is contextually appropriate iff all presuppositions of u are identical to or compatible with all the presuppositions of the context C in which u is uttered, except for any aspect of meaning explicitly thematized and denied in u.[14]

As far as the "context" of utterance of u, a notoriously slippery concept, recall the notion of "common ground" (Clark 1996; cf. section 3.1.2 above) which will help clarify what is meant: speakers negotiate and continuously update a record of propositions which they hold to be mutually known (held, manifest), including, let us note in passing, information about which parts of the common ground are

---

[13] Note that as per Attardo's (1997) two stage approach to implicatures, it is perfectly acceptable for the speaker to violate the maxim of relevance in the first stage and then follow it in the second. Thus, the definition in the text should be understood as "maintaining relevance" in the second stage of processing.

[14] The last clause is necessary to handle certain more or less metalinguistic utterances of the type "This table is not a Duncan Phyfe" which presupposes (roughly) that the hearer has the belief that the table is a Duncan Phyfe.

6.2. IRONY

focalized and relevant to the ongoing interaction.[15] This record is the background upon which the utterances of a discourse are produced. Thus the appropriateness of u is determined in relation to the context of u.

In light of the previous discussion, we can state the theory of irony that we are proposing as follows: an utterance u is ironical if

1. u is contextually inappropriate,

2. u is (at the same time) relevant,

3. u is construed as having been uttered intentionally and with awareness of the contextual inappropriateness by the speaker, and

4. the speaker intends that (part of) his/her audience recognize points 1 – 3

5. unless the hearer construes u as being unintentional irony, in which case 3 – 4 do not apply.

Usually, irony is used to express an evaluative judgment about a given event/situation which is commonly, but not exclusively, negative.

I believe that most of the aspects of this proposal are fairly obvious (at least to those with some familiarity with Gricean pragmatics). Further theoretical issues are dealt with in Attardo (forthcoming), but a few points are better addressed immediately. The proviso on point (4) that at least part of the audience recognize the ironical intent of the speaker, is meant to account for a situation in which, as Clark and Carlson (1982) point out, the speaker addresses two different audiences at the same time, one who is essentially the "butt" of the irony and another audience who is "in" to the ironical intent and appreciates the irony (or at least appreciates the fact that the speaker intends to be ironical). Consider for example, the situation in which a child is pestering his/her parents for ice cream and the speaker, one of the parents, says to him/her

(56) Are you sure you want ice cream?

intending the other parent to understand the ironical intent, but clearly aware that this will be lost on the child. Point (3) is meant to remind the reader of Grice's reflexive intention. Point (5) introduces the possibility of the hearer taking upon him/herself full responsibility for the intentional aspects of irony. Essentially, in that case, the hearer behaves as if the speaker had uttered u ironically, while knowing full well that the speaker did not.

As we have seen, irony is recognized by its inappropriateness. However, being ironical is risky (since the hearer may miss the irony and take the speaker at face

---

[15]Thus, for example, both you, the reader, and I, the author, share the assumption that, I at the time of writing, and you at the time of reading, am/are alive. However, this bit of information was not, presumably, focalized before the occurrence of this sentence.

value). To hedge the speaker's bet, he/she may use a number of clues, to point out to the hearer his/her ironical intention. In the following section, we examine some of the most common markers of irony. It should however be kept in mind that there exists a completely non-marked, signal-free delivery, the so-called "deadpan delivery."

Irony markers vs. factors

Simple-minded as it may seem, it is necessary to distinguish between indices of irony and irony itself. There has been some confusion between ironical markers and ironical utterances, if not entirely explicitly, at least in the practice of some scholars who have come to identify irony with irony that is explicitly marked as such by some ironical indicator. However, irony cannot be identified with its markers. See for example, the following quote, which sums up several of the points we have been making:

> It is possible to be ironic or sarcastic without any overt sign of the speaker's insincerity. The put-on, or deadpan act of sarcasm, still differs from a lie in that the speaker wants his or her actual meaning to be understood at least by some happy few members of the target audience (...) (Haiman 1998: 18)

Muecke (1978) argues that "irony markers cannot be defined as infallible pointers to irony" (365) and that irony needs to be defined in terms of "intention and communication." (ibid.) The latter is defined as "marking" the speaker's utterance "in such a way as to provide [his/]her addressee with grounds for a correct interpretation." (ibid.) Gibbs (1994: 381) notes that "Readers do not simply establish ironic intentions by recognizing certain textual features that conventionally mark irony."

An irony marker/indicator alerts the reader to the fact that a sentence is ironical. The sentence would, however, be ironical even without the marker. For example, a wink, before, during or after a sentence meant as ironical will alert the hearer to the fact that the speaker does not mean literally what he/she is saying. The sentence would, however, still be ironical even if the speaker had not provided the hearer with the indication of its ironical status. Therefore, we may distinguish between irony *markers* and irony *factors*: a marker may be removed without affecting the presence of the irony (only, perhaps, its ease of recognition), while a factor may not be removed without destroying the irony.

It is perhaps possible to speculate that the confusion between marking the irony and being part of it has arisen because those factors which are part of the irony (e.g., exaggeration and/or understatement, or the other forms of co(n)textual inappropriateness) do also, as a side effect, alert the hearer to the presence of the irony. (For further examples see section 6.2.2 below.)

Review of some indices of irony

The following is a partial review of some of the most frequent and/or clear markers of irony. A broader discussion and references can be found in Attardo (forthcoming)

- **Intonation** The most common index of ironical intent is intonation. The ironical intonation has been described as a flat (neither rising, nor falling) contour. Other ironical intonations reported are: question intonation (i.e., rising), lowering of pitch on the normally stressed syllable, exaggerated intonational patterns (e.g. singsong melody, falsetto, etc.), nasalization, and stress patterns broader than usual.

- **Other Phonological means** Among other phonological markers of irony, the following have been reported: slowed rate of speaking, syllable lenghtening, pauses, and laughter.

- **Morphological means** Expressions such as "so to speak" and "one might say" as well as "as everybody knows" may indicate irony. Haiman (1998: 47-48) reports on the usage of various quotative and evidential moods and of lexicalized quotative particles.

- **Typographical means** The written transcription of spoken language being the rough approximation that it is, typographical conventions are a poor substitute for the ironical intonation. "Scare quotes" are used to convey a certain detachment from a written utterance and hence irony. The exclamation mark is used to express emphasis; in the right context, it can underscore other means to highlight irony. Dots ("...") mark a suspended utterance, thus alerting the reader to potential other meanings left unsaid.

- **Kinesic markers** These are the irony markers that people commonly think of, such as winks, nudges, tongue-in-cheek, etc.

- **Cotext** Irony can be signalled by its cooccurrence with incompatible elements in the same sentence, paragraph, or larger textual unit, in which u occurs.

- **Context** Irony can be signalled by its cooccurrence with incompatible elements in the context of u.

6.2.3 Reasons for using irony

Having considered the markers of irony, used by the speaker to increase the probability of successfully having his/her irony be recognized, we turn to the still problematic question of why should a speaker incur into such a risk. Consider for example, the following passage, from Sperber and Wilson's influential treatment of irony:

> The most obvious problem with the classical account [of irony] — and with its modern variant, the Gricean account — is that it does not explain why a speaker who could, by hypothesis, have expressed [his/]her intended message directly should decide instead to say the opposite of what [he/]she meant. (Sperber and Wilson 1986: 240).

Nonetheless, while this facet of irony has not received nearly as much attention as other aspects, several interesting suggestions have been put forth. These are reviewed in what follows.

Social Factors

Group Affiliation   Irony may have two opposed purposes: an inclusive and an exclusive one. On the one hand, irony builds in-group solidarity through shared play; on the other hand, it can be used to express a negative judgment about someone or to exclude them.

Sophistication   As another clue to the reason why speakers should prefer an ironical utterance to a literal one, we can note that an ironical utterance connotes its being ironical (and indirect), and hence its being sophisticated and requiring some mental dexterity to process it. Being associated with humor adds yet another prized connotation to irony, at least in Western society.

One of the purposes of irony seems to be that of showing off the speaker's detachment and hence superiority and the speaker's ability to "play" with language (saying one thing, while meaning another). Dews *et al.* (1995: 347) show that speakers use irony to "show themselves to be in control of their emotions."

Evaluation   Grice (1978: 124; 1989: 53) notes that irony is "intimately connected with the expression of a feeling, attitude, or evaluation." This is a common claim within the literature. Note that the expression of feeling, attitude, etc. is not incompatible with the detachment of sophistication: it is precisely the (affected) detachment that is (part of) the attitude communicated.

Sperber and Wilson (1986: 239), as we have seen, echo this claim (though strangely in an attack on Grice's account) and seek to establish the relevance of the ironical utterance on the basis of its expressing a (negative) attitude towards something. The expression of this attitude would then be the point of using irony. Dews *et al.* (1995: 349) mention aggression as one of the reasons to use irony. However, they also note that irony does, in fact, mute both the negative effect of ironical criticism and the positive effect of ironical praise (Dews *et al.* 1995: 349; Dews and Winner 1995: 15). Thus, Dews and Winner (1995) propose the "tinge" theory, i.e., that the literal meaning tinges the intended meaning of the irony, by muting both criticism and praise, for example. This muting function would then be the point of using irony.

6.2. IRONY

Politeness strategy   Irony has been seen as a face-saving strategy. Dews and Winner's "tinge" theory asserts that irony mitigates the face-threatening aspect of direct criticism. Chen (1990) argues that the desire to avoid being impolite to the hearer (on the assumption that this may cause unpleasant reactions by the hearer) and the desire to convey the speaker's intended meaning (with special reference to the speaker's attitude towards a given situation) motivate the violation of the CP (1990: 172-173) and the use of irony. Dews *et al.* (1995) emphasize face saving function of irony. Specifically, Dews *et al.* (1995: 364) show that ironical criticisms "serve to mute the level of criticism," thus allowing the hearer to save face; the speaker saves face as well, being seen as less angry and more in control.

The idea of irony being motivated by politeness is one of the central tenets of Barbe's work. In fact, she repeatedly (e.g., 1995: 73; 79; 94; 107) summarizes her position on irony as a critical purpose on the speaker's part mitigated by politeness. Consider, for example, the following passage:

> When employing irony (...) speakers are not as obviously aggressive and can thwart counter-attacks. Irony, therefore, turns conflict aside. A critical statement, once clothed in an inoffensive way, helps speakers and hearers to save face. (1995: 90)

As seen above, a critical attitude is not always necessary. As far as the motivation of politeness goes, the use of irony strikes me as a fairly aggressive behavior, especially when coupled with critical intent. While I can imagine the speaker and the hearer looking at the rain outside the window and mellowly contemplating the irony of "Nice weather, isn't it?", I have a much harder time imagining the hearer assuming that the speaker is being polite if after the hearer spilled his/her drink on the speaker's carpet and the speaker says "That was clever of you." However, as Barbe (personal communication) points out, the ironical remark is more polite than a direct criticism.

Rhetorical Factors

Rhetorical   An interesting insight into the rhetorical function of irony comes from Carston (1981:30). She notes that irony is a powerful rhetorical tool because it presupposes the truth of the presupposed proposition to be self-evident. For example, in

(57) S: "John is such a good friend." (When the speaker and the hearer know that John just stole the speaker's car, stereo, collection of rare LPs, etc.),

we see that the set of propositions (P) "John is a bad friend" and/or "John is not a friend" must be presupposed by the speaker and the hearer for them to correctly process the irony. Thus, irony can presumably be used to indirectly incorporate a proposition in the common ground of belief that the speaker and the hearer share about a given situation, even if the hearer does not necessarily share the belief that P is true.

Kreuz *et al.* (1991: 161), note that irony is memorable and therefore it offers "highly effective ways for speakers to achieve their communicative ends," which include "to mock, to insult and to be funny" (ibid.). Giora (1995) sees irony as having two basic functions: a) to provide a highly informative utterance, and b) as a politeness strategy, which takes us to the most significant claim about irony, on which below (section 6.2.3).

Retractability Berrendonner (1981: 238) claims that irony, because it allows one to state something and its opposite at the same time, allows the speaker to avoid any sanctions that may follow from stating directly what he/she thinks. From this perspective, irony allows the speaker to take a non-committal attitude towards what he/she is saying; irony is similar in this lack of commitment to humor (see Attardo 1993, 1994).

6.2.4 Irony and Humor

The relationship between irony and humor is subtle. Quite clearly, irony and humor intersect, since there are cases of humorous irony. Also quite obviously, there are cases of humor which are not ironical. Less obviously, but again quite clearly, there are cases of irony which are not (perceived as) humorous. In other words, humor and irony overlap significantly, but are distinct. Dews *et al.* (1995: 348) speculate that the element of surprise "yielded by the disparity between what is said and what is meant" may trigger humor. Giora (1995: 256-257) argues that humor and irony share some basic mechanisms. Namely, they both violate the "graded informativeness requirement," but they do so differently: a joke goes from an unmarked meaning to a marked one, while irony does the opposite.

Also, if irony is a form of indirect negation and humor is based (in part) on local antonymy, it follows that both humor and irony include negation as a significant consituent of the phenomenon. The connection between irony and humor is borne out by empirical results obtained by Kreuz *et al.* (1991: 153-154) who report that, among the goals listed by speakers in ironical utterances, being funny or witty and to play or be silly were listed much more frequently than in the case of non-ironical utterances. Along the same lines, Dews *et al.* (1995: 363) show that ironical statements are rated as funnier than literal ones. Therefore, it stands to reason that one of the "payoffs" of being ironical is that of being perceived as humorous. (265) On the connections between humor and irony, see also Mizzau (1984: 40-41) and Jorgensen (1996), who sees less of a connection.

With the proviso that irony need not be humorous, when it is so, it is clear that irony may contribute to the perception of humor in a text. Irony shares with register humor the feature that it does not have a clear, unique disjunctor located in a

6.2. IRONY

predictable position in the text, as jokes do. The following section presents an reworking of an analysis of a fragment from Voltaire's *Candide* from Attardo (1994). The fragment exemplifies register humor and hyperdetermination via irony.

6.2.5 A Passage from Voltaire's *Candide*

Consider the following passage, taken from the beginning of *Candide*:

(58) Un jour, Cunégonde en se promenant auprès du château, dans le petit bois qu'on appelait *parc*, vit entre des broussailles le docteur Pangloss qui donnait une leçon de physique expérimentale à la femme de chambre de sa mère, petite brune très jolie et très docile. Comme Mlle Cunégonde avait beaucoup de disposition pour les sciences, elle observa, sans souffler, les expériences réitérées dont elle fut témoin; elle vit clairement la raison suffisante du docteur, les effets et les causes, et s'en retourna tout agitée, toute pensive, toute remplie du désir d'être savante, songeant qu'elle pourrait bien être la raison suffisante du jeune Candide, qui pouvait être la sienne.

(One day, Cunegonde, taking a walk near the castle, in the little wood they called *parc*, saw among the bushes Doctor Pangloss giving a lesson in experimental physics to her mother's maid, a little brunette, very good looking and docile. As Miss Cunegonde had great dispositions for the sciences, she observed, without a breath, the repeated experiences she witnessed; she saw clearly the doctor's sufficient reason, the effects and the causes, and returned, agitated and thoughtful, filled with the desire of being knowledgeable, thinking that she might well be the sufficient condition for the young Candide, and he for her.)

The humorous effect of the scene comes from the inappropriateness of the register of philosophical discourse used to describe sexual intercourse. Sexual intercourse as subject matter greatly restrains the available registers. As a matter of fact, only three variants are possible; medical, euphemistic, and obscene. Either one uses words such as "copulate" or "intercourse" or one is forced to use shorter and more colorful synonyms. A third possibility is that of euphemism ("do it," "make love"), but that raises different issues (basically avoidance of the tabooed subject).

The clash between register instantiated by the text and register normally associated with the subject matter creates an opposition similar to that of a script opposition, thus creating a humorous effect.

In this short passage the text introduces two subject matters which require two distinct registers: philosophy and sexual intercourse. We can list some of the triggers that activate the philosophical register, with the corresponding sexual reality being described:

philosophical register	sexual reality
give a lesson in experimental physics	have intercourse
to have a disposition for science	to be interested in sex
repeated experiments	repeated intercourse (?)
doctor's sufficient reason	penis (?)
effects and causes	orgasms and intercourse (?)
desire of being knowledgeable	sexual desire
being the sufficient reason	be a sexual partner

As noted in Attardo (1994: 267), the philosophical register can hardly be considered appropriate to describe sexual intercourse, thus there is a clash between the choice of register in the text and the subject matter, which would require a different register (for example, a medical one, as above, or an obscene one). Thus this passage displays a register clash *in absentia*, as the second register is implicit (no medical or obscene terms, concerning the sexual intercourse of Pangloss and the chamber maid, are used in the passage). A register clash *in praesentia*, as we saw, would be the occurrence of terms form to incompatible register within the text. Note also that traditionally sexual intercourse has been associated with low, informal varieties of language, whereas philosophy has the opposite associations.

It should be noted that the humorous nature of the text is not limited to the clash between the actual and implied registers; for example, there is a sexual/voyeuristic theme in the episode that may be perceived as humorous. More significantly, there is an ironical satire of Leibnizian philosophy that was almost certainly the direct "butt of the joke." As a matter of fact, it is precisely the hyperdetermination of the humorous effect that makes the text interesting. Let us note how the ironical intent of Voltaire is made apparent by the inappropriateness of the register selection for the text, while the satirical put down of Leibniz is achieved via the presumption of relevance (i.e., why is Voltaire using philosophical jargon from the Leibnizian tradition, rather than, say, the scholastic one?).[16]

Let me conclude this chapter with a small digression: by the definition of irony as relevant inappropriateness and the definition of register humor as a clash (inappropriateness) between either a given register and the one generally associated with its *designata* (*in absentia*) or between two registers (*in praesentia*) one may wonder what exactly the difference between irony and register humor is. The answer is, alas, far from simple. Irony generates much more explicit (strong) implicatures, governed by the maxim of relevance, but also by the negation aspect of irony (Giora 1995). So, in this sense, irony is much more specific than register humor. Register humor is satisfied, so to speak, to generate a much vaguer incongruous clash which may have

---

[16]To be noted is also the fact that Leibnizian philosophy and sex are *local antonyms* and so it may appear strange that the above is classified as irony, since it does not appear that the text is saying the opposite of what it means. In fact, this is precisely what Voltaire is doing, because for the purposes of this text, sex and philosophy are opposites; on local antonymy and its problems, see Attardo (1997) and section 1.3.2.

6.2. IRONY

some degree of resolution/justification, but need not do so. Therefore, irony has a higher degree of resolution (insofar as irony must "mean" something).

However, it seems to be the case that irony and register humor are not entirely distinct phenomena. In fact, the same can be said of many other tropes: one can interpret understatements and exaggerations as inappropriateness corrected (resolved) by relevance. Once we get on this slippery slope it is easy to try to extend the inappropriateness and relevance formula to all indirect/figurative discourse. This temptation will be resisted presently, due to the fact that it would obviously take us too far afield. I will however return to this questions in further publications.

Chapter 7

Case Studies

In what follows, I present an analysis of several cases studies, as follows:

- the opening sequence of the *Chuckles Bites the Dust* episode of the *Mary Tyler Moore Show*, a popular US TV sitcom of the seventies;

- an analysis of the poem *Cinderella* by Anne Sexton, and an outline of the central strands of the *Transformations* collection, of which the poem is part;

- an analysis of Henry Peacham's *A Merry Discourse of Meum and Tuum*;

- an analysis of one strand in Umberto Eco's novel *Il nome della rosa*; and finally

- an analysis of *Han Rybeck ou le coup de l'étrier* by Alphonse Allais.

The next chapter contains the analysis of Wilde's *Lord Arthur Savile's Crime*. Together these case studies are intended as concrete examples of the method presented in the previous chapters. Their purpose is to show both how to concretely perform the analyses and also of their explanatory power.

HRCI and ROSE do not have full analyses of te jab lines; CBTD, the *Cinderella* poem from TRAN, and LASC have a full analysis of the jab and punch lines using the usual abbreviations, here repeated for ease of reference:

SO Script Opposition	LM Logical Mechanism
SI Situation	NS Narrative Strategy
TA Target	LA Language

The cases studies show a variety of notations: all lines will be numbered sequentially (in Roman numerals, except in HRCI and LASC) in the order in which they appear. We will not distinguish between punch and jab lines in the numbering. In

CBTD, jab lines are numbered, but only the last addition is numbered. Punch lines are numbered throughout. Lines are numbered separately inside different narratives.

It is clear that a close analysis is best followed if the reader can check it for him/herself against the original. Ideally, the reader should have the text analyzed at hand. To this end, the text of HRCI and of LASC are reproduced in their entirety.[1] When we could not reproduce the actual text for copyright reasons (as well as space constraints) we provide a brief paraphrase and a page number, of the source text used, to let the reader identify the actual text, if necessary.

A vector representation is given for CBTD and for HRCI. Graph representation are provided for TRAN. A chart of the density of lines in LASC appears in the last chapter. Special numbering systems, page numbers of the originals, etc. are indicated in a footnote at the beginning of the text.

This apparent notational exuberance is on the contrary one of the positive sides of the approach we have been developing: each text is presented using the method that best highlights its significant features. For example, LASC has 253 definite lines, with a few more problematic ones. The text is about 12400 words. To produce a graph such as those used in TRAN would have required drawing a graph 12 meters long (some 37 feet). The vector representation used for CBTD and for HRCI works well for narratives that involve embedded narratives and are not too long (at 61 units, the HRCI one borders unreadability). Other representations are possible (e.g., Hemplemann 2000).

A few conventions have been used. The following two abbreviations: *irr* = irrelevant, and *na* = not applicable. When SI = cotext, the situation is idiosyncratic to the text (and therefore it makes no sense to try to characterize it generally). When indicated, narratives are framed upon completion. The symbol ¬ indicates that the text is not finished.

7.1 *Chuckles Bites the Dust*: the opening sequence

Our first example is the opening part of the *Chuckles Bites the Dust* episode of the Mary Tyler Moore Show. The MTM Show ran on CBS from 1970 to 1977. The Chuckles episode was the 127th in the 168-show run of the series. The setting is the newsroom of WJM, a small (imaginary) TV station in Minneapolis, MI, in which Mary, played by Mary Tyler Moore, works.[2]

The initial setup is in the newsroom, where Murray (a journalist and friend of the main character) is reading a teletype printout. He says, to Mary:

The "teletype must be broken, or else G. Ford [then president] held up a liquor store with a toy pistol"

---

[1] They are available in electronic form at http://unix1.cc.ysu.edu/sattardo/humtxt/index.html.

[2] The initial numbers refer to the progressive numbering of the lines and to the page number where the line appears. The structure of the text, up to the given line, is noted after these.

7.1. CHUCKLES BITES THE DUST: THE OPENING SEQUENCE.

I–79–[↦-P→]¬
SO *president/criminal*
LM *teletype is broken–mechanical failure*
SI *hold up*
TA *technology (?) Pres. Ford*
NS *joke*
LA *irr.*

The continuation of the narrative is structured as follows:

$$[\mapsto\text{-}P\rightarrow]\text{-}\neg$$

namely, the first joke about president Ford is followed by a serious sequence of text in which Sue Ann (a collague) enters the scene, greets Murray and Mary and asks Mary to shut her eyes. Clearly, this is preparatory for a joke, but it is not in itself, humorous. The text proceeds with a jab line, delivered by Murray, in which he pretends to believe that the reason Sue Ann is asking Mary to close her eyes is because Sue Ann is not wearing make up and is presumably ashamed of being seen in that condition, again presumably because she does not look good.

II–79–[↦-P→]-J-¬
SO *ugly/beautiful; surprise/shame*
LM *Murray misinterprets Sue Ann's behavior clued by her vanity*
SI *cotextual*
TA *Sue Ann (possibly, women at large)*
NS *request adjacency pair*
LA *irr*

Sue Ann dismisses Murray's implied insult and replies with another jab, attacking Murray's age. She then reiterates her request that Mary close her eyes.

III–79–[↦-P→]-J-J2-¬
SO *young/old; smart/stupid*
LM *Murray's appearance*
SI *cotext*
TA *Murray*
NS *statement*
LA *irr*

After Mary complies, Sue Ann brings in a mobile made of plastic food. This is an entirely visual jab.

IV–79–[↦-P→]-J-J-J3¬
SO *art/trash*
LM *unresolved (resolved by J 5)*

SI *cotext*
TA *none*
NS *visual*
LA *visual*

After Mary opens her eyes she produces a jab asking if she can close them again. She then asks what the object is.

V–80–[↦-P→]-J-J-J-J4¬
SO *overreaction (losing the use of sight)/normal reaction*
LM *mobile is ugly, not wanting to see an ugly thing*
SI *cotext*
TA *mobile and its owner (Sue Ann)*
NS *question*
LA *irr*

Sue Ann's answer to Mary's question consists of a description and explanation of the mobile.

VI–80–[↦-P→]-J-J-J-J-J5¬
SO *food/art*
LM *four food groups are educational (?)*
SI *cotext*
TA *mobile/Sue Ann*
NS *second half of adjacency pair in the previous turn*
LA *irr*

Sue Ann proceeds to explain that she used the mobile as a prop for a show titled "What's all this fuss about famine"

VII–80–[↦-P→]-J-J-J-J-J6¬
SO *high/low status*
LM *Sue Ann is superficial*
SI *cotext*
TA *Sue Ann*
NS *title*
LA *"fuss" connotes triviality, "famine" connotes seriousness*

Mary replies that Sue Ann "shouldn't have"

VIII–80–[↦-P→]-J-J-J-J-J-J7¬
SO *true/false; polite/impolite*
LM *mobile is ugly*
SI *cotext*

7.1. CHUCKLES BITES THE DUST: THE OPENING SEQUENCE. 131

TA *Sue Ann*
NS *second turn of adjacency pair (receive gift)*
LA *pragmatic pun (idiomatic vs. literal)*

Mary then continues by noting that her lease may forbid her from "hanging food"

IX–80–[↦-P→]-J-J-J-J-J-J-J-J8¬
SO *decoration/food*
LM *mobile represents food*
SI *cotext*
TA *Sue Ann*
NS *irr*
LA *irr*

A discussion of where the mobile may be best placed follows. Sue Ann concludes it by suggesting that Mary place the mobile in her bedroom to "relieve the tedium"

X–80–[↦-P→][↦-J-J-J-J-J-J-J-P2]¬
SO *sex/no sex or conventional vs. exotic sex*
LM *Mary's sex life is not rich (as Sue Ann's)*
SI *contextual*
TA *Mary*
NS *irr*
LA *irr (but latinism may add to the humor)*

This ends the first scene (Sue Ann exits; Ted enters). Note that the narrative gets enclosed by the brackets and the ↦ symbol is added at the beginning, for consistency.

On his way in, Ted greets individually all the staff. This is a mannerism of his. The jab is intertextual. (indicated by ˆ)

XI–80–[↦-P→][↦-J-J-J-J-J-J-J-P2]-J1ˆ-¬
SO *normal/abnormal*
LM *Ted is weird*
SI *greeting*
TA *Ted*
NS *greeting*
LA *irr*

Ted then proceeds to greet the mobile.

XII–81–[↦-P→][↦-J-J-J-J-J-J-J-P2]-Jˆ-J2¬
SO *human/object*
LM *Ted is absent-minded*
SI *cotext*

TA *Mary (as owner of the mobile?)*
NS *greeting*
LA *irr*

Ted sings the title line from the song "happy days are here again." Mary asks if he made it up and Ted answers that it is a line of a song, the title of which he has forgotten. I choose to ignore, for the time being, that both Ted's and Mary's remarks are incongruous. I only code as a jab the fact that Ted does not realize that the title of the song is what he has just sung.

XIII–81–[↦-P→][↦-J-J-J-J-J-J-J-P2]-J^-J-J3¬
SO *actual/non-actual*
LM *self-defeating statement (paradox); Ted is stupid*
SI *cotext*
TA *Ted*
NS *irr*
LA *quotation*

Murray questions Ted as to the reason of his good mood. Ted's answer resolves the incongruity of his singing (see above). Ted is happy (and was demonstrating it) because the circus is in town and "they want me." I choose to ignore the fact that this behavior is childish, and hence could be seen as incongruous. Ted's explanation is greeted by Murray's asking if Ted has to provide his own shovel. The implicatures are fairly complex: if the circus wants Ted that means that he is supposed to perform some task for them. Murray infers that the task to be performed by Ted is that to clean the animals' manure (the script for circus contains information about circus animals).

XIV–81–[↦-P→][↦-J-J-J-J-J-J-J-P2]-J^-J-J-J4...¬
SO *excrement/no excrement*
LM *Murray's low opinion of Ted/shoveling excrement is a low job*
SI *circus*
TA *Ted*
NS *question*
LA *irr*

Ted ignores Murray's insult and relates that he is the parade's Marshall and that he has wanted this role for a long time but that his desire has been thwarted before when the job went to the meteorologist from another TV station. He then expresses joy at the fact that something went wrong with the parade on that occasion. Murray inquires what went wrong and Ted reveals that the parade was adversely affected by rain ("it rained on their parade").

XV–81–[↦-P→][↦-J-J-J-J-J-J-J-P2]-J^-J-J-J-J5...¬
SO *figurative/literal*

7.1. CHUCKLES BITES THE DUST: THE OPENING SEQUENCE. 133

    LM *pun; also "meteorologist" is associated with rain*
    SI *parade*
    TA *none (the parade organizers? the meteorologist?)*
    NS *second turn of adjacency pair (Q&A)*
    LA *idiom*

Ted proceeds to relate another incident in which a basketball player got stuck in a little car the year before. Mary ends the recollection of the event by saying that the player had to be freed by taking the car apart and that that "kind of spoiled the effect." We have two lines: one in the embedded narrative about the basketball player (the situation of being stuck in the car), and one in Mary's discourse.

    XVI–81–[↦-P→][↦-J-J-J-J-J-J-J-P2]-J⌒-J-J-J-J-[↦-J-]¬
    SO *big/small control/loss of control*
    LM *confusion (got in the wrong car)*
    SI *parade*
    TA *basketball player*
    NS *irr*
    LA *irr*

    XVII–81–[↦-P→][↦-J-J-J-J-J-J-J-P2]-J⌒-J-J-J-J-[↦-J-]-J5¬
    SO *actual/non-actual*
    LM *none (?)*
    SI *irr*
    TA *Mary*
    NS *irr*
    LA *understatement*

Murray comments that the parade has "a history of disaster" and when Ted replies that this year he will be in charge, Murray replies "I rest my case."

    XVIII–81–[↦-P→][↦-J-J-J-J-J-J-J-P2]-J⌒-J-J-J-J-[↦-J-]-J-J6...¬

    SO *good/bad*
    LM *Ted is prone to errors*
    SI *cotext*
    TA *Ted*
    NS *irr*
    LA *idiom*

As Ted is telling Murray that nothing can ruin his day, Lou enters and tells Ted that he cannot go to the parade.

    XIX–81–[↦-P→][↦-J-J-J-J-J-J-J-P2]-J⌒-J-J-J-J-[↦-J-]-J-J7...¬
    SO *likely/unlikely*

LM *coincidence*
SI *cotext*
TA *Ted*
NS *irr*
LA *irr*

The (feeble) humor is generated by the fortuitous coincidence that Lou would dash Ted's hopes just when Ted has just finished stating that nothing can ruin his day. A possible interpretation of the humor in this scene is that this is a case of situational irony.

Lou explains that the reason he does not want Ted to go is that if the anchorman marches with a chimp, "it gives him an undignified image." When Ted replies that it will not give Ted an undignified image, Lou replies he was talking about the monkey.

XX–81–[↦-P→][↦-J-J-J-J-J-J-J-J-P2]-J^-J-J-J-J-[↦-J-]-J-J-J8¬
SO *actual/non-actual human/monkey*
LM *antecedent reference assignment error*
SI *cotext*
TA *Ted*
NS *Q&A*
LA *antecedent must be ambiguous*

The scene ends on Ted's protest. Overall, the scene looks as follows:

[↦-P→][↦-J-J-J-J-J-J-J-J-P2] [↦-J^-J-J-J-J-[↦-J-]-J-J8-]

We can now turn to the next case study.

7.2 Sexton's *Cinderella*

This section[3] presents an analysis of the *Cinderella* poem from TRAN (Sexton 1981: 221-295). As is well known, *Transformations* is a collection of poems by Anne Sexton[4] which reinterpret seventeen fairy tales by the Brothers Grimm.

Sexton's reinterpretations are organized similarly throughout the collection. Each piece begins with a prologue in which the narrator (presumably Sexton herself) discusses contemporary/realistic notions. The fairy tale follows the prologue, identifiable to the audience by one of several clues (*once, there once was,* etc.) which

---
[3] Written with Cynthia Vigliotti. Vigliotti (forthcoming) will present an analysis of all the poems of *Transformations*.

[4] Often considered a writer whose work defined the genre of "Confessional poetry," Anne Sexton (1928-1974) published eight books of poetry: *To Bedlam and Part Way Back* (1960), *All My Pretty Ones* (1962), *Live or Die* (1966) which one the Pulitzer Prize for Poetry, *Love Poems* (1969), *Transformations* (1971), *The Book of Folly* (1972), *The Death Notebooks* (1974), and *The Awful Rowing Toward God* (1975). Two collections, *45 Mercy Street* (1976) and *Words for Dr. Y: Uncollected Poems* (1978) were published posthumously.

7.2. SEXTON'S CINDERELLA

signify entrance into the mythical world. An epilogue, in which Sexton reenters the modern world, closes each piece. Often the prologue and epilogue serve to emphasize the relationships between reality and the fairy tale. In what follows, we discuss the various strands found in the text of *Cinderella* and then present a list of all the humorous lines found in the text, with a full GTVH analysis of each.

Three SO strands can be found in *Cinderella*: REALITY/FAIRY TALE, EXCREMENT/NON-EXCREMENT, and HIGH/LOW STATURE (see figure 7.1). The first of these SOs, REALITY/FAIRY TALE, illustrates the incongruity which arises when contemporary real world notions such as "Bonwit Teller" and "real estate" are thrust into the world of the fairy tale. The next SO, EXCREMENT/NON-EXCREMENT, focuses at one level, on the literal opposition between such items as "diapers" and "Dior." On another level, however, Sexton uses this opposition to echo the one found in the REALITY/FAIRY TALE SO. In the real world, diapers and toilets are a necessary, if often unpleasant, reality. In the world of the fairy tale, however, there is rarely any mention of bodily functions: princes and princesses, and even evil stepmothers, rarely (if ever) express the need to relieve themselves. Finally, the SO HIGH/LOW STATURE represents the opposition between a "high" notion, such as a royal wedding, and a "low" notion, such as a market (cf. line XIV, verse 42).

One of the most significant strands in the poem emerges from parallelization. The LM strand, "parallelization," features two substrands, "that story," and "...never..." (both of which consist of the verbatim repetition of a fragment of text). The "that story" substrand distinguishes a parallelism between the prologue and the four individual stories contained therein which appear, at first glance, to have little or nothing to do with the tale of Cinderella and the fairy tale proper. This strand further emphasizes the parallelisms between reality and the fairy tale. In other words, while reading the prologue the audience is reminded after each new tale is introduced (the plumber's, the nursemaid's, the milkman's and the charwoman's tales) that the story they are about to hear is not at all novel (*"that* story"), that they have heard it all before. What follows is Sexton's retelling of the original tale. It is not until the last few lines of the poem that the reader is reminded of the prologue and thus the link between prologue and tale is revealed. The parallelisms at work in this substrand would appear as the following:

5	plumber	:	winning lottery	::	Cinderella	:	marrying Prince
10	nursemaid	:	capturing oldest son	::	Cinderella	:	marrying Prince
21	charwoman	:	winning lawsuit	::	Cinderella	:	marrying Prince
109	Cinderella	:	marrying Prince	::	prologue's characters	:	becoming rich

Finally, in the closing of the poem, Sexton illustrates that Cinderella's tale is no different from those we read in the prologue, that it is after all, "that story." Like the aforementioned substrand, the "...never..." substrand serves as an echo to the tales in the prologue. Thus, line 103 recalls both the nursemaid and the charwoman ("...diapers or dust..."), line 104 recalls the milkman ("...the timing of an egg..."), and line 105 reminds us that we have heard these stories before ("...telling the same story twice..."), thereby establishing a link between the contemporary characters and Cinderella, the real world and the fairy tale.

Other LM strands include:

- *pun* (see figure 7.2) which consists of four instances of a play on the familiar phrase, "from rags to riches."

- *analogy/parallelism* which operates in several humorous similes featuring Cinderella or the Prince (e.g., Cinderella is like Al Jolson, because her face is blackened by soot, verse 32)

- *anachronistic juxtaposition* which is used to describe the incongruity which arises with the appearance of contemporary characters or notions such as Al Jolson (verse 32), shoe salesmen (verse 91), and the Bobbsey Twins (verse 108).

We have identified one SI strand, "sudden wealth." The situation featured in each of these humorous instances is that of the character becoming wealthy quite suddenly and unexpectedly, taking him or her from a low prestige to a high prestige status: for example, the characters in the prologue all become wealthy for reasons outside their professional occupation (e.g., the plumber hitting the lottery, verse 4).

There are three NS strands found in *Cinderella*. The first, "metanarrative commentary," identifies those humorous instances wherein the author either addresses her audience directly or interrupts the fairy tale narrative to comment sardonically on the events taking place. For example, Sexton uses phrases like "my dears" (40) and "you all" (41) to speak to her audience from within the fairy tale. Likewise, she comments drolly on events and characters like the evil stepmother (55) and amputation (86). This technique affords Sexton a narrative distance which, when combined with the ridiculousness of the events being described, results in a humorous contrast.

The second NS strand "framing device" includes two classes of items:

- "that story" (see figure 7.2 and above), and

- "...never..." (see figure 7.2 and above)

Both classes serve as framing devices because the occurrence of "that story" links the prologue to the epilogue (via echoic repetition) while also linking the *Cinderella* narrative to both the prologue and epilogue, by explicitly introducing a similarity between the fairy tale and the real world. The "never" substrand (cf. the comb strand at the end of the LM strands graph in figure 7.2) functions similarly by echoing features related to the characters found in the prologue, e.g., "never arguing over the timing of an egg" (104) and the milkman character (16), or "never bothered by diapers or dust" (103) and the nursemaid (9) and charwoman (20), respectively (diapers/dust).

7.2. SEXTON'S CINDERELLA

The third NS strand "similes" corresponds to the "analogy/parallelism" LM, not reproduced in figure (7.2):

    32   Cinderella looks like Al Jolson
    57   Cinderella cries like a gospel singer
    91   the Prince feels like a shoe salesman

We further noted three TA strands:

- class, which targets class differences (cf. "toilets to riches" (4))

- fairy tale, in which Sexton makes fun of the lack of novelty of the story she is *re*telling, e.g., "next came the ball, as you all know" (41), characters in the story, etc. e.g., "the bird is important, my dears, so heed him" (40), "that's the way with stepmothers" (55).

- marriage as happy ending of fairy tales (cf. the "never" LM and NS strand).

The following are the humorous lines in the text of *Cinderella*, with their GTVH analysis, in footnote. The Roman and Arabic numbers preceding the quotation indicate line number and verse in the poem, respectively.

I-3 "...who wins the Irish Sweepstakes."[5]
II-4 "From toilets to riches."[6]
III-5 "That story."[7]
IV-9 "From diapers to Dior."[8]
V-10 "That story."[9]
VI-14 "...who goes into real estate..."[10]
VII-15 "...and makes a pile."[11]
VIII-16 "From homogenized to martinis at lunch."[12]
IX-20 "From mops to Bonwit Teller."[13]
X-21 "That story."[14]

---

[5] SO *reality/myth; high/low stature;* LM *none;* SI *sudden wealth;* TA *class;* NS *none;* LA *irr.*

[6] SO *reality/myth; high/low stature; excrement/non-excrement;* LM *pun;* SI *sudden wealth;* TA *class;* NS *none;* LA *irr.*

[7] SO *novelty/familiarity;* LM *parallelization;* SI *narration;* TA *fairy tale;* NS *framing device;* LA *irr.*

[8] SO *reality/myth; high/low stature; excrement/non-excrement;* LM *pun;* SI *sudden wealth;* TA *class;* NS *none;* LA *irr.*

[9] SO *novelty/familiarity;* LM *parallelization;* SI *narration;* TA *fairytale;* NS *framing device;* LA *irr.*

[10] SO *reality/myth;* LM *none;* SI *sudden wealth;* TA *class;* NS *none;* LA *irr.*

[11] SO *excrement/non-excrement;* LM *none;* SI *sudden wealth;* TA *class;* NS *none;* LA *idiomatic.*

[12] SO *reality/myth; high/low stature;* LM *pun;* SI *sudden wealth;* TA *class;* NS *none;* LA *irr.*

[13] SO *reality/myth; high/low stature;* LM *pun;* SI *sudden wealth;* TA *class;* NS *none;* LA *irr.*

[14] SO *novelty/familiarity;* LM *parallelization;* SI *narration;* TA *fairytale;* NS *framing device;* LA *irr.*

XI-32 "...and walked around looking like Al Jolson."[15]
XII-40 "The bird is important, my dears, so heed him."[16]
XIII-41 "Next came the ball, as you all know."[17]
XIV-42 "It was a marriage market."[18]
XV-55 "That's the way with stepmothers."[19]
XVI-57 "...cried forth like a gospel singer."[20]
XVII-62 "Rather a large package for a simple bird."[21]
XVIII-63 "So she went. Which is no surprise."[22]
XIX-86 "That's the way with amputations."[23]
XX-91 "He began to feel like a shoe salesman."[24]
XXI-103 "...never bothered by diapers or dust,"[25]
XXII-104 "...never arguing over the timing of an egg,"[26]
XXIII-105 "...never telling the same story twice,"[27]
XXIV-106 "...never getting a middle-aged spread."[28]
XXV-108 "Regular Bobbsey Twins."[29]

---

[15] SO *reality/myth*; LM *analogy; anachronistic juxtaposition*; SI *cotextual*; TA *Cinderella*; NS *simile*; LA *irr.*

[16] SO *narrative/metanarrative*; LM *none*; SI *narration*; TA *fairytale*; NS *metanarrative commentary*; LA *irr.*

[17] SO *narrative/metanarrative*; LM *none*; SI *narration*; TA *fairytale*; NS *metanarrative commentary*; LA *irr.*

[18] SO *reality/myth; high/low stature*; LM *none*; SI *cotextual*; TA *marriage/class*; NS *none*; LA *alliterative/idiomatic.*

[19] SO *narrative/metanarrative*; LM *none*; SI *narration*; TA *fairytale*; NS *metanarrative commentary*; LA *irr.*

[20] SO *reality/myth*; LM *analogy/anachronistic juxtaposition*; SI *cotextual*; TA *Cinderella*; NS *simile*; LA *evangelistic register.*

[21] SO *narrative/metanarrative*; LM *reasoning from false premises*; SI *none*; TA *fairytale*; NS *metanarrative commentary*; LA *irr.*

[22] SO *narrative/metanarrative*; LM *none*; SI *narration*; TA *fairytale*; NS *metanarrative commentary*; LA *irr.*

[23] SO *serious/glib*; LM *none*; SI *narration*; TA *fairytale*; NS *metanarrative commentary*; LA *irr.*

[24] SO *reality/myth; high/low stature*; LM *analogy/anachronistic juxtaposition*; SI *cotextual*; TA *Prince*; NS *simile*; LA *alliterative.*

[25] SO *excrement/non-excrement*; LM *parallelization*; SI *cotextual*; TA *marriage*; NS *framing device*; LA *alliterative.*

[26] SO *domesticity/non-domesticity*; LM *parallelization*; SI *cotextual*; TA *marriage*; NS *framing device*; LA *irr.*

[27] SO *novelty/familiarity*; LM *parallelization*; SI *cotextual*; TA *marriage*; NS *framing device*; LA *irr.*

[28] SO *attractive/unattractive*; LM *parallelization*; SI *cotextual*; TA *marriage*; NS *framing device*; LA *colloquial.*

[29] SO *reality/fairy tale*; LM *anachronistic juxtaposition*; SI *cotextual*; TA *marriage*; NS *none*; LA *idiomatic ("regular x").*

7.2. SEXTON'S CINDERELLA

XXVI-109 "That story."[30]

7.2.1 Graphs

The analysis of the poem *Cinderella* above is quite detailed, yet it may be difficult to grasp the interplay of strands in the poem. Representing strands is more easily done in graphical form and thus we have elaborated a technique to chart strands in graphs.

The technique, pioneered in Vigliotti (1998), consists of representing the text of the poem using a straight line, which represents the vector of the text. The line is carefully drawn so as to be proportional to the length of the text. In this case, we have somewhat arbitrarily chosen to use the verse (line of the poem) as the basic unit of analysis. Each verse corresponds to one millimeter on the vector. Thus, by observing the scale on the vector itself, the reader can locate with sufficient accuracy each jab line on the vector and therefore in the text itself. All jab lines are indicated on the graph as a short line perpendicular to the vector. Strands are represented by a thick straight line connecting the perpendicular jabs. All strands are labeled.

The graphs lend themselves well to the visualization of the relative positions of the jabs within the text. The names *combs* and *bridges* are metaphors derived from their visual appearance on the graphs.

As a convention, we reserve position 0 on the vector for the title of the poem. A small triangle having the base parallel to the vector and its vertex touching the vector ($\triangledown$) indicates the end of the poem.

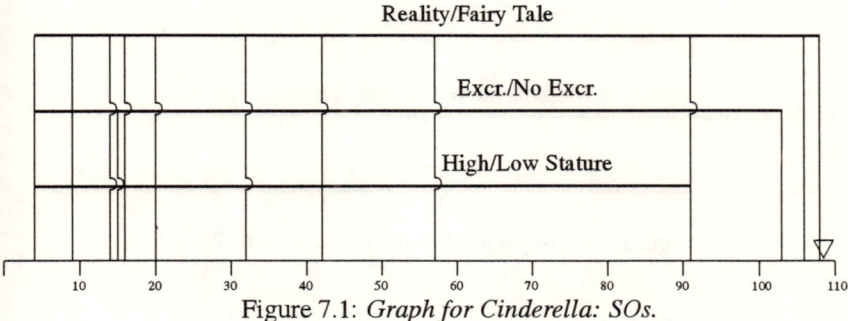

Figure 7.1: *Graph for Cinderella: SOs.*

Figure (7.1) represents the SOs of the poem *Cinderella*. Note that lines that belong to different strands are attached to several horizontal lines.

---

[30]SO *novelty/familiarity*; **LM** *parallelization*; **SI** *cotextual*; **TA** *fairytale*; **NS** *framing device*; **LA** *irr.*

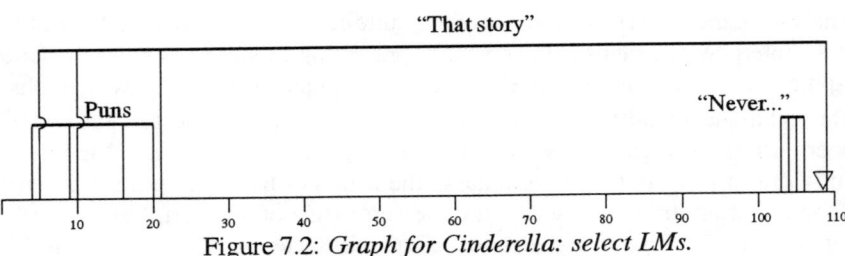

Figure 7.2: *Graph for Cinderella: select LMs.*

Figure (7.2) presents a selection of LMs. Note the comb of puns at the beginning of the poem, and the comb playing on "Never..." towards the end. Note also the comb-bridge combination, with the repetiton of "that story."

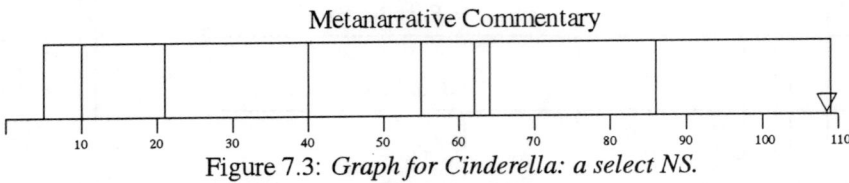

Figure 7.3: *Graph for Cinderella: a select NS.*

Finally, figure (7.3) presents one of the NS strands in the poem, chosen because of its interest in the text (see above) and to illustrate a more or less unmarked distribution (compare it to the combs and bridges of the previous graph). An idea of the complexity of a total graph for the poem can be gathered by overlapping these three partial graphs.

7.2.2 Stacks

Since the concept of stack has been proposed (Wilson 1997) no serious applications have been developed, no doubt due to the labor intensive nature of the work. To give an idea of the procedure to identify stacks, let us consider the list of select SOstrands, as they appear in the various poems in TRAN.[31] To do so consider the data in the following chart, which lists TRAN's poems and their relevant SO strands. In order to be included in the chart, a strand must occur in at least two different poems.

	R/FT	N/M	Food	Sex	Excr.
Briar Rose	•	•	•		
Godfather Death	•	•	•	•	
Snow White	•	•	•		
The White Snake	•	•			
Rumpelstiltskin	•	•	•	•	
The Little Peasant	•	•	•	•	•
Iron Hans	•	•	•		
Rapunzel	•	•	•	•	
One Eyes, Two Eyes...	•	•	•	•	
The Wonderful Musician	•	•	•		
Red Riding Hood	•	•	•	•	
Maiden Without Hands	•	•	•		
The Frog Prince	•	•	•	•	•
Hansel and Gretel	•	•	•		
12 Dancing Princesses	•	•			
Cinderella	•	•	•		•
The Gold Key	•	•	•		

The following key clarifies the abbreviations in the chart above:

	TRAN (Select SO Strands)
R/FT	Reality/Fairy Tale
N/M	Narrative/Metanarrative
Food	Food/No Food
Sex	Sex/No Sex
Excr.	Excrement/No Excrement

Even a cursory glance at the chart reveals that there are three SO strands that occur in virtually all of the poems (namely, R/FT, N/M, and Food/No Food). As the reader will recall, the fact that one particular strand occurs in different texts identifies it as an intertextual strand. These three are the central SO strands of the collection (cf. section 5.3.3). Note that the FOOD/NO FOOD SO occurs in all but two of the

---
[31] Details on the establishment of the strands in each poem will be found in Vigliotti (forthcoming).

poems. Hence one could question the centrality of the strand. By the definition given in (5.3.3), we would be perfectly right to label a strand that occurs in 14 out of 17 poems as central. However, to distinguish between strands that occur in all the parts of a text and those that occur only in a majority thereof, we may choose to indicate them as *strong* central strands and *weak* central strands, respectively.

The analysis of TRAN allows us to locate sequences of lines which are thematically or formally linked (strands), and then to identify various strands which are similarly related (stacks). Clearly, the *Reality/Fairy Tale* SO strand and the NARRATIVE/METANARRATIVE SO strand are closely related, as the narrator is writing from within the world of "reality" while the narratives proper (the retellings of the original tales) are mythical. What results is a stack uniting the two strands.

We now turn to the next case study, which differs very significantly from the previous two.

7.3 *A Merry Discourse of Meum and Tuum*

Peacham's MDMT[32] is an example of the picaresque genre in English literature. It relates the adventures of two litigious brothers (oddly named *Meum* and *Tuum*) who set out to travel from their hometown to London and back. The narrative consists of little else than a sequence of episodes, connected by the presence of the two main characters (rarely, only one of them). There is one excursus, in which the narrator relates a personal anecdote (p. 31 of the 1639 edition).

The text presents significant interest from a literary and sociological point of view (see Locatelli 1998), but from the humorous content it is somewhat "flat." The picaresque genre requires that the fabula consist of a series of episodes more or less independent from one another, loosely connected by a chronological sequence (so, roughly speaking, fabula and plot coincide). The distribution of humor throughout the text is consistent with this organization: we find a virtually random distribution of lines throughout the text (see picture 7.3), with no page of the original edition including more than three lines and a few without any. Comparing these figures to Wilde's LASC virtuoso numbers (cf. chapter 8 and the chart 9.1) one gets a very clear feeling of the differences in artistry, control over the medium, and general

---

[32] Henry Peacham Jr. (1578-1644?) was a minor author in the late Elizabethan and Stuart periods. He published several collections of emblems, a treatise on courtly manners (*The Compleat Gentleman*, 1622), elegies, political pamphlets, and humorous texts, such as *Coach and Sedan* (1636), a dialogue, *The More the Merrier* (1608), a collection of epigrams, and *A Merry Discourse of Meum and Tuum* (MDMT) (1639). Towards the end of his life, Peacham published several political pamphlets in which he sided with the royalists (i.e., the supporters of Charles I) and against the parlimentary rebels. He also published a book about living in London (*The Art of Living in London*) which is reflected in MDMT's familiarity with London life. The text of MDMT was critically edited from the 1639 copy (Folger Shakespeare Library, Washington, DC, *Rare Books* Call number: 19510) by Locatelli (1998) who reproduces the original texts respecting the pagination. This edition has been used in the analysis. On Peacham, see also Cawley (1971) and Young (1979).

7.3. A MERRY DISCOURSE OF MEUM AND TUUM 143

sophistication between the authors.[33]

The previous observations notwithstanding, there are some interesting configurations within MDMT: first and foremost we note a significant strand involving the "litigiousness" of the two brothers, which occurs 12 times within the text, thus probably qualifying for the status of default central strand. We also note a comb configuration of lines (jab lines 6-8) involving the paper clothes that the brothers wear at the beginning of the story. Finally, we can note an "attack by animal" bridge (lines 31 and 51) enriched by the detail that the victim is first one and the the other brother. These can be observed in figure (7.3), while a complete list of the lines with their location in the text can be found in tables (7.3) and (7.2).

A Jab against a doctor in the Renaissance

The reader will recall the script for DOCTOR, see in section (1.1). MDMT gives us the possibility to see a second example of humor based on the exploitation of that script, besides the canonical doctor's wife joke (7). Consider the following exerpt from MDMT:

(59) if any patient should demand of him [Meum] the name and quality of his disease, and what were the Symptomes of the same, hee could not tell (jab 43, page 29)

Now, the following inferential chain takes place: if one has studied a subject, it follows that one knows about it. Hence, if one has studied medicine, one should know about it. The script for MEDICINE includes knowledge of symptoms of diseases, their names, and the nature thereof.

STUDY→ KNOW (MEDICINE → DISEASE → SYMPTOM, NAME, NATURE)

Since the text of MDMT tells us that Meum cannot provide his patients with this information, we can draw the additional inference that he is not a (good) doctor. Note how example (59) is clearly a jab line and not a punch line, the text continues indeed as follows:

(60) wherefore he held it the best course of professing, to cure all at once (jab 44, page 29-30)

In this continuation, we find an amusing reversal of the logical conclusions to which Meum should have arrived, i.e., that he should stop practicing medicine, since he is not capable of doing so. On the contrary, Meum decides that, since he cannot tell for which disease his potions may be helpful, he might as well claim that they are helpful for all of them.

---

[33] We limit ourselves to these impressionistic considerations as it is obviously too early to venture detailed analyses comparing authors when so few texts have been analyzed; see also 9.1.

$[\mapsto J^1 - J^2_\bullet - J^3 - J^4 - J^5 - J^6_\bullet - J^7_p - J^8_p - J^9_p - J^{10}_\bullet - J^{11} - J^{12} - J^{13}_\bullet - J^{14} - J^{15} - J^{16}_\bullet$

$- J^{17} - J^{18}_\bullet - J^{19} - J^{20}_\bullet - J^{21} - J^{22} - J^{23} - J^{24}_p - J^{25}_\bullet - J^{26} - J^{27} - J^{28} - J^{29} - J^{30}_\bullet -$

$J^{31}_a - J^{32} - J^{33} - J^{34} - J^{35} - J^{36} - J^{37} - J^{38} - J^{39} - J^{40} - J^{41}_\bullet - J^{42} - J^{43} - J^{44} -$

$J^{45} - J^{46} - [\mapsto J^{47}] - J^{48} - J^{49} - J^{50} - J^{51}_a - J^{52} - J^{53} - J^{54}_\bullet - J^{55}_\bullet \to]$

Legenda:

litigiousness	•
paper clothes	p
attack by animal	a

Figure 7.4: *The Merry Discourse of Meum and Tuum by Henry Peacham, Jr.*

7.3. A MERRY DISCOURSE OF MEUM AND TUUM

#	p.	Jab
1	A3	Fannius' Nettle
2	1	Wrangle
3	2	Plutus' 4 sons fight
4	3	Butter price too high
5	4	Suit made with dogs' skins
6	5	"they will raise a mutinie"
7	5	parchment suite
8	6	black lines = lace
9	6	waxen seals = buttons
10	6	fight over shoehorn
11	7	church steeple = room
12	7	bells do not trouble study
13	9	gentleman laboured to make all parties friends but for M & T
14	9	"sute" ceases as parson dies
15	10	Sitomagnum = bigplace
16	10	M & T stay 4/5 days, lawyers work 12 months
17	10	Bailiff's trick about cattle
18	11	M & T sue one another's client
19	11	Hostess pacifies everybody M & T leave
20	12	Baker and Hostess in Qui
21	13	M gets bread and cheese
22	13	T gets roast pork and beer
23	14	Land of Pronounes
24	14	M & T sell paper clothes
25	14	M & T lodge at the Two Wrestlers
26	15	M & T learn logic in 1 day (?)
27	16	pear tree
28	17	M & T lodging at Theeving Lane and Hell
29	17	spell in Westminster bridge
30	18	Brawl btw Beareward and M
31	18	T and bull
32	19	Cornish and Devonshire law students "make much of them"
33	20	Cobwebs in Westminster
34	22	M & T "like the Whetstone"
35	23	M "physitian"
36	23	T "gypsy"
37	24	"honest and substantial people dwell in that lane"
38	24	T = mine; M = thine
39	24	"empty purses a legall way"
40	25	two earses and 3 feete
41	26	"by no means (...)yet (...) held the parish to it for one seven years"
42	29	Master Lime witholds money gathered
43	29	M doctor but does not know names of diseases
44	30	best course "professing to cure all at once"
45	30	Leveret and "veriest Asse" = M

Table 7.1: *List of Jab Lines in Peacham's The Merry Discourse of Meum and Tuum*

#	p.	Jab
46	30	M herborist
47	31	excursus: Dr. John in Utrecht
48	32	Lime + Twig
49	33	"never saw you" "we are those you mean"
50	34	"Interest, a fierce, a cruel Mastive"
51	34	M attacked by dog
52	34	Littleton
53	36	pregnant women
54	37	quarrelsomeness spreads
55	38	return ro Wrangle, more fights

Table 7.2: *List of Jab Lines in Peacham's The Merry Discourse of Meum and Tuum; continued.*

The difference with the doctor's wife joke analyzed by Raskin cf. example (7) is striking: in the doctor's wife joke, the script for doctor is discarded, once the punch line reveals that the presumed patient is in fact the doctor's wife's lover. In the doctor's jab line in Peacham's text, the script is not discarded at all, instead it is used to create another jab, and continue the narrative. Our next case study is a contemporary novel, by Umberto Eco.

7.3. A MERRY DISCOURSE OF MEUM AND TUUM

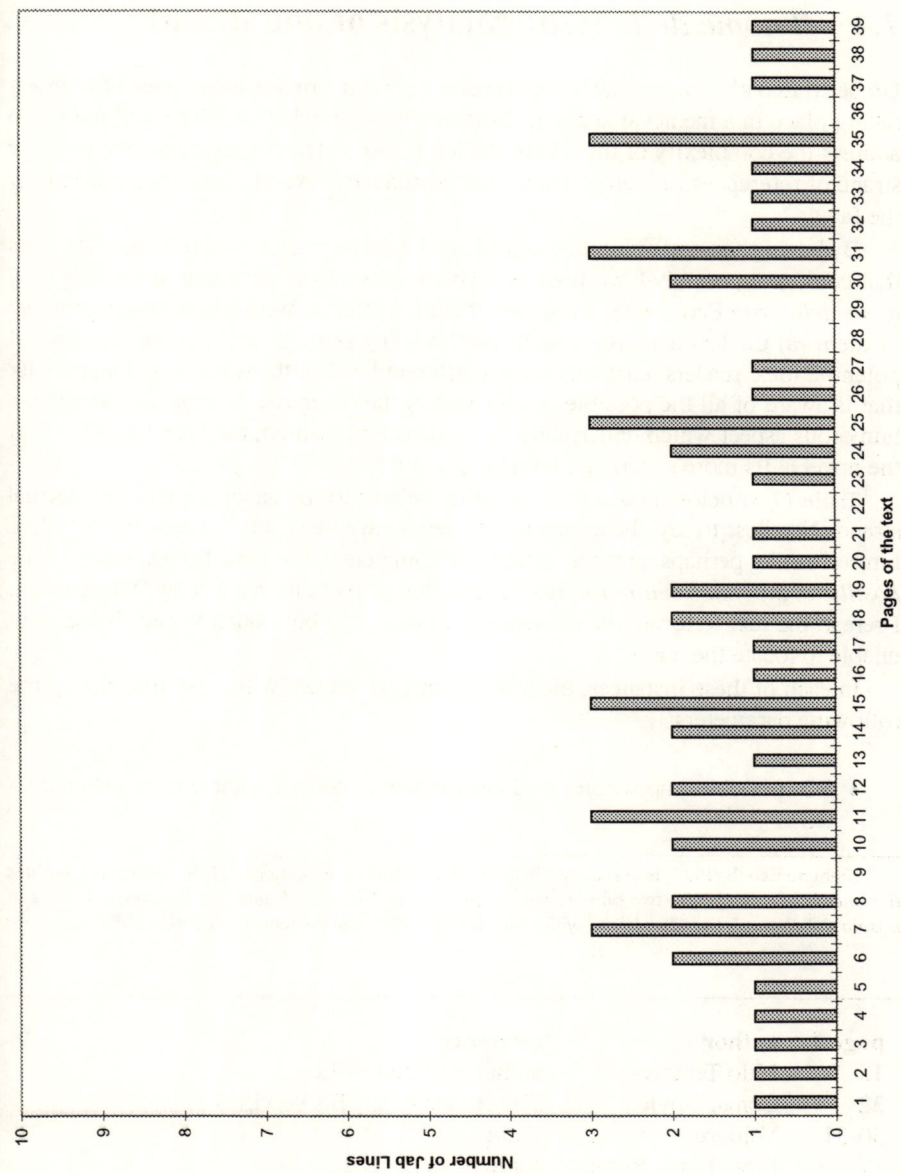

Figure 7.5: *MDMT segmentation chart*

7.4 *Il nome della rosa*: **Analysis of one strand**

Umberto Eco's[34] *Il nome della rosa* revolves around a mysterious series of murders taking place in a medieval abbey in Northern Italy. In what follows I will not try to address the complexity of the text in the least, and instead focus on on one peculiar strand of references to literary works that postdate by several centuries the events of the fabula.

By having a strand of humorous jab lines based on intertextual references to texts that could not possibly have been available to any of the personae in the text of *Il nome della rosa* Eco creates a number of textual effects. We are concerned with two of them: a) the text acquires a multi-level reading setting, i.e., it postulates several potential ideal readers, each enjoying a different level of the text (or an ideal reader that is aware of all the possible levels), and b) the otherwise serious text acquires a humorous aspect which undermines, in postmodern fashion, the very foundation of the novel at its more superficial levels (e.g., as a whodunit).

Table (7.3) below lists all the jabs that belong to the anachronistic intertextual strand. Needless to say, those are only the few I have been able to identify. Only Eco himself could, perhaps, provide us with the complete list of jabs. For example, in the *Postille* to the *Nome della rosa*, Eco tells us that he included a quote by Wittgenstein. I reread the text to locate the references in table (7.3) but, much to my shame, was unable to locate the quote.

In each of these instances, the text presents its readers with a jab line having the following parameters:

- SO: possible/impossible; medieval/modern; modern author/medieval character.

---

[34]Umberto Eco (b. 1932) is best known in academic circles as a semiotician. He has published, besides *Il nome della rosa* (1980), two other novels: *Il pendolo di Foucault* (*Foucault's Pendulum*, 1988) and *L'isola del giorno prima* (*The Island of the Day Before*, 1994), and the recent *Baudolino* (2000).

---

page #	author	reference
13	Milo Temesvar	author invented by Eco
32	Conan Doyle	The Hound of the Baskervilles
30-31	Voltaire	Zadig
87	Jorge Louis Borges	Jorge from Burgos
266	Alphonse Allais	"la logique mène à tout..."
?	Wittgenstein	

Table 7.3: *Some of the anachronistic/intertextual jabs of ROSE.*

7.4. IL NOME DELLA ROSA: ANALYSIS OF ONE STRAND 149

- LM: none, or some appropriateness to context (e.g., Jorge is a librarian, so was Borges.)

- SI: text written in the middle ages

- TA: naive model reader (?)

- NS: intertextual allusion

- LA: irr

7.4.1 A text with more than one model reader

Each text assumes a model reader for whom the text is written (cf. section 1.6.1). It is therefore clear that when a text is structured in such a way that it is possible to derive two or more distinct TWRs from the processing of the text the text is thereby postulating different possible model readers. In our specific case, ROSE assumes at least two model readers: a naive reader, who does not get any of the intertextual allusions, and a sophisticated one, who gets them all.[35]

Since the sophisticated reader is the one who gets the anachronistic jabs which undermine the realistic illusion (3.3) we may assume, as I did in the text above, that the target of the humor is the naive model reader who does not understand that the realistic illusion has been breached (since a monk writing in the 14th century could not have known Voltaire, Alphonse Allais, or Borges) and "misses the joke."

7.4.2 A Serious Novel with a Humor Strand

Il nome della rosa is not a funny novel, by any stretch of the imagination. Nonetheless, there are some humorous instances (e.g., those listed in Table 7.3). As we saw, they can be linked in a strand. This is a prototypical example of a serious text in which a humorous strand appears without touching the largest part of the text, i.e., a best-case scenario for Palmer's idea of the serious plot upon which humor is attached (cf. section 2.2.3).

We turn now to the next case study, a text that could not be more different from the present one, except of course for the prolonged attention that Eco has given to its author, Alphonse Allais.

---

[35] I resisted the temptation to name the naive model reader Adso, and the sophisticated one Guglielmo, only after a week of prayer and fasting.

7.5 Han Rybeck ou le coup de l'étrier

This short story[36] by Alphonse Allais[37] appeared in a newspaper, *Le journal*, and was then published in a collection in *Pas de bile* (1893). At first brush, HRCI can be segmented in five sections, as per the following chart:

Paragraph	Section
3-9	Authorial introduction
10-13	establishment of the situation
14-22	main excursus: the "loup-phoques" incident
23-30	Han Rybeck's fishing
31-61	principal story: fight and marriage of Han Rybeck

Let us note immediately that the first four sections are roughly as long as the last one. The intuitively central narrative does not start until well into the text (about half way, par. 31). Thus it seems that HRCI does not fit easily the tripartite characteristics of narratives, or that at least the onset of the central complication of the fabula is systematically delayed by the plot and/or digressions.

There occurs in HRCI an excursus "narrative" which ends in a punch line:

(61) 3-4 A celle-là seule que j'aime (...) faire plaisir à cinq ou six personnes

The main narrative (level$_0$) is in fact very short, and serves only to introduce the longer, more significant narrative (10-61) at level$_{-1}$. An interesting aspect of the short story is that the level$_0$ narrative keeps intruding in the level$_1$ narrative, via authorial metanarrative comments (see below). A further complication is that within the level$_{-1}$ narrative is a "parasitic" narrative (par. 14-23 and 33-34) which is in fact a deliberately poorly camouflaged pretext for a pun. Technically, the parasitic narrative is not an embedded narrative, however, it violates too clearly the standards of realistic plot construction that we have marked it in the text as distinct.[38]

---

[36]Numbering is by paragraph of the text, in what seems like a "natural" segmentation unit: the paragraphs are very short, some of them consist of only one sentence. This analysis supersedes and amends Attardo (1997b).

[37]Alphonse Allais, (1854-1905) wrote primarily short stories which were published in newspapers, but he also produced some book-lengths works: *L'affaire Blaireau* (1899), and *Captain Cap* (1902, *Le parapluie de l'escouade*). Most of his short stories were collected in book form. His complete works have been published in two volumes: *Oeuvres anthumes* and *Oeuvres postumes* (Allais' own titles). On Allais, see Caradec (1994) and Defays and Rosier (1997).

[38]Allais is not someone who can be trusted when it comes to plots and fabulae (see section 5.5.2). It is possible that the peculiar organization, which includes a serious husteron-proteron (i.e., the presentation of something that happened before after other events; in our case, Han's departure for fishing which took place days before Polalek's attempt at breeding *loupfoques*), may be deliberately confusing.

7.5.1 Overall Analysis

We find four strands in the text:

1. sexual prowess, with a phallic substrand

2. Onomastic puns, e.g., Han Rybeck = Henri Becque.

3. Parody of the naturalistic French novels of the *fin de siècle* and particularly of *Pêcheur d'Islande*, by Pierre Loti.

4. Metanarrative comments of the narrator. Out of eleven occurrences, ten are humorous. In one very peculiar instance of metanarrative commentary, the implied narrator makes fun of the narrator's poor quality humor.

In what follows we will consider these strands one by one.

Sexual prowess strand

The main strand (in narrative terms, in the sense that it is tied to the central SO) in HRCI is the "sexual prowess" strand. The tyrant Polalek VI has sentenced to death Han Rybeck, but graces him after he sees the effects of intercourse with his fiancée on the latter (this having been Han's last wish):

(62) 57-59
Paule, transfigurée, une grande roseur épandue sur sa jolie physionomie, ses cheveux plus chauds de ton on eut dit, ébouriffés pas mal. Et ses grands yeux qui luisaient comme d'une récente extase! Cette fois, Polalek ne put réprimer son admiration. (...) ça, c'est épatant! (...) il gracia Han Rybeck"

(Paule, transfigured, and all awash in the blush that had washed over her pretty physionomy, her hair of a warmer hue, one would have said, not a bit disheveled. And her large eyes shining as if of a recent ecstasy! This time Polalek could not refrain his admiration. (...) Now, that's astonishing! (and) he graced Han Rybeck.)

An interesting issue is the fact that properly speaking some of the effects of intercourse on Paule Norr are impossible (hence incongruous): one does not change color of the hair that easily. Also the simile "her large eyes shining as if of a recent ecstasy!" is peculiar since Paule Norr has just experencied precisely a sexual ecstasy and hence this would not qualify at all as a simile. However, the presence of the connector *comme* (as if) forces a reinterpretation whereby we interpret ecstasy as mystical ravishment. Note how the interpretive path goes from sexual intercourse to religious rapture, thus providing an excellent counterexample of those theories which see in debasement an essential element of humor.

Several jab lines from other strands sustain this strand: among these let's note the allusions in

(63) 18 la presqu'île de Lagrenn-Houyer
   25 pêche à la morue

which refer to the argotic meaning of the terms "morue" (prostitute) and "grenouille" (easy woman, prostitute).

Phallic substrand   HRCI contains several phallic references catalogued below (along with references to copulation):

(64) 1 Coup de l'étrier
   18 terre en forme de phallus
   33 infames copulations
   43 godes
   49 elle est raide celle-là!
   57 récente extase
   60 croître et multiplier
   61 se [anaphoric reference to "multiply" from the line above]

It is possible that the text harbors other references to sex, but these are hidden under argotic terms, otherwise unflagged.

Onomastic Puns

There occurs in HRCI a strand based on proper names with a SO FRENCH/ICE-LANDIC. Interestingly, and somewhat unusually, this strand is "announced" by the narrator at the beginning of the text:

(65) "Laissez-moi vous (...) conter une [histoire islandaise], à peine dérangée au goût de Paris" (Let me tell you an Icelandic story, only a little adapted [lit. disturbed] according to Parisian taste.)

Under the guise of an unfamiliar spelling the reader recognizes easily familiar toponyms (the North Pole, the *Grenouillère*, a familiar place for Parisians) and familiar names of writers and journalists.

	Iceland	France
1	Han Rybeck	Henri Becque
10	Polalek VI	Paul Alexis
18	Lagrenn-Houyer	La Grenouillère
39	Paule Norr	Pôle Nord
40	Fern Anxo	Fernand Xau

7.5. HAN RYBECK OU LE COUP DE L'ÉTRIER

In general, there is an aspect of "inside joke" to these onomastic jabs. Henri Becque (1837-1899) and Paul Alexis (1847-1901) were well known writers and journalists. They were members of the naturalist movement, and friends of Emile Zola. Fernand Xau was the editor of *Le journal* (1892-1944), the newspaper in which Allais published HRCI for the first time. Allais knew both Becque and Alexis: both of them published on *Le matin* another Parisian newspaper. Allais and Becque both wrote for *La revue illustrée*. Alexis wrote also for *Le journal*.

Technically, each instance of the name *Polalek VI* or *Han Rybeck* should count as a jab line. However, I feel that this would be excessive, as after the initial humor has been experienced, the text sets up a TWR in which there is a character whose name is *Polalek* and who is the sixth descendent in that dynastic line. In other words, once the initial SO has been assumed as part of the TWR it is, so to speak, neutralized. The same phenomenon can be seen in Eco's ROSE: upon first encountering the names of *Guglielmo di Baskerville* and *Jorge da Burgos* one is aware of the anachronistic incongruity, but after encountering the names virtually on every page of the text for some 600 pages, the incongurity is no longer felt.[39] It should be noted that the strand of onomastic jokes reinforces the strand of literary parody (see below).

Parody of the naturalist novel of the *fin de siècle*.

A parodic strand runs throughout HRCI. Allais' main target is *Pêcheur d'Islande* a novel by Pierre Loti[40], but in general the exotism of much late-Romantic writing is targeted. The parody of Loti's novel is clear: Allais' subtitle *Conte d'Islande* closely matches Loti's. Loti's main character is called Yann, while Allais' is Han. Most significantly, both stories are about marriages to be arranged.

In fact, Allais, perhaps to make sure that all his readers got the joke, makes no mystery of who is his target:

(66) 25 "(car la pêche à la morue existait à cette époque et M. Pierre Loti n'a rien inventé)" (Cod fishing existed in that period and Mr. Loti has invented nothing)

Furthermore, the sexual prowess strand is itself parodic, since it creates a striking opposition between Allais' Icelandic sexual mores and Loti's very chaste description: a textbook case of the SEX/NO SEX SO.

We should also add to this literary parody strand, the onomastic jabs on Henri Becque and Paul Alexis, both of whom were naturalist writers, which we saw in the

---

[39]The attentive reader might see an apparent contradiction with the claim in section (5.3.4) that repetition is a source of humor. There are two main differences: one is that most repetition in longer texts is based on the "repetition with variation" paradigm, i.e., several KRs are repeated, but some aspects of the line are variated to keep the humor fresh. The second, and perhaps more significant, is that in the case of onomastic jabs, very often the repetition is no longer a full one: Allais uses *Polalek*, Eco *Jorge* and *Guglielmo*. These names are not humorous in the least. Thus, in fact, no repetition of the jab has taken place, at least in those cases.

[40]Pierre Loti [pseud. of Julien Viaud] (1850-1923) published successful exotic novels beginning 1879, which include *Pêcheur d'Islande (1886)*. He was a member of the prestigious *Académie française*.

previous strand (so this would be a case of hyperdetermination, as the jabs are active in more strands simultaneously).

Let us note, in passing, that this kind of literary attack is farly rare in Allais' work (cf. Defays 1992: 109). Conversely, this is not the only attack against Loti's in Allais' opus: Loti is attacked again, among many others, in 1899 (cf. Caradec 1994: 374-376). Thus there is an intertextual "anti-Loti" strand within Allais' production.

Finally, let us note that Allais predates by almost a century the postcolonial critique of exotism, the noble savage myth, and attendant paternalism, not to mention racist ideologies, Loti being a prime example of this "orientalist" aesthetizing exotism in French letters.

Metanarrative Comments of the Narrator

There are eleven cases of metanarrative comments in the text. Out of the eleven, ten are humorous.[41] Defays (1992: 21-54) notes that it is very common in Allais. Let us note that metanarrative comments allows the narrator to introduce lines within the text without having to develop a setup.

All metanarrative comments are listed below:

(67) 3-9 Introduction.
  4: [note] Dédicace commode, que je ne saurais trop recommander...
  18: (ce qui signifie, en langue finnoise, terre en forme de phallus)
  22 Le vrai loup-phoque, entre nous, n'était-ce point lui!
  25 (car la pêche à la morue existait à cette époque et M. Pierre Loti...
  31 Ah! ce fut bientôt fait! [non-humorous]
  35 (le cheval arabe est, dans ces parages, d'une élève difficile)
  36 (surtout quand on a une mauvaise plume et presque...
  43 [note] Même aux plus durs temps de la domination norvégienne...
  48 (Cette conversation s'accomplissait, bien entendu, en dialecte ...
  55 (le manuscrit que j'ai sous les yeux ne précise pas ce laps)

Among these examples of metanarrative intervention, one (occurring in par. 21-22) is particularly interesting. It is examined immediately below.

The *loup-phoque* narrative The largest of the excursus narratives covers paragraphs 14-21. Within it, Allais describes the failed attempt by Polalek VI to breed wolf-seals by having wolves and seals copulate (Han Rybeck intervenes and scatters the animals). The completely nonsensical plan is justified by the existence of the argotic word *loufoque* (meaning "crazy") which is a homonym of *loup + phoque* (wolf+seal). It should be emphasized that the narrative is a joke embedded in the text, as it ends on a punch line.

---
[41] During discussion at the conference where this analysis was first presented it was suggested that the eleventh instance is also funny. While this would be neat and symmetrical, I feel it is a stretch of the text.

Immediately after the occurrence of the punch line of the excursus narrative there occurs another metanarrative comment, which evaluates the narrative which just took place (22)

(68) "Le vrai loup-phoque, entre nous, n'était-ce point lui!" (In confidence, wasn't he the real crazy person/wolf-seal?)

This comment is incongruous in a peculiar way: the narrator has just finished relating a story which we can therefore assume he endorses to a certain degree. However, by pointing out the absurdity of the punning LM (i.e., the fact that Polalek VI wanted to breed a new animal based on the fact that the name of wolves and seals in French put one after the other sounds like the word for "crazy person") the narrator is distancing himself from his own joke (in fact, judging it negatively). In order to account for this, we need to postulate two narrative levels: we have the narrative in which Polalek VI is attempting an absurd cross-species breeding experiment (level$_0$), then we have the narrator telling the story (level$_1$) and finally another narrator making fun of the first narrator (level$_2$).

Since, of course, both narrators are personae of Allais' it follows that he is making fun of himself, i.e., that the jab in par. 22 is autoironical. We will find this peculiar type of humor again in Wilde's LASC.

7.5.2 Schematic representation of HRCI

Considering that HRCI consists of 61 paragraphs, and that each is fairly short, it seemed like a reasonable approach to take the paragraph as the unit of analysis, especially so that we could represent the textual vector as a single line of text of 61 "positions" in which each marker stood for a paragraph. We can now represent on the line the occurrence of any jab/punch lines, using the notation introduced in ch. (7.1): each dash ("–") equals one pararaph; the superscript indicates the paragraph number, the subscript indicates the strand, according to the legenda in figure (7.5.2).

Square brackets indicate the beginning and ending of the narratives. Round parentheses indicate the "parasitic narrative" discussed in the text. The resulting schema for HRCI as follows:

$$[\mapsto J^1_{\bullet\triangle\square}J^2_\square[\mapsto-{}^3P^4_\diamond \to][\mapsto J^5_\square J^6_\square J^7_{\diamond\square}-{}^8-{}^9[\mapsto J^{10}_{\triangle\square}-{}^{11}-{}^{12}-{}^{13}(-{}^{14}-{}^{15}$$

$$-{}^{16}-{}^{17}J^{18}_{\triangle\flat\bullet}-{}^{19}-{}^{20}J^{21}_\sharp[J^{22}_\flat]-{}^{23})-{}^{24}J^{25}_{\flat\bullet\square}[-{}^{26}]-{}^{27}-{}^{28}-{}^{29}-{}^{30}[-{}^{31}]-{}^{32}$$

$$(J^{33}_{\flat\bullet}-{}^{34})-{}^{35}J^{36}_\flat-{}^{37}-{}^{38}J^{39}_\triangle J^{40}_\triangle-{}^{41}-{}^{42}J^{43}_{\flat\bullet\square}-{}^{44}J^{45}_\bullet-{}^{46}-{}^{47}J^{48}_{\flat\square}J^{49}_\bullet-{}^{50}$$

$$-{}^{51}-{}^{52}-{}^{53}-{}^{54}J^{55}_\flat-{}^{56}J^{57}_\bullet J^{58}_\square-{}^{59}J^{60}_\bullet J^{61}_\bullet \to]]$$

Legenda

sexual prowess	•
embedded narrative	◇
onomastic puns	△
naturalistic parody	□
metanarrative comments	♭
loup+phoques	♯

Figure 7.6: *Han Rybeck ou le coup de l'étrier by Alphonse Allais*

7.5.3 The text of Han Rybeck ou le coup de l'étrier
Han Rybeck ou le coup de l'étrier₁

Conte islandais₂

A celle-là seule que j'aime et qui le sait bien.₃ ⁴²

Je suis loin de regretter le voyage que je viens d'accomplir en Islande. J'y fus reçu par de candides gens, coeurs simples, flairant la rogue bien plus que l'ail, ce qui n'est pas fait pour me déplaire.₅

Les habitants ne sont pas plus bêtes que dans le midi de l'Europe et ils crient moins fort.₆

La nourriture, peu variée, y est saine et abondante, et on a toutes les peines du monde à obtenir sa facture. Pays béni!₇

Et puis les belles légendes qu'on y trouve, et aussi les amusantes histoires!₈

Laissez-moi vous en conter une, à peine dérangée au goût de Paris.₉

C'ètait au XIVe siècle. L'Islande gémissait alors sous le joug du rude duc norvegien Polalek VI.₁₀

Altérés d'indépendance, les jeunes Islandais avaient juré de se débarasser des ces étrangers indiscrets et brutaux.₁₁

Parmi les révoltés, il y en était un qui se faisait remarquer par l'âpreté des ses revendications et par la peu commune énergie des ses actes: on l'appelait Han Rybeck.₁₂

Han Rybeck! Quand les Islandais vraiment dignes de ce nom avaient dit *Han Rybeck*, ils avaient tout dit.₁₃

Le duc norvégien Polalek VI faisait, en quelque sorte, exprès d'attirer sur lui la dèfaveur de ce brave peuple.₁₄

Paillard et ivrogne, il se faisait un jeu d'offenser les moeurs chastes et tempérantes des gens d'Islande, accoutumés d'aimer seulement leur femme et d'étancher leur soif à la fonte des neiges.₁₅

Évidemment, cet état de choses ne pouvait durer longtemps.₁₆

Imagina-t-il pas, en une heure d'ivresse, cette entreprise ridicule, digne à peine de faire hausser les èpaules du plus paisible:₁₇

Sur ses ordres, des loups furent amenés dans la presqu-île du Lagrenn-Houyer (ce qui signifie en langue finnoise, *terre en forme de phallus*).₁₈

A l'entrée de la presqu-île, des hommes commandés faisaient la garde avec des piques et des frondes, pour empêcher de s'évader les loups.₁₉

---

⁴²Dèdicace commode, que je ne saurais pas trop recommender à mes confrères. Elle ne coûte rien, et peut, du même coup, faure plaisir à cinq ou six personnes.₄

Du côté de la mer, des pêcheurs, en grande quantité, avaient mission de rabattre sur le littoral de la presqu-île, le plus de phoques qu'ils pourraient.[20]

Dans l'imagination déréglée de Polalek VI, il devait survenir de la rencontre des loups et des phoques une sorte de métissage produisant des bêtes étranges qu'il nommait déjà des *loup-phoques*.[21]

Le vrai *loup-phoque*, entre nous, n'était-ce point lui![22]

Les pauvres Islandais, terrorisés, n'oserent point résister à cette consigne burlesque, et tous se mirent à l'oeuvre.[23]

Précisément, Han Rybeck ne se trouvait point dans le pays.[24]

Parti depuis quelques jours pour la pêche à la morue (car la pêche à la morue existait à cette époque et M. Pierre Loti n'a rien inventé), Han Rybeck n'était pas attendu de sitôt.[25]

Heureusement les choses tournèrent mieux qu'on espérait.[26]

Une nuit, le hardi morutier avait rencontré un sloop anglais, chargé de cabillauds, qui se disposait à rallier sa patrie.[27]

Tout l'équipage était saoul, mais comme les Anglais sont saouls quand ils se mettent à être saouls.[28]

De quelque coups de hache habilement distribués, Han Rybeck mit cesse aux criailleries de ces sales poivrots. En un tour de main, il fit passer dans sa barque la pêche des Englishmen. Le lendemain soir, il entrait, vent arrière, dans le port de Reykjavik.[29]

Des femmes le mirent au courant de la dernière fantaisie de Polalek, et le supplièrent d'intervenir.[30]

Ah! ce fut bientôt fait![31]

D'un bond il arrivait à Lagrenn-Houyer.[32]

D'un autre bond, et muni d'une terrible barre d'anspect, il éparpillait les infâmes copulations des loups et des phoques.[33]

Perdant la tête, les bête s'enfuyaient, les phoques du côté terre, les loups vers l'océan.[34]

Ranimés par la présance de leur chefs, les Islandais reprenaient courage. Cependant, Polalek VI, averti de ces désordres, accourait au galop de son petit poney (le cheval arabe est, dans ces parages, d'une élève difficile).[35]

En moins de temps qu'il n'en faut pour l'écrire (surtout quand on a une mauvaise plume et presque pas d'encre, tel moi, en ce moment), Han Rybeck était saisi, garrotté et jeté dans la prison du château.[36]

Polalek VI, jugeant en premier ressort et sans appel, le condamna à mort et décida que son exécution aurait lieu le lendemain matin sur la place même du crime.[37]

Han ne protesta pas.[38]

Il demandat seulement qu'on lui permît, avant sa mort, d'épouser sa fiancée, une des plus jolies filles de l'île, et qu'on appelait Paule Norr.[39]

Sur les instances du bailli de Reykjavik, un brave homme dont l'histoire a conservé le nom, Fern Anxo, Polalek consentit à cette cérémonie.[40]

7.5. HAN RYBECK OU LE COUP DE L'ÉTRIER

Au petit matin, une heure avant l'exécution, la jeune fille fut introduite dans le cachot du condamné.₄₁

Le bailli, représentant l'état civil⁴³, inscrivit les noms des jeunes époux.₄₃

Complètement ivre, Polalek VI consacra religieusement leur union, et tout le monde allait se retirer, y compris la jeune fiancée, quand Han Rybeck se récria violamment:₄₄

— Pardon, pardon! Ce n'est pas seulement au point de vue formalitaire que j'ai demandé `a épouser ma blonde fiancée, Paule Norr.₄₅

— Comment! s'étonna Polalek VI, vous voudriez...₄₆

— Mais pourquoi pas?₄₇

(Cette conversation s'accomplissait, bien entendu, en dialecte finnois.)₄₈

— Eh bien! elle est raide, della là, reprit le rude duc.₄₉

— C'est bien le cas de le dire, observa spirituellement un courtisan.₅₀

Et un gros rire secoua ces brutes.₅₁

Pas trop mauvais homme, dans le fond, Polalek VI accéda au dernier voeu du condamné.₅₂

— Qu'on les laisse seuls! commanda-t-il.₅₃

Et, discrètement, tous se retirèrent.₅₄

Après quelques instants (le manuscript que j'ai sous les yeux ne précise pas ce laps), on rouvrait la porte du cachot, et les jeunes gens en sortaient fièrement:₅₅

Han Rybeck, la tête haute, enlaçant d'un bras tendre la taille de la belle Paule.₅₆

Paule, transfigurée, une grande roseur épandue sur sa jolie physionomie, ses cheveux plus chauds de ton, on eût dit, ébouriffés pas mal. Et ses grand yeux qui luisaient comme d'une récente extase!₅₇

Cette fois Polalek ne put réprimer son admiration.₅₈

— Ah! par exemple! ça c'est épatant! s'écria-t-il dans sa rude langue du Nord.₅₉

Faisant sur les époux, le geste auguste du bénisseur, il gracia Han Rybeck, lui offrit la propre presqu'île de Lagrenn-Hoyer et invita les jeunes gens à croître et à multiplier.₆₀

Les jeunes gens ne se le firent pas dire deux fois.₆₁

---

⁴³Même aux plus dur temps de la domination Norvégienne, les agglomerations islandaises conservèrent leurs privileges municipaux. Les *godes* norvégiens n'exerçaient que des droits militaires et ecclésiastiques.₄₂

7.5.4 English Translation of HRCI
Han Rybeck or one for the road.₁
Icelandic tale₂

To the one I love and who knows.₃ [44]

I am far from regretting the trip I just took in Iceland. I was greeted by innocent people, simple hearts, smelling more of fish than of garlic, which is far from displeasing me.₅

The inhabitants are not dumber than in the south of Europe and they shout less.₆

The food, which lacks in variety, is healthy and plentiful, and one has the hardest time getting one's bill. Blessed country!₇

Moreover, what beautiful legends one finds there, and also what amusing stories!₈

Let me tell you one, barely altered to a Parisian flavor.₉

It was in the 14th century. Iceland bemoaned the yoke of the harsh Norwegian duke, Polalek the Sixth.₁₀

Drunk on independence, the young Icelanders had sworn to get rif of these indiscreet and brutal strangers.₁₁

Among the rebels was one who stood out by the harshness of his claims and the uncommon energy of his actions: he was called Han Rybeck.₁₂

Han Rybeck! When Icelanders who were worthy of that name had said *Han Rybeck*, they had said everything.₁₃

The Norwegian duke Polalek the Sixth was practically trying to draw upon himself the disfavor of this brave people.₁₄

A ribald and a drunkard, he made a game of offending the chaste and temperant behavior of the Icelandic people, accustomed to love only their wife and the quench their thrirst to the melting snow.₁₅

Obviously, this state of affairs could not last long.₁₆

Didn't he imagine, in a time of drunkenness, this ridiculous enterprise, barely worthy of the shrugging of the most peaceful:₁₇

Upon his orders, wolves were brought in the peninsula of Lagenn-Houyer (which means, in Finnish, phallus-shaped land).₁₈

At the peninsula's entrance, ordered men stood guard with spears and slings to stop the wolves from escaping.₁₉

From the sea's end, fishermen in great numbers had for mission to corral on the beach of the peninsula the greatest number of seals they could.₂₀

In the deranged imagination of Polalek the Sixth from the meeting of wolves and seals a sort of hybrid was to be born, producing strange animals he already called wolve-seals [goof].₂₁

---

[44] Handy dedication, which I cannot recommend enough to my colleagues. It doesn't cost anything and can, in one shot, please five or six people.₄

7.5. HAN RYBECK OU LE COUP DE L'ÉTRIER

Between us, wasn't he the real goof!₂₂

The poor terrorized Icelanders did not dare resist these burlesque orders and they all got to work.₂₃

Precisely, Han Rybeck was not in the country.₂₄

Having left since a few days before for a cod fishing trip (since cod fishing existed at this time, and Mr. Pierre Loti invented nothing), Han Rybeck was not expected any time soon.₂₅

Luckily, things turned out better than was hoped.₂₆

One night the daring cod-fisher had encountered an English *sloop*, loaded with haddock, which was getting ready to return to its homeland.₂₇

All the crew was drunk, like Englishmen are drunk when they set out to be drunk.₂₈

With a few axe blows skillfully distributed, Han Rybeck ended the shouts of those dirty drunks, In a flash, he moved to his boat the Englishmen' catch. The next evening he entered, wind in his sails, the harbor of Reykjavik.₂₉

Some women informed him of Polalek's latest fantasy and begged him to intervene.₃₀

Ah! Was it ever done fast!₃₁

In a jump he was at Lagrenn-Houyer.₃₂

With another jump, and armed of a terrible lever bar he scattered the foul copulations between the wolves and the seals.₃₃

Panicked, the animals ran away, the seals towards the land, the wolves towards the sea.₃₄

Reinvigorated by the presence of their chiefs, the Icelanders took heart. However, Polalek, made aware of these disorders, arrived racing his little poney (the Arabian mare is, in these countries, of difficult breeding).₃₅

In less time one needs to write it (especialy if one has a bad pen and almost no ink, such as me, in this moment) Han Rybeck was caught, tied up, and thrown in the prison of the castle.₃₆

Polalek the Sixth, judging in the first resort and without appeal condemned him to death and decided that his execution would take place the next morning on the very spot of the crime.₃₇

Han did not protest.₃₈

He asked only to be allowed, before his death, to marry his fiancèe, one of the prettiest girls of the island, who was called Paule Norr.₃₉

On the authority of the bailiff of Reykjavik, a good man whose name history has preserved, Fern Anxo, Polalek consented to the ceremony.₄₀

At dawn, an hour before the execution, the young woman was brought into the cell of the convict.₄₁

The bailiff, representing Registrar,[45] inscribed the names of the young couple.₄₃

---

[45] Even during the harshest time of the Norwegian domination, the Icelandic settlements kept their municipal privileges. the Norwegian *godes* only exerted military and ecclesiastical rights.₄₂

Completely drunk, Polalek the Sixth consecrated religiously their union. As everybody was about to retire, including the young fiance, Han Rybeck complained violently:[44]

Excuse me, excuse me. It was not purely formal point of view that I asked to marry my blonde fiance, Paule Norr.[45]

—What? marveled Polalek the Sixth, you'd like to...[46]

—And why not?[47]

(This conversation took place, of course, in Finnish dialect.)[48]

—Well, that's a hard one, said the rude duke.[49]

—I'd say, cleverly observed a courtesan.[50]

And those brutes laughed heartily.[51]

Not too evil a man, at the bottom, Polalek the Sixth agreed to the convict's last wish.[52]

—Let them be alone! he commanded.[53]

And, discretely, they all withdrew.[54]

After a few moments (the manuscript which I have under my eyes does not specify the extent) the door was opened and out came the proud young couple.[55]

Han Rybeck his head held high, holding tenderly the waist of the beautiful Paule.[56]

Paule, transfigured, and all awash in the blush that had washed over her pretty physionomy, her hair of a warmer hue, one would have said, not a little disheveled. And her large eyes shining as if of a recent extasy! This time Polalek could not refrain his admiration.[57]

—Ah! Look at this! Now, that's astonishing! said he in his rough northern language.[58]

Doing over the couple the blessing gesture he graced Han Rybeck, gave him the peninsula of Lagrenn-Hoyer and invited the young people to grow and multiply.[59]

The young people got to it, without asking for more.[60]

Chapter 8

"Lord Arthur Savile's Crime" by Oscar Wilde

8.1 CHAPTER I

IT[1] was Lady Windermere's last reception before Easter, and Bentinck House was even more crowded than usual. Six Cabinet Ministers had come on from the Speaker's Levee in their stars and ribands, all the pretty women wore their smartest dresses, and at the end of the picture-gallery stood the Princess Sophia of Carlsruhe, a heavy Tartar[2]-looking lady, with *tiny black eyes and wonderful emeralds* [3], talking *bad French*[4] at the *top of her voice,*[5] and *laughing immoderately* [6] at everything that was said to her. It was certainly a wonderful medley of people. *Gorgeous peeresses chatted affably to violent Radicals*[7], popular *preachers* brushed coat-tails with eminent

---

[1] The text analyzed was obtained on the Internet. Each jab line is marked by italicizing the text (for the first fifty jab lines) and with an associated footnote which contains a description of the jab line in the six KR. Within KRs elements separated by semi-colons are alternatives, those separated by commas are elaborations. Comments follow the 6 KRs listing.

[2] SO *beautiful/ugly; good/bad*; LM *none*; SI *NA*; TA *Princess Sophia*; NS *irr*; LA *irr.*

[3] SO *human feature/stone; normal/abnormal*; LM *coordination*; SI *NA*; TA *Princess Sophia*; NS *irr*; LA *coordinating conj..*

[4] SO *good/bad French*; LM *none*; SI *NA*; TA *Princess Sophia*; NS *irr*; LA *irr.*

[5] SO *soft/loud; appropriate/inappropriate; normal/abnormal*; LM *none*; SI *NA*; TA *Princess Sophia*; NS *irr*; LA *irr.*

[6] SO *appropriate/inappropriate; normal/abnormal*; LM *none*; SI *NA*; TA *Princess Sophia*; NS *irr*; LA *irr.* Note the comb strand with the "Princess Sophia" TA.

[7] SO *peeress/radical; normal/abnormal (?)*; LM *physical proximity (?)*; SI *party, conversation*; TA *none (?)*; NS *irr*; LA *irr.*

sceptics[8], *a perfect bevy of bishops kept following a stout prima-donna*[9] from room to room, on the staircase stood *several Royal Academicians, disguised as artists,*[10] and it was said that at one time the supper-room was absolutely *crammed with geniuses.*[11] In fact, *it was one of Lady Windermere's best nights,*[12] and *the Princess stayed till nearly half-past eleven.*[13]

As soon as she had gone, Lady Windermere returned to the picture-gallery, where *a celebrated political economist was solemnly explaining the scientific theory of music to an indignant virtuoso*[14] from Hungary, and began to talk to the Duchess of Paisley. She looked *wonderfully beautiful*[15] with her *grand* ivory throat, her *large* blue forget-me-not eyes, and her *heavy*[16] coils of golden hair. OR PUR they were

---

[8]SO *preacher/sceptic;* normal/abnormal (?); LM *physical proximity; marginal;* SI *party, conversation;* TA *none (?);* NS *irr;* LA *irr.*

[9]SO *bishops/prima-donna; normal/abnormal;* LM *physical proximity (?);* SI *party, conversation;* TA *bishops;* NS *irr;* LA *irr.* Consider also the alliteration of "*pe*rfect *be*vy of *bi*shops" which may be a separate jab line. Not to mention the *stout* prima-donna may be considered a jab (FAT/BEAUTIFUL SO); however, opera singers are stereotypically fat, hence it is ignored in the analysis.

[10]SO *academician/artist; normal/abnormal;* LM *none;* SI *party, conversation;* TA *academicians, artists;* NS *irr;* LA *irr.* The jab lines 7-10 establish a comb strand, with the following features: SO NORMAL/ABNORMAL, SI "party," and LM "physical proximity." Consider also the alliteration of "*sta*ircase *sto*od *se*veral" which may be a separate jab line.

[11]SO *genius/people; normal/abnormal;* LM *physical proximity (?);* SI *party;* TA *geniuses (?);* NS *irr;* LA *idiom: "crammed with people".*

[12]SO *best/worst; serious/ironical; normal/abnormal;* LM *none;* SI *party [the party cannot have been that good, cf. next line];* TA *implied author;* NS *metanarrative commentary;* LA *irr.* This line needs perhaps some explanation: we have here an example of metanarrative irony in which the implied narrator (cf. section 5.2) is saying something that the reader can tell is inappropriate. Therefore we have to either assume lack of control of the author, or postulate an intermediate implied author being made fun of by the author (cf. also the same phenomenon in Allais' HRCI; see section 7.5).

[13]SO *early/late; serious/ironical; normal/abnormal;* LM *none;* SI *party [leaving at 11:30 is hardly late];* TA *implied author;* NS *metanarrative commentary;* LA *irr.*

[14]SO *economy/music;true/false;* LM *faulty reasoning [presumption];* SI *conversation;* TA *political economists; character;* NS *irr;* LA *irr [but see below].* Possibly there is an interesting stylistic jab line, consisting in the four modifiers: "celebrated," "solemnly," "scientific," "indignant" which may be seen as paralleling the incongruity in the jab line above (and thus as reinforcing factors). Note how the jab line would function perfectly well without the modifiers: *a political economist was explaining the theory of music to a virtuoso,* which preserves the incongruity of the economist explaining musical theory to a musician. Note also that the first modifier ("celebrated") introduces very discreetly an element of social critique: who is doing the celebrating? Obviously newspapers, socialites, possibly government officials, etc. However, we are told that the economist is ridiculous (presumptuous). Hence, it follows that the social opinion is wrong.

[15]SO *beautiful/fat; serious/ironical; actual/non-actual;* LM *none;* SI *[according to stereotype, large women are not beautiful];* TA *Lady Windermere, character; narrator (?);* NS *irony;* LA *irr.* Note that the reconstruction of the irony is done *ex post hoc* after the detection of the next line. Note also that in this case, the implied narrator may be ironical himself (I assume implied narrators share the sex of the empirical narrator).

[16]SO *slim/fat; normal/abnormal;* LM *none;* SI *physical aspect;* TA *Lady Windermere, character;* NS *NA;* LA *irr.* Note again the subtlety of the line: the humorous effect of the description of Lady Windermere is obtained by the accumulation of three modifiers ("grand," "large," and "heavy") which

8.1. CHAPTER I 165

- *not that pale straw colour that nowadays usurps the gracious name of gold*,[17] but such gold as is woven into sunbeams or hidden in strange amber; and they gave to her face something of the frame of a *saint*, with not a little of the fascination of a *sinner*.[18] She was a curious psychological study. Early in life she had discovered *the important truth*[19] that *nothing looks so like innocence as an indiscretion*;[20] and by a series of *reckless escapades, half of them quite harmless*,[21] she had acquired all the *privileges of a personality*.[22] She had more than once changed her husband; indeed, Debrett credits her with three marriages; but *as she had never changed her lover*,[23] the world had long ago ceased to talk *scandal*[24] about her. She was now forty years of age, childless, and with that inordinate passion for pleasure which is the secret of remaining young.[25]

Suddenly she looked eagerly round the room, and said, in her clear contralto[26] voice, 'Where is my cheiromantist?'

'Your what, Gladys?' exclaimed the Duchess, giving an involuntary start.

'My cheiromantist, Duchess; *I can't live without him at present.*'[27]

'Dear Gladys! you are always so original,' murmured the Duchess, *trying to*

---

activate the script FAT while one could argue that in fact no such inference is legitimate as "large eyes" and "heavy coils of hair" are positive features. If this is correct, the previous ironical jab line would of course disappear.

[17] SO *complain/not complain; normal/abnormal*; **LM** *none*; **SI** *NA*; **TA** *narrator*; **NS** *NA*; **LA** *irr*. A complex jab line in which the narrator complains about something that is not obviously wrong, which again forces the postulation of an implied narrator who is dissociating himself from the statement of the narrator. A subtle form of irony which seems to have no precise target, except the undermining of the authorial credibility.

[18] SO *saint/sinner; good/bad*; **LM** *none [possibly, sin is interesting]*; **SI** *description*; **TA** *narrator*; **NS** *irr*; **LA** *irr [idiom: saints and sinners]*.

[19] SO *true/false*; **LM** *none*; **SI** *metanarrative comentary*; **TA** *narrator*; **NS** *irr*; **LA** *irr*. An interesting, if hard to interpret, incongruity between the conservative attitude of the narrator, only a few words above, and the dandysm of the present statement.

[20] SO *innocence/indiscretion; good/bad*; **LM** *false reasoning [trusting apparences]*; **SI** *NA*; **TA** *those mistaking indiscretion for innocence(?)*; **NS** *NA*; **LA** *NA*.

[21] SO *reckless/harmless; good/bad*; **LM** *none*; **SI** *NA*; **TA** *none (?)*; **NS** *irr*; **LA** *irr*.

[22] SO *privileges/duties(?); real/unreal*; **LM** *reasoning from false premises [i.e., the previous three jab lines]*; **SI** *Lady Windermere's life*; **TA** *those granting her the privileges*; **NS** *irr*; **LA** *irr*. Note how granting *the privileges* of a personality, presupposes that the grantee does not have one (otherwise, he/she would automatically have them).

[23] SO *change husband/lover; normal/abnormal*; **LM** *none*; **SI** *marriage and unfaithfullness*; **TA** *Lady Windermere*; **NS** *irr*; **LA** *irr*. Note the etsablishment, with 15 and 16 of a strand with TA "Lady Windermere."

[24] SO *scandal/no scandal; normal/abnormal*; **LM** *chiastic reversal*; **SI** *marriage and unfaithfullness*; **TA** *Lady Windermere*; **NS** *irr*; **LA** *irr*. The chiastic reversal is particularly clever: one wife and three lovers would be a scandal, three husbands and one lover are therefore (!) not a scandal.

[25] One could arguably maintain that this last epigram is a jab line as well.

[26] One could argue that the description of Lady Windermere's voice is too positive to be serious.

[27] SO *possible/impossible*; **LM** *exaggeration*; **SI** *NA*; **TA** *Lady Windermere*; **NS** *irr*; **LA** *irr*.

remember[28] what a cheiromantist really was, and hoping it was not the same as a cheiropodist.[29]

'He comes to see my hand twice a week regularly,' continued Lady Windermere, 'and is most interesting about it.'

'Good heavens!' said the Duchess to herself, '*he is a sort of cheiropodist after all*.[30] How very dreadful. *I hope he is a foreigner at any rate. It wouldn't be quite so bad then.*'[31]

'I must certainly introduce him to you.'

'Introduce him!' cried the Duchess; 'you don't mean to say he is here?' and she began looking about for a small tortoise-shell fan and a very tattered lace shawl, *so as to be ready to go at a moment's notice*.[32]

'Of course he is here; *I would not dream of giving a party without him*.[33] He tells me I have a *pure psychic hand*,[34] and that *if my thumb had been the least little bit shorter*,[35] I should have been a confirmed *pessimist*,[36] and *gone into a convent*.'[37]

'Oh, I see!' said the Duchess, *feeling very much relieved*;[38] 'he tells fortunes, I suppose?'

---

[28] SO *ignorance/knowledge; good/bad*; LM *none*; SI *NA*; TA *Duchess of Paisley*; NS *irr*; LA *irr*.

[29] SO *cheiropodist/cheiromantist; normal/abnormal*; LM *paronymy*; SI *NA*; TA *Duchess of Paisley*; NS *irr*; LA *paronyms*.

[30] SO *ignorance/knowledge; good/bad*; LM *none [possibly established ignorance]*; SI *NA*; TA *Duchess of Paisley*; NS *irr*; LA *irr*. A strand based on TA "Duchess of Paisley" is hereby established; cf. jabs 28 and 29. Note the comb structure.

[31] SO *foreigner/British; good/bad*; LM *reasoning from false premises*; SI *NA*; TA *Duchess of Paisley; foreigners; British citizens*; NS *irr*; LA *irr*. The inclusion of British citizens among the targets of the joke may be in need of some explanation: since the Duchess is clearly being made fun of and she is British, they may be seen as targeted by association.

[32] SO *normal/abnormal*; LM *exaggeration*; SI *conversation*; TA *Duchess of Paisley*; NS *irr*; LA *irr*.

[33] SO *possible/impossible*; LM *exaggeration*; SI *NA*; TA *Lady Windermere*; NS *irr*; LA *irr*. Essentially the same jab line as line 25, above.

[34] SO *sense/nonsense; normal/abnormal*; LM *none*; SI *psychic reading*; TA *cheiromantist; Lady Windermere*; NS *irr*; LA *irr*.

[35] SO *short thumb/actual thumb; possible/impossible*; LM *none*; SI *?*; TA *cheiromantist; Lady Windermere*; NS *irr*; LA *irr*. Note that nothing can follow from such a trivial fact. Note also the allusion to the famous saying that if Cleopatra's nose had been shorter momentous consequences would have followed.

[36] SO *possible/impossible*; LM *nonsequitur*; SI *psychic reading*; TA *cheiromantist, Lady Windermere*; NS *irr*; LA *irr*.

[37] SO *possible/impossible*; LM *nonsequitur*; SI *psychic reading*; TA *cheiromantist, Lady Windermere*; NS *irr*; LA *irr*. Note the stablishment of a strand "cheiromantist's nonsense" in three jab lines immediately following one another. A pure comb configuration, in 33 words. Note also the concurrent jab based on the equivalence "nun = pessimist": SO *religious/not religious*; LM *coordination*; SI *psychic reading*; TA *cheiromantist, Lady Windermere*; NS *irr*; LA *coordinating conjunction*.

[38] SO *normal/abnormal*; LM *exaggeration*; SI *conversation*; TA *Duchess of Paisley*; NS *irr*; LA *irr*. Cf. lines 29 and 30. The strand "The duchess of Paislye has negative feelings towards cheiromantists" is established. It is a comb: 3 jabs within about 150 words.

8.1. CHAPTER I

'And misfortunes, too,'[39] answered Lady Windermere, 'any amount of them. Next year, for instance, I am in great danger, both by land and sea, so *I am going to live in a balloon*,[40] and *draw up my dinner in a basket every evening*.[41] It is all written down on my little finger, or on the palm of my hand, *I forget which*.'[42]

'But surely that is tempting Providence, Gladys.'

'My dear Duchess, surely *Providence can resist temptation*[43] by this time. I think every one should have their hands told once a month, so as to know what not to do. Of course, *one does it all the same*,[44] but it is so pleasant to be warned. Now if some one doesn't go and fetch Mr. Podgers at once, I shall have to go myself.'

'Let me go, Lady Windermere,' said a tall handsome young man, who was standing by, listening to the conversation with an amused smile.

'Thanks so much, Lord Arthur; but I am afraid you wouldn't recognise him.'

'If he is as wonderful as you say, Lady Windermere, *I couldn't well miss him*.[45] Tell me what he is like, and I'll bring him to you at once.'

'Well, he is not a bit like a cheiromantist. I mean he is not mysterious, or esoteric, or romantic-looking. He is a little, stout man, with a funny, bald head, and great gold-rimmed spectacles; something between a family doctor and a country attorney. I'm really very sorry, but it is not my fault. People are so *annoying*.[46] *All my pianists look exactly like poets, and all my poets look exactly like pianists*;[47] and I remember last season asking a *most dreadful conspirator* to dinner, a man who had blown up ever so many people, and always wore a coat of mail, and carried a dagger up his shirt-sleeve; and do you know that when he came he *looked just like a nice old clergyman*,[48] and cracked jokes all the evening? Of course, *he was very amusing*,

---

[39]Lady Windermere seems to be interpreting the generic *fortunes* as meaning only "good" fortune. Possibly a jab line.

[40]SO *live at home/in a balloon; normal/abnormal*; LM *reasoning from false premises*; SI *living quarters*; TA *Lady Windermere*; NS *irr*; LA *irr*.

[41]SO *live at home/in a balloon; normal/abnormal*; LM *reasoning from false premises; follows from previous jab line*; SI *living quarters*; TA *Lady Windermere*; NS *irr*; LA *irr*.

[42]SO *trivial/important; normal/abnormal*; LM *none*; SI *danger*; TA *Lady Windermere*; NS *irr*; LA *irr*. Note how Lady Windermere's casual attitude to the cheiromantist's prediction is inconsistent with her taking it so seriously (previous lines).

[43]SO *god/human; normal/abnormal*; LM *false parallelism [human : temptation :: god : temptation]*; SI *cotext*; TA *Lady Windermere; god*; NS *irr*; LA *irr*.

[44]SO *logical/illogical; normal/abnormal*; LM *nonsequitur*; SI *danger*; TA *Lady Windermere*; NS *irr*; LA *irr*. More of Lady Windermere's contradictory attitude to the cheiromantist's prediction. This begins a strand in which Lady Windermere oscillates between believeing in Podgers and considering him a fraud.

[45]SO *logical/illogical; normal/abnormal*; LM *nonsequitur; takes metaphor literally*; SI *conversation*; TA *Lord Arthur*; NS *irr*; LA *irr*.

[46]SO *annoying/not annoying; normal/abnormal*; LM *none [but see below]*; SI *cotext*; TA *Lady Windermere*; NS *irr*; LA *irr*. The reasons people are annoying is given in the next pair of jab lines.

[47]SO *expected/unexpected; normal/abnormal*; LM *reasoning from false premises; chiasmus*; SI *cotext*; TA *Lady Windermere*; NS *irr*; LA *irr*.

[48]SO *expected/unexpected; normal/abnormal; good/bad*; LM *reasoning from false premises*; SI *cotext*;

and all that, but I was awfully disappointed;⁴⁹ and when I asked him about the coat of mail, he only laughed, and said *it was far too cold to wear in England*.⁵⁰ Ah, here is Mr. Podgers! Now, Mr. Podgers, I want you to tell the Duchess of Paisley's hand. Duchess, you must take your glove off. No, not the left hand, the other.'

'Dear Gladys, I really don't think it is quite right,' said the Duchess, feebly unbuttoning a rather soiled⁵¹ kid glove.

'Nothing interesting ever is,' said Lady Windermere: 'ON A FAIT LE MONDE AINSI. But I must introduce you. Duchess, this is Mr. Podgers, my pet cheiromantist. Mr. Podgers, this is the Duchess of Paisley, and if you say that she has a larger mountain of the moon than I have, I will never believe in you again.'⁵²

'I am sure, Gladys, there is nothing of the kind in my hand,'⁵³ said the Duchess gravely.

'Your Grace is quite right,' said Mr. Podgers, glancing at the little fat hand with its short square fingers, 'the mountain of the moon is not developed. The line of life, however, is excellent. Kindly bend the wrist. Thank you. Three distinct lines on the RASCETTE! You will live to a great age, Duchess, and be extremely happy. Ambition - very moderate, line of intellect not exaggerated, line of heart - '

'Now, do be indiscreet, Mr. Podgers,' cried Lady Windermere.

'Nothing would give me greater pleasure,' said Mr. Podgers, bowing, 'if the Duchess ever had been, but I am sorry to say that I see great permanence of affection, combined with a strong sense of duty.'

'Pray go on, Mr. Podgers,' said the Duchess, looking quite pleased.

'Economy is not the least of your Grace's virtues,' continued Mr. Podgers, and Lady Windermere went off into fits of laughter.⁵⁴

TA *Lady Windermere*; **NS** *irr*; **LA** *irr*. Note how the jab about people failing to fulfill Lady Windermere's expectations is established as a strand (comb). The present jab is enhanced by the opposition "dreadful" vs. "nice."

⁴⁹**SO** *disappointed/not disappointed; expected/unexpected; normal/abnormal; good/bad*; **LM** *reasoning from false premises*; **SI** *cotext*; **TA** *Lady Windermere*; **NS** *irr*; **LA** *irr*. Note how this jab about people failing to fulfill Lady Windermere's expectations is enhanced by the opposition "disappointed" vs. "very amusing." Note also that we have here a double reversal, whereby the conspirator is a nice and funny person and this is a source of disappointment for Lady Windermere. In this case, the readers share Lady Windermere's expectations about conspirators, but not her expectations about dinner guests.

⁵⁰**SO** *clothing/weapon; normal/abnormal*; **LM** *reasoning from false premises*; **SI** *cotext*; **TA** *Lady Windermere (?); conspirator (?)*; **NS** *irr*; **LA** *irr*.

⁵¹**SO** *clean/dirty; normal/abnormal*; **LM** *none*; **SI** *clothing description*; **TA** *Duchess of Paisley*; **NS** *irr*; **LA** *irr; euphemistic*.

⁵²This is arguably an exaggeration; however, given the fairly unusual—although not always humorous—behavior of Lady Windermere, one cannot rule out that she is meaning the last sentence seriously.

⁵³**SO** *ignorance/knowledge; mountain/hand*; **LM** *reasoning from false premises; ignorance*; **SI** *hand reading*; **TA** *Duchess of Paisley*; **NS** *irr*; **LA** *irr*.

⁵⁴**SO** *laughable/serious; normal/abnormal*; **LM** *none (see comments)*.; **SI** *cotext*; **TA** *Podgers; Lady Windermere (?)*; **NS** *irr*; **LA** *irr*. It is unclear why lady Windermere is laughing. From the ensuing dialogue it seems reasonable to assume that Podgers is wrong or lying and that the Duchess of Paisley is

8.1. CHAPTER I

'Economy is a very good thing,' remarked the Duchess complacently; 'when I married Paisley he had eleven castles, and not a single house fit to live in.'

'And now he has twelve houses, and not a single castle,'[55] cried Lady Windermere.

'Well, my dear,' said the Duchess, 'I like - '

'Comfort,' said Mr. Podgers, 'and modern improvements, and hot water laid on in every bedroom. Your Grace is quite right. Comfort is the only thing our civilisation can give us.

'You have told the Duchess's character admirably, Mr. Podgers, and now you must tell Lady Flora's'; and in answer to a nod from the smiling hostess, a tall girl, with sandy Scotch hair, and high shoulder-blades, stepped awkwardly from behind the sofa, and held out a long, bony hand with spatulate fingers.

'Ah, a pianist! I see,' said Mr. Podgers, 'an excellent pianist, but perhaps hardly a musician.[56] Very reserved, very honest, and with a great love of animals.'

'Quite true!' exclaimed the Duchess, turning to Lady Windermere, 'absolutely true! Flora keeps two dozen collie dogs at Macloskie, and would turn our town house into a menagerie if her father would let her.'

'Well, that is just what I do with my house every Thursday evening,' cried Lady Windermere, laughing, 'only I like lions better than collie dogs.'[57]

'Your one mistake,[58] Lady Windermere,' said Mr. Podgers, with a pompous bow.

'If a woman can't make her mistakes charming, she is only a female,' was the answer. 'But you must read some more hands for us. Come, Sir Thomas, show Mr. Podgers yours'; and a genial- looking old gentleman, in a white waistcoat, came forward, and held out a thick rugged hand, with a very long third finger.

'An adventurous nature; four long voyages in the past, and one to come. Been ship-wrecked three times. No, only twice, but in danger of a shipwreck your next journey. A strong Conservative, very punctual, and with a passion for collecting curiosities. Had a severe illness between the ages sixteen and eighteen. Was left a fortune when about thirty. Great aversion to cats and Radicals.'

'Extraordinary!' exclaimed Sir Thomas; 'you must really tell my wife's hand, too.'

'Your second wife's,' said Mr. Podgers quietly, still keeping Sir Thomas's hand in his. 'Your second wife's. I shall be charmed'; but Lady Marvel, a melancholy-

---

all but a spendthrift. However, Lady Windermere's attitude is incomprehensible if she believes in Podgers' skills.

[55] SO *house/castle; noble/common; good/bad*; LM *the Duchess thinks like a commoner*; SI *cotext*; TA *Duchess of Paisley*; NS *irr*; LA *repetition with variation*.

[56] A baffling remark, as "pianist" implies "musician." Possibly a jab based on the period's connotations of the word *musician*.

[57] A perplexing passage in the text, since it emerges from the developments of the text that Lady Windermere is here metaphorical, as her "lions" are in fact interesting people (young men?). It is unclear if this is intended as a jab line.

[58] Obscure witticism. It is unclear what Podgers means.

looking woman, with brown hair and sentimental eyelashes, entirely declined to have her past or her future exposed; and nothing that Lady Windermere could do would induce Monsieur de Koloff, the Russian Ambassador, even to take his gloves off. In fact, many people seemed afraid to face the odd little man with his stereotyped smile, his gold spectacles, and his bright, beady eyes; and when he told poor Lady Fermor, right out before every one, that she did not care a bit for music, but was extremely fond of musicians,[59] it was generally felt that cheiromancy was a most dangerous science, and one that ought not to be encouraged, except in a TETE-A-TETE.

Lord Arthur Savile, however, who did not know anything about Lady Fermor's unfortunate story, and who had been watching Mr. Podgers with a great deal of interest, was filled with an immense curiosity to have his own hand read, and feeling somewhat shy about putting himself forward, crossed over the room to where Lady Windermere was sitting, and, with a charming blush, asked her if she thought Mr. Podgers would mind.

'Of course, he won't mind,' said Lady Windermere, 'that is what he is here for. All my lions, Lord Arthur, are performing lions, and jump through hoops whenever I ask them. But I must warn you beforehand that I shall tell Sybil everything. She is coming to lunch with me to-morrow, to talk about bonnets, and if Mr. Podgers finds out that you have a bad temper, or a tendency to gout, or a wife living in Bayswater, I shall certainly let her know all about it.'

Lord Arthur smiled, and shook his head. 'I am not afraid,' he answered. 'Sybil knows me as well as I know her.'

'Ah! I am a little sorry to hear you say that. The proper basis for marriage is a mutual misunderstanding.[60] No, I am not at all cynical, I have merely got experience, which, however, is very much the same thing.[61] Mr. Podgers, Lord Arthur Savile is dying to have his hand read. Don't tell him that he is engaged to one of the most beautiful girls in London, because that appeared in the MORNING POST a month ago.[62]

'Dear Lady Windermere,' cried the Marchioness of Jedburgh, 'do let Mr. Podgers stay here a little longer. He has just told me I should go on the stage, and I am so interested.'

'If he has told you that, Lady Jedburgh, I shall certainly take him away.[63] Come over at once, Mr. Podgers, and read Lord Arthur's hand.'

'Well,' said Lady Jedburgh, making a little MOUE as she rose from the sofa, 'if I

---

[59] SO *sex/music; good/bad*; LM *none*; SI *cheiromantic reading*; TA *Lady Fermor*; NS *irr*; LA *irr*.

[60] SO *understanding/musinderstanding; normal/abnormal*; LM *none*; SI *irr*; TA *marriage (?)*; NS *aphorism*; LA *irr*. Note the possible presence of an institutional target. A typical Wildean aphorism.

[61] SO *experience/cynicism; good/bad*; LM *experience leads to cynicism*; SI *irr*; TA *naiveté* ; NS *irr*; LA *irr*.

[62] SO *Podgers is a fraud/is genuine*; LM *none*; SI *irr*; TA *Podgers/Lady Windermere*; NS *irr*; LA *irr*.

[63] Unclear reponse, perhaps lady Windermere objects to the fact that Podgers is not telling her guests shocking things. Another interpretation is that Lady Windermere objects to Podgers' erroneous/flattering reading, which she knows to be false.

8.1. CHAPTER I

am not to be allowed to go on the stage, I must be allowed to be part of the audience at any rate.'

'Of course; we are all going to be part of the audience,' said Lady Windermere; 'and now, Mr. Podgers, be sure and tell us something nice. Lord Arthur is one of my special favourites.'

But when Mr. Podgers saw Lord Arthur's hand he grew curiously pale, and said nothing. A shudder seemed to pass through him, and his great bushy eyebrows twitched convulsively, in an odd, irritating way they had when he was puzzled. Then some huge beads of perspiration broke out on his yellow forehead, like a poisonous dew, and his fat fingers grew cold and clammy.

Lord Arthur did not fail to notice these strange signs of agitation, and, for the first time in his life, he himself felt fear. His impulse was to rush from the room, but he restrained himself. It was better to know the worst, whatever it was, than to be left in this hideous uncertainty.

'I am waiting, Mr. Podgers,' he said.

'We are all waiting,' cried Lady Windermere, in her quick, impatient manner, but the cheiromantist made no reply.

'I believe Arthur is going on the stage,' said Lady Jedburgh, 'and that, after your scolding, Mr. Podgers is afraid to tell him so.'[64]

Suddenly Mr. Podgers dropped Lord Arthur's right hand, and seized hold of his left, bending down so low to examine it that the gold rims of his spectacles seemed almost to touch the palm. For a moment his face became a white mask of horror,[65] but he soon recovered his SANG-FROID, and looking up at Lady Windermere, said with a forced smile, 'It is the hand of a charming young man.

'Of course it is!' answered Lady Windermere, 'but will he be a charming husband? That is what I want to know.'

'All charming young men are,'[66] said Mr. Podgers.

'I don't think a husband should be too fascinating,' murmured Lady Jedburgh pensively, 'it is so dangerous.'

'My dear child, they never are too fascinating,' cried Lady Windermere. 'But what I want are details. Details are the only things that interest. What is going to happen to Lord Arthur?'

'Well, within the next few months Lord Arthur will go a voyage - '

'Oh yes, his honeymoon, of course!'

'And lose a relative.'

'Not his sister, I hope?' said Lady Jedburgh, in a piteous tone of voice.

---

[64] SO *fear/no fear; normal/abnormal*; LM *parallelism*; SI *cotext*; TA *Lady Windermere; Podgers*; NS *irr*; LA *irr*.

[65] In the light of the developments of the plot, a legitimate question arises: did Podgers foresee his own death? Is it the reason for his pallor? Or did he merely foretell someone's death? Or, if he is a fake, why is he so affected?

[66] SO *true/false*; LM *none*; SI *none*; TA *young men*; NS *aphorism*; LA *irr*.

'Certainly not his sister,' answered Mr. Podgers, with a deprecating wave of the hand, 'a distant relative merely.'

'Well, I am dreadfully disappointed,' said Lady Windermere. 'I have absolutely nothing to tell[67] Sybil to-morrow. No one cares about distant relatives nowadays. They went out of fashion years ago.[68] However, I suppose she had better have a black silk by her; it always does for church, you know. And now let us go to supper. They are sure to have eaten everything up, but we may find some hot soup. François used to make excellent soup once, but he is so agitated about politics[69] at present, that I never feel quite certain about him. I do wish General Boulanger would keep quiet. Duchess, I am sure you are tired?'

'Not at all, dear Gladys,' answered the Duchess, waddling[70] towards the door. 'I have enjoyed myself immensely, and the cheiropodist, I mean the cheiromantist, is most interesting. Flora, where can my tortoise-shell fan be? Oh, thank you, Sir Thomas, so much. And my lace shawl, Flora? Oh, thank you, Sir Thomas, very kind, I'm sure'; and the worthy creature finally managed to get downstairs without dropping her scent-bottle more than twice.[71]

All this time Lord Arthur Savile had remained standing by the fireplace, with the same feeling of dread over him, the same sickening sense of coming evil. He smiled sadly at his sister, as she swept past him on Lord Plymdale's arm, looking lovely in her pink brocade and pearls, and he hardly heard Lady Windermere when she called to him to follow her. He thought of Sybil Merton, and the idea that anything could come between them made his eyes dim with tears.

Looking at him, one would have said that Nemesis had stolen the shield of Pallas, and shown him the Gorgon's head. He seemed turned to stone, and his face was like marble in its melancholy. He had lived the delicate and luxurious life of a young man of birth and fortune, a life exquisite in its freedom from sordid care, its beautiful boyish insouciance; and now for the first time he became conscious of the terrible mystery of Destiny, of the awful meaning of Doom.[72]

How mad and monstrous it all seemed! Could it be that written on his hand, in characters that he could not read himself, but that another could decipher, was some fearful secret of sin, some blood-red sign of crime? Was there no escape possible? Were we no better than chessmen, moved by an unseen power, vessels the potter fashions at his fancy, for honour or for shame? His reason revolted against it, and

---

[67] SO *death/gossip; normal/abnormal*; LM *none*; SI *cheiromantic reading*; TA *Lady Windermere*; NS *irr*; LA *irr.*

[68] SO *fashion/family; normal/abnormal*; LM *none*; SI *none*; TA *relatives (?)*; NS *aphorism*; LA *irr.*

[69] SO *politics/cooking; high/low; normal/abnormal*; LM *none*; SI *cotext*; TA *François*; NS *irr*; LA *irr.*

[70] SO *duck/human; normal/abnormal*; LM *false analogy*; SI *cotext*; TA *Duchess*; NS *irr*; LA *irr.*

[71] SO *clumsy/adroit; good/bad; normal/abnormal*; LM *analogy (the Duchess is absent minded)*; SI *Guests at the party are moving to another room*; TA *Duchess*; NS *irr*; LA *irr.*

[72] SO *high/low style; normal/abnormal*; LM *none*; SI *Lord Arthur Savile (LAS) is struck by fear*; TA *LAS*; NS *register humor*; LA *register markers: mythological names, personifications, "freedom from sordid care," "beautiful boyish insouciance"*. Note that this is an example of diffuse disjunction.

8.1. CHAPTER I

yet he felt that some tragedy was hanging over him, and that he had been suddenly called upon to bear an intolerable burden. Actors are so fortunate. They can choose whether they will appear in tragedy or in comedy, whether they will suffer or make merry, laugh or shed tears. But in real life it is different. Most men and women are forced to perform parts for which they have no qualifications. Our Guildensterns play Hamlet for us, and our Hamlets have to jest like Prince Hal. The world is a stage, but the play is badly cast.[73]

Suddenly Mr. Podgers entered the room. When he saw Lord Arthur he started, and his coarse, fat face became a sort of greenish-yellow colour. The two men's eyes met, and for a moment there was silence.

'The Duchess has left one of her gloves here, Lord Arthur, and has asked me to bring it to her,' said Mr. Podgers finally. 'Ah, I see it on the sofa! Good evening.'

'Mr. Podgers, I must insist on your giving me a straightforward answer to a question I am going to put to you.'

'Another time, Lord Arthur, but the Duchess is anxious. I am afraid I must go.'

'You shall not go. The Duchess is in no hurry.'

'Ladies should not be kept waiting, Lord Arthur,' said Mr. Podgers, with his sickly smile. 'The fair sex is apt to be impatient.'

Lord Arthur's finely-chiselled lips curled in petulant disdain. The poor Duchess seemed to him of very little importance at that moment. He walked across the room to where Mr. Podgers was standing, and held his hand out.

'Tell me what you saw there,' he said. 'Tell me the truth. I must know it. I am not a child.'

Mr. Podgers's eyes blinked behind his gold-rimmed spectacles, and he moved uneasily from one foot to the other, while his fingers played nervously with a flash watch-chain.

'What makes you think that I saw anything in your hand, Lord Arthur, more than I told you?'

'I know you did, and I insist on your telling me what it was. I will pay you. I will give you a cheque for a hundred pounds.'

The green eyes flashed for a moment, and then became dull again.

'Guineas?' said Mr. Podgers at last, in a low voice.

'Certainly. I will send you a cheque to-morrow. What is your club?'

'I have no club. That is to say, not just at present.[74] My address is -, but allow me to give you my card'; and producing a bit of gilt-edge pasteboard from his waistcoat pocket, Mr. Podgers handed it, with a low bow, to Lord Arthur, who read on it,

---

[73] SO *quotation/non-quotation; actual/non-actual*; LM *reasoning from false premises*; SI *see previous*; TA *LAS*; NS *irr*; LA *quotation*.

[74] SO *dissimulating/non-dissimulating; good/bad*; LM *inference*; SI *Podgers cannot afford a club and wants to hide this fact*; TA *Podgers*; NS *irr*; LA *irr*. The almost complete absence of jabs in this section of the text qualifies it for a stretch of "serious relief" in which Wilde gets around to establishing the development of the story. Note the acceleration in the plot.

MR. SEPTIMUS R. PODGERS PROFESSIONAL CHEIROMANTIST 103A WEST MOON STREET

'My hours are from ten to four,' murmured Mr. Podgers mechanically, 'and I make a reduction for families.'[75]

'Be quick,' cried Lord Arthur, looking very pale, and holding his hand out.

Mr. Podgers glanced nervously round, and drew the heavy PORTIERE across the door.

'It will take a little time, Lord Arthur, you had better sit down.'

'Be quick, sir,' cried Lord Arthur again, stamping his foot angrily on the polished floor.

Mr. Podgers smiled, drew from his breast-pocket a small magnifying glass, and wiped it carefully with his handkerchief

'I am quite ready,' he said.

8.2 CHAPTER II

TEN minutes later, with face blanched by terror, and eyes wild with grief,[76] Lord Arthur Savile rushed from Bentinck House, crushing his way through the crowd of fur-coated footmen that stood round the large striped awning, and seeming not to see or hear anything. The night was bitter cold, and the gas-lamps round the square flared and flickered in the keen wind; but his hands were hot with fever,[77] and his forehead burned like fire.[78] On and on he went, almost with the gait of a drunken man.[79] A policeman looked curiously at him as he passed, and a beggar, who slouched from an archway to ask for alms, grew frightened, seeing misery greater than his own.[80] Once he stopped under a lamp, and looked at his hands. He thought he could detect the stain of blood already upon them, and a faint cry broke from his trembling lips.[81]

Murder! that is what the cheiromantist had seen there. Murder! The very night seemed to know it,[82] and the desolate wind to howl it in his ear. The dark corners of the streets were full of it. It grinned at him from the roofs of the houses.[83]

---

[75] SO *doctor/cheiromantist; normal/abnormal*; LM *false analogy*; SI *irr*; TA *Podgers*; NS *irr*; LA *irr*.

[76] SO *upset/calm; normal/abnormal*; LM *LAS believes in cheiromancy, inference; exaggeration*; SI *LAS was told he will murder someone*; TA *LAS*; NS *irr*; LA *irr*. Note that the entire chapter II of LASC is an expansion of this basic overreaction jab.

[77] cf. 76

[78] cf. 76

[79] cf. 76

[80] cf. 76. Note however that here the narrator has taken upon himself to agree that LAS is feeling genuine misery, or else is being ironical.

[81] cf. 76

[82] cf. 76. Note the Romantic stereotype that nature reflects the emotion of the characters.

[83] cf. 76. As above, with a late-Romantic extension to urban landscape.

8.2. CHAPTER II   175

First he came to the Park,[84] whose sombre woodland seemed to fascinate him. He leaned wearily up against the railings, cooling his brow against the wet metal,[85] and listening to the tremulous silence of the trees. 'Murder! murder!' he kept repeating, as though iteration could dim the horror of the word. The sound of his own voice made him shudder, yet he almost hoped that Echo might hear him, and wake the slumbering city from its dreams. He felt a mad desire to stop the casual passer-by, and tell him everything.

Then he wandered across Oxford Street into narrow, shameful alleys. Two women with painted faces mocked at him as he went by.[86] From a dark courtyard came a sound of oaths and blows, followed by shrill screams, and, huddled upon a damp door-step, he saw the crook- backed forms of poverty and eld. A strange pity came over him. Were these children of sin and misery predestined to their end, as he to his? Were they, like him, merely the puppets of a monstrous show?

And yet it was not the mystery, but the comedy of suffering that struck him; its absolute uselessness, its grotesque want of meaning. How incoherent everything seemed! How lacking in all harmony! He was amazed at the discord between the shallow optimism of the day, and the real facts of existence. He was still very young.[87]

After a time he found himself in front of Marylebone Church. The silent roadway looked like a long riband of polished silver, flecked here and there by the dark arabesques of waving shadows. Far into the distance curved the line of flickering gas-lamps, and outside a little walled-in house stood a solitary hansom, the driver asleep inside. He walked hastily in the direction of Portland Place, now and then looking round, as though he feared that he was being followed. At the corner of Rich Street stood two men, reading a small bill upon a hoarding. An odd feeling of curiosity stirred him, and he crossed over. As he came near, the word 'Murder,' printed in black letters, met his eye. He started, and a deep flush came into his cheek. It was

---

[84]**SO** *long/short; normal/abnormal*; **LM** *none*; **SI** *LAS is wandering in London the prey of emotions*; **TA** *LAS*; **NS** *irr*; **LA** *irr*. A simple joke completely lost on those not familiar with the topography of London: LAS is supposedly walking all night, but his itinerary, detailed by Wilde, is ridiculously short: the location of Bentinck House is not directly given but we know it is located on a square reasonably close to (Hyde) park. From there, LAS goes to Oxford Street, and to Portland Place, a few blocks away, and ends up in Piccadily Circus, again a few blocks down Regent Street. I would estimate the distance between Hyde Park and Piccadilly to about 1.5 miles which is a leisurely stroll of about one hour. Note also that LAS' home is in Belgrave Square, on the other side of Hyde Park.

[85]cf. 76. Jabs 76 through 83 and 85 establish the "night of the soul" strand. Note the obvious comb structure.

[86]This (farily explicit) allusion to prostitution may give us a clue as to what LAS did in the hours he was supposedly walking around London. Note that if this allusion is taken seriously the plot collapses: LAS would have spent the night with prostitutes, therefore he would not at all have been affected by Podgers' foretelling. Quite possibly LAS could have believed Podgers and have been affected, but have recovered from the emotion very fast (cf. the waking up scene next). It remains that the Romantic "night of the soul" stereotype Wilde is mocking is undermined.

[87]**SO** *naive/experienced; normal/abnormal*; **LM** *none*; **SI** *irr*; **TA** *LAS*; **NS** *irr*; **LA** *irr*. Note the isolated occurrence of this jab from this strand (metanarrative comments on LAS).

an advertisement offering a reward for any information leading to the arrest of a man of medium height, between thirty and forty years of age, wearing a billy-cock hat, a black coat, and check trousers, and with a scar upon his right cheek. He read it over and over again, and wondered if the wretched man would be caught, and how he had been scarred. Perhaps, some day, his own name might be placarded on the walls of London. Some day, perhaps, a price would be set on his head also.

The thought made him sick with horror. He turned on his heel, and hurried on into the night.

Where he went he hardly knew. He had a dim memory of wandering through a labyrinth of sordid houses, of being lost in a giant web of sombre streets, and it was bright dawn when he found himself at last in Piccadilly Circus. As he strolled home towards Belgrave Square, he met the great waggons on their way to Covent Garden. The white-smocked carters, with their pleasant sunburnt faces and coarse curly hair, strode sturdily on, cracking their whips, and calling out now and then to each other; on the back of a huge grey horse, the leader of a jangling team, sat a chubby boy, with a bunch of primroses in his battered hat, keeping tight hold of the mane with his little hands, and laughing; and the great piles of vegetables looked like masses of jade against the morning sky, like masses of green jade against the pink petals of some marvellous rose. Lord Arthur felt curiously affected, he could not tell why.[88] There was something in the dawn's delicate loveliness that seemed to him inexpressibly pathetic, and he thought of all the days that break in beauty, and that set in storm. These rustics, too, with their rough, good-humoured voices, and their nonchalant ways, what a strange London they saw! A London free from the sin of night and the smoke of day, a pallid, ghost-like city, a desolate town of tombs! He wondered what they thought of it, and whether they knew anything of its splendour and its shame, of its fierce, fiery- coloured joys, and its horrible hunger, of all it makes and mars from morn to eve. Probably it was to them merely a mart where they brought their fruits to sell, and where they tarried for a few hours at most, leaving the streets still silent, the houses still asleep. It gave him pleasure to watch them as they went by. Rude as they were, with their heavy, hob-nailed shoes, and their awkward gait, they brought a little of a ready with them. He felt that they had lived with Nature, and that she had taught them peace. He envied them all that they did not know.

By the time he had reached Belgrave Square the sky was a faint blue, and the birds were beginning to twitter in the gardens.

8.3 CHAPTER III

WHEN Lord Arthur woke it was twelve o'clock, and the midday sun was streaming through the ivory-silk curtains of his room. He got up and looked out of the window.

---

[88]This could be an allusion to the gay subculture, the kind of which has been argued to permeate certain Wildean texts.

8.3. CHAPTER III

A dim haze of heat was hanging over the great city, and the roofs of the houses were like dull silver. In the flickering green of the square below some children were flitting about like white butterflies, and the pavement was crowded with people on their way to the Park. Never had life seemed lovelier to him, never had the things of evil seemed more remote.

Then his valet brought him a cup of chocolate on a tray. After he had drunk it, he drew aside a heavy PORTIERE of peach-coloured plush, and passed into the bathroom. The light stole softly from above, through thin slabs of transparent onyx, and the water in the marble tank glimmered like a moonstone. He plunged hastily in, till the cool ripples touched throat and hair, and then dipped his head right under, as though he would have wiped away the stain of some shameful memory. When he stepped out he felt almost at peace. The exquisite physical conditions of the moment had dominated him, as indeed often happens in the case of very finely-wrought natures, for the senses, like fire, can purify as well as destroy.

After breakfast, he flung himself down on a divan, and lit a cigarette. On the mantel-shelf, framed in dainty old brocade, stood a large photograph of Sybil Merton, as he had seen her first at Lady Noel's ball. The small, exquisitely-shaped head drooped slightly to one side, as though the thin, reed-like throat could hardly bear the burden of so much beauty; the lips were slightly parted, and seemed made for sweet music; and all the tender purity of girlhood looked out in wonder from the dreaming eyes. With her soft, clinging dress of CREPE-DE-CHINE, and her large leaf-shaped fan, she looked like one of those delicate little figures men find in the olive-woods near Tanagra; and there was a touch of Greek grace in her pose and attitude. Yet she was not PETITE. She was simply perfectly proportioned - a rare thing in an age when so many women are either over life-size or insignificant.[89]

Now as Lord Arthur looked at her, he was filled with the terrible pity that is born of love. He felt that to marry her, with the doom of murder hanging over his head, would be a betrayal like that of Judas, a sin worse than any the Borgia had ever dreamed of. What happiness could there be for them, when at any moment he might be called upon to carry out the awful prophecy written in his hand? What manner of life would be theirs while Fate still held this fearful fortune in the scales? The marriage must be postponed, at all costs. Of this he was quite resolved. Ardently though he loved the girl, and the mere touch of her fingers, when they sat together, made each nerve of his body thrill with exquisite joy, he recognised none the less clearly where his duty lay, and was fully conscious of the fact that *he had no right to marry until he had committed the murder.*[90] This done, he could stand before the

---

[89] SO *complain/not complain; normal/abnormal*; **LM** *none*; **SI** *irr*; **TA** *narrator*; **NS** *irr*; **LA** *irr*. cf. jab line 17

[90] SO *duty/murder; good/bad*; **LM** *reasoning from false premises*; **SI** *cotext*; **TA** *LAS*; **NS** *irr*; **LA** *irr*. Finally, and a full 5100 words into the story, Wilde sets the narrative basis of the story: since LAS believes Podgers' prediction that he will commit a murder he believes that he must commit it *before* the marriage. Hence he sets out to commit a crime out of his sense of duty to his fiance. This is the central narrative complication of LASC.

altar with Sybil Merton, and give his life into her hands without terror of wrongdoing. This done, he could take her to his arms, knowing that she would never have to blush for him, never have to hang her head in shame. But done it must be first; and the sooner the better for both.[91]

Many men in his position would have preferred the primrose path of dalliance to the steep heights of duty;[92] but Lord Arthur was too conscientious to set pleasure above principle.[93] There was more than mere passion in his love; and Sybil was to him a symbol of all that is good and noble. For a moment he had a natural repugnance against what he was asked to do, but it soon passed away. His heart told him that it was not a sin, but a sacrifice;[94] his reason reminded him that there was no other course open.[95] He had to choose between living for himself and living for others,[96] and terrible though the task laid upon him undoubtedly was, yet he knew that he must not suffer selfishness[97] to triumph over love. Sooner or later we are all called upon to decide on the same issue - of us all, the same question is asked. To Lord Arthur it came early in life - before his nature had been spoiled by the calculating cynicism[98] of middle-age, or his heart corroded by the shallow, fashionable egotism[99] of our day, and he felt no hesitation about doing his duty.[100] Fortunately also, for him, he was no mere dreamer,[101] or idle dilettante.[102] Had he been so, he would have hesitated, like Hamlet, and let irresolution mar[103] his purpose. But he was essentially practical. Life to him meant action, rather than thought. He had that rarest of all things, common sense.[104]

---

[91] As above.

[92] As above. With stylistic variation: **SO** *high/low style; normal/abnormal*; **LM** *none*; **SI** *cotext*; **TA** *LAS*; **NS** *irr*; **LA** *register humor*.

[93] **SO** *principle/crime; good/bad*; **LM** *false reasoning*; **SI** *cotext*; **TA** *LAS*; **NS** *irr*; **LA** *irr*. The strand "crime is a duty" is by now firmly established by this variation on a theme comb of jabs. Wilde is obviously enjoying the paradoxical nature of the equation that follows from LAS paralogism.

[94] **SO** *sin/sacrifice; good/bad*; **LM** *false reasoning*; **SI** *cotext*; **TA** *LAS*; **NS** *irr*; **LA** *irr*. See above 93.

[95] **SO** *no course/other courses; actual/non-actual*; **LM** *false reasoning*; **SI** *cotext*; **TA** *LAS*; **NS** *irr*; **LA** *irr*. See above 93: by now the strand is so well established that the implied narrator (not the narrator) can afford to directly call into question the faulty logical reasoning that LAS is using.

[96] **SO** *unselfishness/murder; good/bad*; **LM** *false reasoning*; **SI** *cotext*; **TA** *LAS*; **NS** *irr*; **LA** *irr (but there may be a punning allusion in "living for others" which means "killing someone.")*. See above 93.

[97] As above.

[98] As above.

[99] As above.

[100] As above.

[101] **SO** *dreamer/resolute; good/bad*; **LM** *faulty reasoning*; **SI** *cotext*; **TA** *LAS*; **NS** *irr*; **LA** *irr*. Note that the SO implies no murder/murder.

[102] As above.

[103] **SO** *good/bad*; **LM** *faulty reasoning*; **SI** *cotext*; **TA** *LAS*; **NS** *irr*; **LA** *irr*. "Mar" presupposes that the object being marred is "good," hence the SO.

[104] **SO** *common sense/absurdity; good/bad*; **LM** *false reasoning*; **SI** *cotext*; **TA** *LAS*; **NS** *irr*; **LA** *irr*. The strand that has been driven home by a remarkable comb-structure (15 jab lines in a 372 words text passage, for a ratio of of slightly over one jab per 25 words of text!) ends up establishing a "parallel

8.3. CHAPTER III

The wild, turbid feelings of the previous night had by this time completely passed away, and it was almost with a sense of shame that he looked back upon his mad wanderings[105] from street to street, his fierce emotional agony. The very sincerity of his sufferings made them seem unreal to him now. He wondered how he could have been so foolish as to rant and rave about the inevitable.[106] The only question that seemed to trouble him was, whom to make away with;[107] for he was not blind to the fact that murder, like the religions of the Pagan world, requires a victim as well as a priest. Not being a genius, he had no enemies,[108] and indeed he felt that this was not the time for the gratification of any personal pique or dislike, the mission in which he was engaged being one of great and grave solemnity.[109] He accordingly made out a list of his friends and relatives[110] on a sheet of notepaper, and after careful consideration, decided in favour[111] of Lady Clementina Beauchamp, a dear old lady

---

universe" of LAS's ethics, which is essentially a mirror image of normal ethics:

good	bad
murder	no murder
duty	dalliance
sacrifice	sin
living for others	living for himself
love	selfishness
(no cynicism)	cynicism
(altruism)	egotism
no hesitation	(hesitation)
common sense	(no common sense)

This is LAS's system of beliefs, which motivates his actions. Note how the original inferential error (namely, neglecting to consider the existence of another possibility, i.e., that Podger's prediction was groundless) triggers a cascade of inferences which are themselves consistent with the faulty premise and each other. Incidentally, a good argument could be made to rate these jabs as having a "reasoning from false premises" LM. This is the central strand of the story.

[105] SO *big/small; normal/abnormal*; **LM** *none*; **SI** *LAS' walk around town*; **TA** *LAS*; **NS** *irr*; **LA** *irr*. The presence of this jab is conditional on the restricted knowledge of London toponomastics seen above (84).

[106] SO *real/unreal*; **LM** *none*; **SI** *metanarrative comments of the narrator*; **TA** *narrator*; **NS** *irr*; **LA** *irr*. Passages like these two sentences led to postulate the presence of an implied narrator who is dissociating himself from the naive narrator who is committing the same faulty reasoning of LAS.

[107] SO *one/many; normal/abnormal*; **LM** *false reasoning*; **SI** *cotext*; **TA** *LAS*; **NS** *irr*; **LA** *irr*. The strand of the above paragraphs returns.

[108] SO *genius/enemy; normal/abnormal*; **LM** *none*; **SI** *gnomic phrase*; **TA** *none ?*; **NS** *gnomic*; **LA** *irr*. Typical Wildean pithy saying, which implies that all geniuses have enemies, an eerily cogent claim. Note, on the methodological plane, that another jab has occurred in the text which involves the word "genius" (11) but that it does not trigger a strand.

[109] SO *solemnity/homicide; normal/abnormal*; **LM** *false reasoning*; **SI** *cotext*; **TA** *LAS*; **NS** *irr*; **LA** *irr*. Again the central strand.

[110] SO *friends and relatives/victims; normal/abnormal*; **LM** *none*; **SI** *choice of homicide victims*; **TA** *LAS*; **NS** *irr*; **LA** *irr*.

[111] SO *favor/homicide; normal/abnormal*; **LM** *false reasoning*; **SI** *cotext*; **TA** *LAS*; **NS** *irr*; **LA** *irr*.

who lived in Curzon Street, and was his own second cousin by his mother's side. He had always been very fond of Lady Clem, as every one called her, and as he was very wealthy himself, having come into all Lord Rugby's property when he came of age, there was no possibility of his deriving any vulgar monetary advantage by her death. In fact, the more he thought over the matter, the more she seemed to him to be just the right person, and, feeling that any delay would be unfair[112] to Sybil, he determined to make his arrangements at once.

The first thing to be done was, of course,[113] to settle with the cheiromantist;[114] so he sat down at a small Sheraton writing-table that stood near the window, drew a cheque for 105 pounds, payable to the order of Mr. Septimus Podgers, and, enclosing it in an envelope, told his valet to take it to West Moon Street. He then telephoned to the stables for his hansom, and dressed to go out. As he was leaving the room he looked back at Sybil Merton's photograph, and swore that, come what may, he would never let her know what he was doing for her sake, but would keep the secret of his self-sacrifice[115] hidden always in his heart.

On his way to the Buckingham, he stopped at a florist's, and sent Sybil a beautiful basket of narcissus, with lovely white petals and staring pheasants' eyes, and on arriving at the club, went straight to the library, rang the bell, and ordered the waiter to bring him a lemon-and-soda, and a book on Toxicology.[116] He had fully decided that poison was the best means to adopt in this troublesome business. Anything like personal violence was extremely distasteful to him, and besides, he was very anxious not to murder Lady Clementina in any way that might attract public attention,[117] as he hated the idea of being lionised at Lady Windermere's,[118] or seeing his name fig-

---

[112] SO *delay/haste (of homicide); normal/abnormal*; LM *false reasoning*; SI *cotext*; TA *LAS*; NS *irr*; LA *irr*.

[113] SO *obvious/non-obvious; normal/abnormal*; LM *none*; SI *metanarrative comments of the narrator*; TA *narrator*; NS *irr*; LA *irr*. As 106.

[114] SO *proper behavior/homicide; normal/abnormal*; LM *false reasoning*; SI *cotext*; TA *LAS*; NS *irr*; LA *irr*. The "murder as duty" central strand is here evoked subtly: settling one's debts is of course the sign of a an honest person's behavior, hence the contrast between this action seen as the first step of planning an homicide.

[115] SO *self sacrifice/homicide; normal/abnormal*; LM *false reasoning*; SI *cotext*; TA *LAS*; NS *irr*; LA *irr*.

[116] SO *lemon-and-soda/toxicology; normal/abnormal*; LM *coordination*; SI *things to be brought to LAS*; TA *none*; NS *irr*; LA *coordinating conjunction*.

[117] SO *public attention/prison; good/bad*; LM *understatement (?)*; SI *if discovered, the murder would attract attention*; TA *LAS*; NS *irr*; LA *irr*. It is an interesting feature of this small comb strand (considering the next three jab lines) that prison or even capital punishment is never mentioned as a possible outcome of a murder. This is the source of the incongruity, as noted in the analysis; however, a further aspect, not reflected in the analysis, may be that LAS is so secure that his noble rank will prevent any serious consequences of his behavior from affecting him that he only has to worry about the trivial ones. This aspect could be seen as social satire.

[118] SO *public attention/prison; good/bad*; LM *understatement (?)*; SI *if discovered, the murder would attract attention*; TA *LAS*; NS *irr*; LA *irr*.

8.3. CHAPTER III

uring in the paragraphs of vulgar society - newspapers.[119] He had also to think of Sybil's father and mother, who were rather old-fashioned people, and might possibly object to the marriage if there was anything like a scandal,[120] though he felt certain that if he told them the whole facts of the case they would be the very first to appreciate the motives that had actuated him.[121] He had every reason, then, to decide in favour of poison. It was safe, sure, and quiet, and did away with any necessity for painful scenes, to which, like most Englishmen, he had a rooted objection.[122]

Of the science of poisons, however, he knew absolutely nothing, and as the waiter seemed quite unable to find anything in the library but RUFF'S GUIDE and BAILEY'S MAGAZINE, he examined the book-shelves himself, and finally came across a handsomely-bound edition of the PHARMACOPOEIA, and a copy of Erskine's TOXICOLOGY, edited by Sir Mathew Reid, the President of the Royal College of Physicians, and one of the oldest members of the Buckingham, having been elected in mistake for somebody else;[123] a CONTRETEMPS that so enraged the Committee, that when the real man came up they black-balled him[124] unanimously.[125] Lord Arthur was a good deal puzzled at the technical terms used in both books, and had begun to regret that he had not paid more attention to his classics at Oxford, when in the second volume of Erskine, he found a very interesting and complete account of the properties of aconitine, written in fairly clear English. It seemed to him to be exactly the poison he wanted. It was swift - indeed, almost immediate, in its effect - perfectly painless, and when taken in the form of a gelatine

---

[119] SO *public attention/prison; good/bad*; LM *understatement (?)*; SI *if discovered, the murder would attract attention*; TA *LAS*; NS *irr*; LA *irr*.

[120] SO *scandal/prison; good/bad*; LM *understatement (?)*; SI *if discovered, the murder would attract attention*; TA *LAS*; NS *irr*; LA *irr*.

[121] SO *appreciate motives/object (to homicide); normal/abnormal*; LM *faulty reasoning*; SI *cotext*; TA *LAS*; NS *irr*; LA *irr*.

[122] SO *painful scene/homicide; normal/abnormal*; LM *none (false reasoning?)*; SI *cotext*; TA *LAS; Englishmen*; NS *irr*; LA *irr*. Note that this is a variation on the "murder as duty" strand since the narrator states that LAS has a "rooted objection" towards painful scenes but as we know from the cotext not for homicide. The inferential path that shows the contradiction is for once clear: there is a scalar implicature (cf. Levinson 1983: 132ff) whereby if one objects to painful scenes *a fortiori* one should object to homicide. A further observation: in the anlysis, we do not address the stylistic gems in the text such as the present use of the modifier "rooted" attached to objection. To do so would require an analysis even more detailed than the present one. For the sake of exemplification, let us note that a first approximation might focus on the intensification function of the modifier which is then completely lost in the opposition scene/murder. Thus we might say (metaphorically) that the incongruity between "scene" and "murder" is made more intense, heightened by the modifier. Resolving the metaphor would require too long an analysis.

[123] SO *oldest member/elected by mistake; good/bad*; LM *none*; SI *election to scientific societies*; TA *the Buckingham; scientific societies*; NS *irr*; LA *irr*. The beginning of a very short embedded narrative.

[124] SO *fault/no fault; normal/abnormal*; LM *false reasoning (blame the victim)*; SI *election to scientific society*; TA *scientific societies*; NS *irr*; LA *irr*. The end of the very short embedded narrative. As such, this is a punch line.

[125] An intensifier of the previous punch line.

capsule, the mode recommended by Sir Mathew, not by any means unpalatable.[126] He accordingly made a note, upon his shirt-cuff, of the amount necessary for a fatal dose, put the books back in their places, and strolled up St. James's Street, to Pestle and Humbey's, the great chemists. Mr. Pestle, who always attended personally on the aristocracy, was a good deal surprised at the order, and in a very deferential manner murmured something[127] about a medical certificate being necessary. However, as soon as Lord Arthur explained to him that it was for a large Norwegian mastiff that he was obliged to get rid of, as it showed signs of incipient rabies, and had already bitten the coachman twice in the calf of the leg, he expressed himself as being perfectly satisfied, complimented Lord Arthur on his wonderful knowledge of Toxicology, and had the prescription made up immediately.[128]

Lord Arthur put the capsule into a pretty little silver BONBONNIERE that he saw in a shop window in Bond Street, threw away Pestle and Hambey's ugly pill-box,[129] and drove off at once to Lady Clementina's.

'Well, MONSIEUR LE MAUVAIS SUJET,' cried the old lady, as he entered the room, 'why haven't you been to see me all this time?'

'My dear Lady Clem, I never have a moment to myself,' said Lord Arthur, smiling.

'I suppose you mean that you go about all day long with Miss Sybil Merton, buying CHIFFONS and talking nonsense? I cannot understand why people make such a fuss about being married. In my day we never dreamed of billing and cooing in public, or in private for that matter.'[130]

'I assure you I have not seen Sybil for twenty-four hours, Lady Clem. As far as I can make out, she belongs entirely to her milliners.'[131]

'Of course; that is the only reason you come to see an ugly old woman like myself. I wonder you men don't take warning. ON A FAIT DES FOLIES POUR MOI, and here I am, a poor rheumatic creature, with a false front and a bad temper.[132]

---

[126]SO *unpalatable/lethal; good/bad*; LM *none*; SI *modes of administering poison*; TA *Erskine/LAS/narrator*; NS *irr*; LA *irr*. It is unclear to whom the comment about the not unpalatability of the gelatine capsule of poison is to be attributed to.

[127]SO *polite/excessive deference; normal/abnormal*; LM *Mr. Pestle is a snob*; SI *pharmacy*; TA *Mr. Pestle*; NS *irr*; LA *irr*. Note also the humorous name "Pestle" for a chemist.

[128]SO *polite/excessive deference; normal/abnormal*; LM *Mr. Pestle is a snob*; SI *pharmacy*; TA *Mr. Pestle*; NS *irr*; LA *irr*. Note the three part show of excessive deference.

[129]It is somewhat incongruous to qualify a pill-box as ugly, as it is primarily a functional object; however, there exist elaborate pill-boxes, so we have no evidence of whether the narrator means this as a jab line or whether this is merely an innocent remark. I have chosen not to analyze this as a jab line.

[130]SO *true/false*; LM *Lady Clem is jealous of young people (?)*; SI *public displays of affection*; TA *Lady Clementina*; NS *irr*; LA *irr*. A possible LM here could be that Lady Clementina is old and therefore is making an excessive show of conservatism.

[131]SO *milliners/other activities; true/false*; LM *stereotype; exaggeration*; SI *cotext*; TA *Sybil; women*; NS *irr*; LA *irr*. A stereotypical joke uttered by LAS.

[132]SO *front/temper*; LM *coordination*; SI *old lady's life*; TA *Lady Clementina*; NS *irr*; LA *coordinating conjunction*. A somewhat dubious jab, as it is unclear what a "false front" is; I am assuming it refers to

8.3. CHAPTER III
183

Why, if it were not for dear Lady Jansen, who sends me all the worst French novels she can find, I don't think I could get through the day.[133] Doctors are no use at all, except to get fees out of one.[134] They can't even cure my heartburn.'

'I have brought you a cure for that, Lady Clem,' said Lord Arthur gravely. 'It is a wonderful thing, invented by an American.'

'I don't think I like American inventions, Arthur. I am quite sure I don't. I read some American novels lately, and they were quite nonsensical.'[135]

'Oh, but there is no nonsense at all about this, Lady Clem! I assure you it is a perfect cure.[136] You must promise to try it'; and Lord Arthur brought the little box out of his pocket, and handed it to her.

'Well, the box is charming, Arthur. Is it really a present? That is very sweet of you. And is this the wonderful medicine? It looks like a BONBON.[137] I'll take it at once.'

'Good heavens! Lady Clem,' cried Lord Arthur, catching hold of her hand, 'you mustn't do anything of the kind. It is a homoeopathic medicine, and if you take it without having heartburn, it might do you no end of harm.[138] Wait till you have an attack, and take it then. You will be astonished at the result.'[139]

'I should like to take it now,' said Lady Clementina, holding up to the light the little transparent capsule, with its floating bubble of liquid aconitine. I am sure it is delicious.[140] The fact is that, though I hate doctors, I love medicines. However, I'll keep it till my next attack.'

'And when will that be?' asked Lord Arthur eagerly. 'Will it be soon?'

'I hope not for a week. I had a very bad time yesterday morning with it. But one never knows.'

'You are sure to have one before the end of the month then, Lady Clem?'

---

a piece of clothing and that therefore it is incongruous to describe oneself as having a piece of clothing and a character tendency (note how they both have negative modifiers, reinforcing the parallelism of the coordinating conjunction).

[133] SO *good/bad novel*; LM *none*; SI *Lady Clementina likes to read bad French novels*; TA *Lady Clementina; literary targets?*; NS *irr*; LA *irr*.

[134] SO *cure/charge; good/bad*; LM *none*; SI *doctors*; TA *doctors*; NS *irr*; LA *irr*. Lady Clementina (much like Lady Windermere) produces a stream of paradoxical claims which establish a strand. The present one brings to mind two French works: Molière's *Malade imaginaire* (1673) and Jules Romain's *Knock*. (1923).

[135] SO *inventions/novels; normal/abnormal*; LM *nonsequitur*; SI *cotext*; TA *Lady Clementina*; NS *irr*; LA *irr*.

[136] SO *cure/poison; good/bad*; LM *none*; SI *cotext*; TA *Lady Clementina/LSAS*; NS *irr*; LA *irr*.

[137] SO *bonbon/poison; good/bad*; LM *similarity (of the container)*; SI *cotext*; TA *lady Clementina*; NS *irr*; LA *irr*.

[138] SO *harm/death; good/bad*; LM *false reasoning*; SI *cotext*; TA *Lady Clementina*; NS *irr*; LA *irr*.

[139] SO *astonished/dead; good/bad*; LM *false reasoning*; SI *cotext*; TA *Lady Clementina*; NS *irr*; LA *irr*.

[140] SO *delicious/deadly; good/bad*; LM *reasoning from false premises*; SI *cotext*; TA *Lady Clementina*; NS *irr*; LA *irr*. A new strand built around lady Clementina, buth with the SO death/candy.

'I am afraid so. But how sympathetic you are to-day,[141] Arthur! Really, Sybil has done you a great deal of good. And now you must run away, for I am dining with some very dull people, who won't talk scandal,[142] and I know that if I don't get my sleep now I shall never be able to keep awake during dinner.[143] Good-bye, Arthur, give my love to Sybil, and thank you so much for the American medicine.'[144]

'You won't forget to take it, Lady Clem, will you?' said Lord Arthur, rising from his seat.

'Of course I won't, you silly boy. I think it is most kind of you to think of me,[145] and I shall write and tell you if I want any more.'[146]

Lord Arthur left the house in high spirits, and with a feeling of immense relief.[147]

That night he had an interview with Sybil Merton. He told her how he had been suddenly placed in a position of terrible difficulty,[148] from which neither honour nor duty would allow him to recede. He told her that the marriage must be put off for the present, as until he had got rid of his fearful entanglements,[149] he was not a free man. He implored her to trust him, and not to have any doubts about the future. Everything would come right,[150] but patience was necessary.

The scene took place in the conservatory of Mr. Merton's house, in Park Lane, where Lord Arthur had dined as usual. Sybil had never seemed more happy, and for a moment Lord Arthur had been tempted to play the coward's part,[151] to write to Lady Clementina for the pill, and to let the marriage go on as if there was no such person as Mr. Podgers in the world. His better nature,[152] however, soon asserted itself, and

---

[141] SO *sympathetic/assassin; good/bad*; **LM** *reasoning from false premises*; **SI** *cotext*; **TA** *Lady Clementina*; **NS** *irr*; **LA** *irr*.

[142] SO *dull/interesting (scandal); good/bad*; **LM** *reasoning from false premises*; **SI** *cotext*; **TA** *Lady Clementina (?)*; **NS** *irr*; **LA** *irr*. Note the LM which implies that gossip is interesting, a truism which is however socially inadmissible.

[143] SO *sleep/eat; normal/abnormal*; **LM** *reasoning from false premises; exaggeration*; **SI** *cotext*; **TA** *dull guests*; **NS** *irr*; **LA** *irr*.

[144] SO *poison/medicine; good/bad*; **LM** *reasoning from false premises*; **SI** *cotext*; **TA** *Lady Clementina*; **NS** *irr*; **LA** *irr*.

[145] SO *kind/murderous; good/bad*; **LM** *reasoning from false premises*; **SI** *cotext*; **TA** *Lady Clementina*; **NS** *irr*; **LA** *irr*.

[146] SO *write/die; possible/impossible*; **LM** *reasoning from false premises*; **SI** *cotext*; **TA** *Lady Clementina*; **NS** *irr*; **LA** *irr*. This ends the Lady Clementina episode, hence it is a punch line.

[147] SO *relief/remorse; good/bad*; **LM** *reasoning from false premises*; **SI** *cotext*; **TA** *LAS*; **NS** *irr*; **LA** *irr*.

[148] SO *difficulty/homicide; good/bad*; **LM** *reasoning from false premises*; **SI** *cotext*; **TA** *LAS*; **NS** *irr*; **LA** *irr*.

[149] SO *entanglement/homicide; good/bad*; **LM** *reasoning from false premises*; **SI** *cotext*; **TA** *LAS*; **NS** *irr*; **LA** *irr*.

[150] SO *come right/homicide; good/bad*; **LM** *reasoning from false premises*; **SI** *cotext*; **TA** *LAS*; **NS** *irr*; **LA** *irr*.

[151] SO *coward/courageous; homicide/no homicide; good/bad*; **LM** *reasoning from false premises*; **SI** *cotext*; **TA** *LAS*; **NS** *irr*; **LA** *irr*.

[152] SO *better nature/homicide; good/bad*; **LM** *reasoning from false premises*; **SI** *cotext*; **TA** *LAS*; **NS**

even when Sybil flung herself weeping into his arms, he did not falter. The beauty that stirred his senses had touched his conscience also. He felt that to wreck so fair a life for the sake of a few months' pleasure would be a wrong thing to do.[153]

He stayed with Sybil till nearly midnight, comforting her and being comforted in turn, and early the next morning he left for Venice, after writing a manly,[154] firm letter to Mr. Merton about the necessary postponement of the marriage.

8.4 CHAPTER IV

IN Venice he met his brother, Lord Surbiton, who happened to have come over from Corfu in his yacht. The two young men spent a delightful fortnight together. In the morning they rode on the Lido, or glided up and down the green canals in their long black gondola; in the afternoon they usually entertained visitors on the yacht; and in the evening they dined at Florian's, and smoked innumerable cigarettes on the Piazza.[155] Yet somehow Lord Arthur was not happy. Every day he studied the obituary column in the TIMES, expecting to see a notice of Lady Clementina's death, but every day he was disappointed.[156] He began to be afraid that some accident had happened to her,[157] and often regretted[158] that he had prevented her taking the aconitine when she had been so anxious to try its effect.[159] Sybil's letters, too, though full of love, and trust, and tenderness, were often very sad in their tone, and sometimes he used to think that he was parted from her for ever.

After a fortnight Lord Surbiton got bored with Venice, and determined to run down the coast to Ravenna, as he heard that there was some capital cock-shooting in the Pinetum.[160] Lord Arthur at first refused absolutely to come, but Surbiton, of

---

irr; **LA** *irr*.

[153] **SO** *wreck a life/homicide; good/bad*; **LM** *reasoning from false premises*; **SI** *cotext*; **TA** *LAS*; **NS** *irr*; **LA** *irr*. Note the complex jab, which introduces the moral evaluation upon which the strand rests.

[154] **SO** *manly/weakling; good/abd*; **LM** *none*; **SI** *LAS write a manly letter after having been "comforted" by Sybil*; **TA** *LAS*; **NS** *irr*; **LA** *irr*.

[155] These may be gay flags.

[156] **SO** *disappointed/satisfied; normal/abnormal*; **LM** *reasoning from false premises*; **SI** *cotext*; **TA** *LAS*; **NS** *irr*; **LA** *irr*. The return of the death-as-positive strand.

[157] **SO** *accident/no accident; good/bad*; **LM** *reasoning from false premises*; **SI** *cotext*; **TA** *LAS*; **NS** *irr*; **LA** *irr*. The narrator is again playing on the "death-as-positive" central strand with the following inferential chain: if LAS does not see the notice of her death in the paper, it follows that she has not died, but since this was the "normal" course of events if her life had been undisturbed, it follows that something must have happened to her. Hence LAS' concern for Lady Clementina. Of course, the fact that LAS is expecting the news of her death he has caused is the source of the incongruity.

[158] **SO** *regret/no regret; good/bad*; **LM** *reasoning from false premises*; **SI** *cotext*; **TA** *LAS*; **NS** *irr*; **LA** *irr*.

[159] **SO** *anxious to try/not anxious; good/bad*; **LM** *reasoning from false premises*; **SI** *cotext*; **TA** *Lady Clementina*; **NS** *irr*; **LA** *irr*.

[160] More gay flags?

whom he was extremely fond, finally persuaded him that if he stayed at Danieli's by himself he would be moped to death, and on the morning of the 15th they started, with a strong nor'-east wind blowing, and a rather choppy sea. The sport was excellent, and the free, open-air life brought the colour back to Lord Arthur's cheek, but about the 22nd he became anxious about Lady Clementina, and, in spite of Surbiton's remonstrances, came back to Venice by train.

As he stepped out of his gondola on to the hotel steps, the proprietor came forward to meet him with a sheaf of telegrams. Lord Arthur snatched them out of his hand, and tore them open. Everything had been successful.[161] Lady Clementina had died quite suddenly on the night of the 17th!

His first thought was for Sybil, and he sent her off a telegram announcing his immediate return to London. He then ordered his valet to pack his things for the night mail, sent his gondoliers about five times their proper fare,[162] and ran up to his sitting-room with a light step and a buoyant heart. [163] There he found three letters waiting for him. One was from Sybil herself, full of sympathy and condolence. The others were from his mother, and from Lady Clementina's solicitor. It seemed that the old lady had dined with the Duchess that very night, had delighted every one by her wit and ESPRIT, but had gone home somewhat early, complaining of heartburn. In the morning she was found dead in her bed, having apparently suffered no pain. Sir Mathew Reid[164] had been sent for at once, but, of course, there was nothing to be done, and she was to be buried on the 22nd at Beauchamp Chalcote. A few days before she died she had made her will, and left Lord Arthur her little house in Curzon Street, and all her furniture, personal effects, and pictures, with the exception of her collection of miniatures, which was to go to her sister, Lady Margaret Rufford, and her amethyst necklace, which Sybil Merton was to have. The property was not of much value; but Mr. Mansfield, the solicitor, was extremely anxious for Lord Arthur to return at once, if possible, as there were a great many bills to be paid, and Lady Clementina had never kept any regular accounts.

Lord Arthur was very much touched by Lady Clementina's kind remembrance of him,[165] and felt that Mr. Podgers had a great deal to answer for.[166] His love of Sybil, however, dominated every other emotion, and the consciousness that he had

---

[161] SO *success/failure; life/death; good/bad*; LM *reasoning from false premises*; SI *cotext*; TA *LAS*; NS *irr*; LA *irr*.

[162] Strange behavior, which could be accounted for as a result of the joy of hearing of Lady Clementina's death, or as another gay flag.

[163] SO *happy/sad; good/bad*; LM *reasoning from false premises*; SI *cotext*; TA *LAS*; NS *irr*; LA *irr*.

[164] SO *competent/incompetent; good/bad*; LM *none*; SI *doctor called on the scene*; TA *Sir Mathew Reid*; NS *irr*; LA *irr*. The reader will recall that the doctor had been elected to his office by mistake.

[165] SO *remorse/gratitude; normal/abnormal*; LM *reasoning from false premises*; SI *cotext*; TA *LAS*; NS *irr*; LA *irr*.

[166] SO *guilt/innocence; normal/abnormal*; LM *reasoning from false premises*; SI *cotext*; TA *LAS*; NS *irr*; LA *irr*.

8.4. CHAPTER IV

done his duty[167] gave him peace and comfort. When he arrived at Charing Cross, he felt perfectly happy.[168]

The Mertons received him very kindly. Sybil made him promise that he would never again allow anything to come between them, and the marriage was fixed for the 7th June. Life seemed to him once more bright and beautiful, and all his old gladness came back to him again.

One day, however, as he was going over the house in Curzon Street, in company with Lady Clementina's solicitor and Sybil herself, burning packages of faded letters, and turning out drawers of odd rubbish, the young girl suddenly gave a little cry of delight.

'What have you found, Sybil?' said Lord Arthur, looking up from his work, and smiling.

'This lovely little silver BONBONNIERE, Arthur. Isn't it quaint and Dutch?[169] Do give it to me! I know amethysts won't become me till I am over eighty.'

It was the box that had held the aconitine.

Lord Arthur started, and a faint blush came into his cheek. He had almost entirely forgotten what he had done, and it seemed to him a curious coincidence that Sybil, for whose sake he had gone through all that terrible anxiety,[170] should have been the first to remind him of it.

'Of course you can have it, Sybil. I gave it to poor Lady Clem myself.'

'Oh! thank you, Arthur; and may I have the BONBON too? I had no notion that Lady Clementina liked sweets. I thought she was far too intellectual.'[171]

Lord Arthur grew deadly pale, and a horrible idea crossed his mind.

'BONBON, Sybil? What do you mean?' he said in a slow, hoarse voice.

'There is one in it, that is all. It looks quite old and dusty, and I have not the slightest intention of eating it. What is the matter, Arthur? How white you look!'

Lord Arthur rushed across the room, and seized the box. Inside it was the amber-coloured capsule, with its poison-bubble. Lady Clementina had died a natural death after all!

The shock of the discovery was almost too much for him. He flung the capsule into the fire, and sank on the sofa with a cry of despair.[172]

---

[167] SO *duty/homicide; good/bad*; LM *reasoning from false premises*; SI *cotext*; TA *LAS*; NS *irr*; LA *irr*.

[168] SO *happy/sad; good/bad*; LM *reasoning from false premises*; SI *cotext*; TA *LAS*; NS *irr*; LA *irr*.

[169] SO *quaint/Dutch; normal/abnormal*; LM *coordination*; SI *cotext*; TA *Sybil*; NS *irr*; LA *coordinating conjunction*. There is a possibility that the narrator does not mean this as a jab line, if for example, Dutch art was considered quaint in aristocratic circles in that period.

[170] SO *anxiety/death; good/bad*; LM *reasoning from false premises*; SI *cotext*; TA *LAS*; NS *irr*; LA *irr*. Note the intensifier "terrible."

[171] SO *intellectual/liking sweets; normal/abnormal*; LM *none*; SI *cotext*; TA *Sybil*; NS *irr*; LA *irr*.

[172] SO *despair/relief; normal/abnormal*; LM *reasoning from false premises*; SI *cotext*; TA *LAS*; NS *irr*; LA *irr*. Note how LAS should be relieved of not having killed his aunt, whereas his reaction is the opposite.

8.5 CHAPTER V

MR. MERTON was a good deal distressed at the second postponement of the marriage, and Lady Julia, who had already ordered her dress for the wedding,[173] did all in her power to make Sybil break off the match. Dearly, however, as Sybil loved her mother, she had given her whole life into Lord Arthur's hands, and nothing that Lady Julia could say could make her waver in her faith. As for Lord Arthur himself, it took him days to get over his terrible disappointment, and for a time his nerves were completely unstrung. His excellent common sense,[174] however, soon asserted itself, and his sound, practical mind did[175] not leave him long in doubt about what to do. Poison having proved a complete failure, dynamite, or some other form of explosive, was obviously the proper thing to try.[176]

He accordingly looked again over the list of his friends and relatives,[177] and, after careful consideration, determined to blow up his uncle,[178] the Dean of Chichester. The Dean, who was a man of great culture and learning, was extremely fond of clocks, and had a wonderful collection of timepieces, ranging from the fifteenth century to the present day, and it seemed to Lord Arthur that this hobby of the good Dean's offered him an excellent opportunity for carrying out his scheme. Where to procure an explosive machine was, of course, quite another matter. The London Directory gave him no information on the point,[179] and he felt that there was very little use in going to Scotland Yard about it,[180] as they never seemed to know anything about the movements of the dynamite faction till after an explosion had taken

---

[173] SO *trivial/significant reason; normal/abnormal*; LM *none*; SI *cotext*; TA *Lady Julia*; NS *irr*; LA *irr*.

[174] SO *common sense/absurdity; good/bad*; LM *reasoning from false premises*; SI *cotext*; TA *LAS*; NS *irr*; LA *irr*.

[175] SO *common sense/absurdity; good/bad*; LM *reasoning from false premises*; SI *cotext*; TA *LAS*; NS *irr*; LA *irr*. As above.

[176] SO *proper/improper; good/bad*; LM *reasoning from false premises*; SI *cotext*; TA *LAS*; NS *irr*; LA *irr*. As above, with a variation on the theme ("proper thing to do") and metanarrative intensifier ("obviously") whereby the narrator endorses LAS's reasoning.

[177] Cf. 110.

[178] SO *blow up/not blow up; good/bad*; LM *reasoning from false premises*; SI *cotext*; TA *LAS*; NS *irr*; LA *irr*.

[179] SO *London Directory/bombs; normal/abnormal*; LM *reasoning from false premises*; SI *cotext*; TA *LAS*; NS *irr*; LA *irr*. Another variation on the theme of the central strand: LAS treats blowing up his uncle as any other errand one would run.

[180] SO *police/criminal; normal/abnormal*; LM *reasoning from false premises; false reasoning*; SI *cotext*; TA *LAS*; NS *irr*; LA *irr*. Note the local logic of asking the Police about producing dynamite, since they investigate this kind of action (in order to prevent it, however).

8.5. CHAPTER V

place,[181] and not much even then.[182]

Suddenly he thought of his friend Rouvaloff, a young Russian of very revolutionary tendencies, whom he had met at Lady Windermere's in the winter. Count Rouvaloff was supposed to be writing a life of Peter the Great, and to have come over to England for the purpose of studying the documents relating to that Tsar's residence in this country as a ship carpenter;[183] but it was generally suspected that he was a Nihilist agent, and there was no doubt that the Russian Embassy did not look with any favour upon his presence in London. Lord Arthur felt that he was just the man for his purpose, and drove down one morning to his lodgings in Bloomsbury, to ask his advice and assistance.

'So you are taking up politics seriously?'[184] said Count Rouvaloff, when Lord Arthur had told him the object of his mission; but Lord Arthur, who hated swagger of any kind, felt bound to admit to him that he had not the slightest interest in social questions, and simply wanted the explosive machine for a purely family matter,[185] in which no one was concerned but himself.

Count Rouvaloff looked at him for some moments in amazement,[186] and then seeing that he was quite serious, wrote an address on a piece of paper, initialled it, and handed it to him across the table.

'Scotland Yard would give a good deal to know this address, my dear fellow.'

'They shan't have it,' cried Lord Arthur, laughing; and after shaking the young Russian warmly by the hand he ran downstairs, examined the paper, and told the coachman to drive to Soho Square.

There he dismissed him, and strolled down Greek Street,[187] till he came to a place called Bayle's Court. He passed under the archway, and found himself in

---

[181] SO *know before/after; good bad*; **LM** *reasoning from false premises*; **SI** *Scotland Yard investigating dynamite bombings*; **TA** *Scotland Yard*; **NS** *irr*; **LA** *irr*. Note how LSA's reasoning is logical: to prevent bombings one has to know of them ahead of time. If one learns about them after the fact, then one cannot prevent them. Of course, the premiss is faulty: investigations are much more complex and involve infiltrating terrorist organizations, etc.

[182] SO *knowledge/ignorance; good/bad*; **LM** *none*; **SI** *Scotland Yard's investigations*; **TA** *Scotland Yard*; **NS** *irr*; **LA** *irr*.

[183] SO *Tsar/ship carpenter; normal/abnormal*; **LM** *none*; **SI** *Tsar's occupation during his stay in England*; **TA** *Tsar*; **NS** *irr*; **LA** *irr*.

[184] SO *politics/bombing*; **LM** *stereotype*; **SI** *political bombing*; **TA** *terrorists; Russians*; **NS** *irr*; **LA** *irr*. Note how in Wilde's time this was most likely a jab line; for those who have witnessed the terrorist movements of the late 20th century the idea that being serious about politics might involve securing explosives is no longer necessarily incongruous.

[185] SO *family matter/terrorism; normal/abnormal*; **LM** *reasoning from false premises*; **SI** *cotext*; **TA** *LAS*; **NS** *irr*; **LA** *irr*.

[186] This is not properly a jab line, but it is quite significant nonetheless. Count Rouvaloff sees that LAS is acting crazily. He is the only character in the short story that shares the normal system of belief of the readers (although he does not try to stop LAS). That the only character to think like the (implied) reader is a Nihilist revolutionary is too good a coincidence to think that the implied narrator did not plan it.

[187] Innocent toponyms or gay flags? Note also immediately below "cul" (*bottom*, in French). Note the probable irony that the address (apparently fictitious) is fairly close to Trafalgar Square.

a curious CUL-DE-SAC, that was apparently occupied by a French Laundry, as a perfect network of clothes-lines was stretched across from house to house, and there was a flutter of white linen in the morning air. He walked right to the end, and knocked at a little green house. After some delay, during which every window in the court became a blurred mass of peering faces, the door was opened by a rather rough-looking foreigner, who asked him in very bad English what his business was. Lord Arthur handed him the paper Count Rouvaloff had given him. When the man saw it he bowed, and invited Lord Arthur into a very shabby front parlour on the ground floor, and in a few moments Herr Winckelkopf,[188] as he was called in England, bustled into the room, with a very wine-stained napkin round his neck, and a fork in his left hand.[189]

'Count Rouvaloff has given me an introduction to you,' said Lord Arthur, bowing, 'and I am anxious to have a short interview with you on a matter of business. My name is Smith, Mr. Robert Smith, and I want you to supply me with an explosive clock.'

'Charmed to meet you, Lord Arthur,'[190] said the genial little German, laughing. 'Don't look so alarmed, it is my duty to know everybody, and I remember seeing you one evening at Lady Windermere's.[191] I hope her ladyship is quite well. Do you mind sitting with me while I finish my breakfast? There is an excellent PATE, and my friends are kind enough to say that my Rhine wine is better than any they get at the German Embassy,'[192] and before Lord Arthur had got over his surprise at being recognised, he found himself seated in the back-room, sipping the most delicious Marcobrunner out of a pale yellow hock-glass marked with the Imperial monogram, and chatting in the friendliest manner possible to the famous conspirator.[193]

'Explosive clocks,' said Herr Winckelkopf, 'are not very good things for foreign exportation,[194] as, even if they succeed in passing the Custom House, the train ser-

---

[188] SO *angle(square)head/neutral name; normal/abnormal*; **LM** *none*; **SI** *onomastics*; **TA** *Herr Winckelkopf*; **NS** *irr*; **LA** *irr*. Chlopicki (2000) perceptively argues that Herr Winckekopf and Princess Sophia of Carlsruhe (jabs 2 to 6) share a German origin and there is therefore a "German stereotype" strand.

[189] SO *food/explosives; good/bad*; **LM** *none*; **SI** *Herr Winckelkopf is eating*; **TA** *Herr Winckelkopf; LAS; implied reader*; **NS** *irr*; **LA** *irr*. It is not clear who is targeted here: a serious possibility are the expectations of the reader that a terrorist behave stereotypically (cf. Lady Windermere's disappointment at her conspirator: .

[190] SO *incognito/recognized; good/bad*; **LM** *none*; **SI** *LAS is recognized*; **TA** *LAS*; **NS** *irr*; **LA** *irr*.

[191] SO *socialites/terrorist; normal/abnormal*; **LM** *Lady Windermere's strange habit of inviting terrorists*; **SI** *cotext*; **TA** *Lady Windermere*; **NS** *irr*; **LA** *irr*. Note how this jab line also explains how Herr Winckelkopf knew LAS and perhaps that he is the conspirator who disappointed Lady Windermere.

[192] SO *embassy guests/terrorist's guests; normal/abnormal*; **LM** *none, but see previous jab*; **SI** *cotext*; **TA** *none?*; **NS** *irr*; **LA** *irr*. Lady Windermere is thus not the only person who likes to mix socialites and their enemies: in this case, the terrorist shares friends with the ambassador.

[193] SO *friend/conspirator; good/bad*; **LM** *none*; **SI** *cotext*; **TA** *LAS*; **NS** *irr*; **LA** *irr*. This third jab establishes a mini-strand (comb configuration) "friendly terrorist."

[194] SO *explosive clocks/export goods; normal/abnormal*; **LM** *none*; **SI** *cotext*; **TA** *Herr Winckelkopf*; **NS** *irr*; **LA** *irr*. It is debatable (here as elsewhere) that this jab really targets the character. However, if

8.5. CHAPTER V

vice is so irregular, that they usually go off before they have reached their proper destination.[195] If, however, you want one for home use, I can supply you with an excellent article, and guarantee that you will he satisfied with the result. May I ask for whom it is intended? If it is for the police, or for any one connected with Scotland Yard, I am afraid I cannot do anything for you.[196] The English detectives are really our best friends,[197] and I have always found that by relying on their stupidity, we can do exactly what we like.[198] I could not spare one of them.'[199]

'I assure you,' said Lord Arthur, 'that it has nothing to do with the police at all. In fact, the clock is intended for the Dean of Chichester.'

'Dear me! I had no idea that you felt so strongly about religion,[200] Lord Arthur. Few young men do nowadays.'[201]

'I am afraid you overrate me, Herr Winckelkopf,' said Lord Arthur, blushing. 'The fact is, I really know nothing about theology.'

'It is a purely private matter then?'

'Purely private.'

Herr Winckelkopf shrugged his shoulders, and left the room, returning in a few minutes with a round cake of dynamite about the size of a penny, and a pretty little French clock, surmounted by an ormolu figure of Liberty trampling on the hydra of Despotism.[202]

Lord Arthur's face brightened up when he saw it. 'That is just what I want,' he cried, 'and now tell me how it goes off.'

'Ah! there is my secret,' answered Herr Winckelkopf, contemplating his invention with a justifiable[203] look of pride; 'let me know when you wish it to explode, and I will set the machine to the moment.'

'Well, to-day is Tuesday, and if you could send it off at once - '

---

anyone, the only targetable entity is that one, hence the choice in the notation.

[195] SO *effective/ineffective*; LM *missing link*; SI *cotext*; TA *Herr Winckelkopf*; NS *irr*; LA *irr*.

[196] SO *police/terrorist target; normal/abnormal*; LM *reasoning from false premises*; SI *cotext*; TA *police (?)*; NS *irr*; LA *irr*.

[197] SO *friends/enemies of terrorists; normal abnormal*; LM *none*; SI *cotext*; TA *police*; NS *irr*; LA *irr*.

[198] SO *freedom of movement/restriction; good/bad*; LM *reasoning from false premises*; SI *cotext*; TA *police*; NS *irr*; LA *irr*.

[199] SO *freedom of movement/restriction; good/bad*; LM *reasoning from false premises; missing link*; SI *cotext*; TA *police*; NS *irr*; LA *irr*.

[200] SO *religion/terrorism; normal/abnormal*; LM *faulty inference*; SI *LAS wants to blow up the Dean of Chichester*; TA *Herr Wincklekopf*; LAS; NS *irr*; LA *irr*.

[201] SO *religion/no religion; good/bad*; LM *none*; SI *cotext*; TA *Herr Wincklekopf*; NS *irr*; LA *irr*. This jab establishes a subtle, bridge configured, strand with the 17 and the 89 jabs, which could be labeled "stereotyped grumbling."

[202] SO *stereotypical/non-stereotypical*; LM *false reasoning (French clock, hence Liberty*; SI *description of the clock*; TA *France*; NS *irr*; LA *irr*.

[203] SO *justifiable/unjustifiable; normal/abnormal*; LM *none*; SI *pride of Winckelkopf over his bomb*; TA *narrator*; NS *matanarrative comment*; LA *irr*.

'That is impossible; I have a great deal of important work on hand for some friends of mine in Moscow. Still, I might send it off tomorrow.'

'Oh, it will be quite time enough!' said Lord Arthur politely, 'if it is delivered to-morrow night or Thursday morning. For the moment of the explosion, say Friday at noon exactly. The Dean is always at home at that hour.'

'Friday, at noon,' repeated Herr Winckelkopf, and he made a note to that effect in a large ledger that was lying on a bureau near the fireplace.

'And now,' said Lord Arthur, rising from his seat, 'pray let me know how much I am in your debt.'

'It is such a small matter, Lord Arthur, that I do not care to make any charge. The dynamite comes to seven and sixpence, the clock will be three pounds ten, and the carriage about five shillings.[204] I am only too pleased to oblige any friend of Count Rouvaloff's.'

'But your trouble, Herr Winckelkopf?'

'Oh, that is nothing! It is a pleasure to me. I do not work for money; I live entirely for my art.'[205]

Lord Arthur laid down 4 pounds, 2s. 6d.[206] on the table, thanked the little German for his kindness, and, having succeeded in declining an invitation to meet some Anarchists[207] at a meat-tea on the following Saturday, left the house and went off to the Park.

For the next two days he was in a state of the greatest excitement, and on Friday at twelve o'clock he drove down to the Buckingham to wait for news. All the afternoon the stolid hall-porter kept posting up telegrams from various parts of the country giving the results of horse-races, the verdicts in divorce suits, the state of the weather, and the like, while the tape ticked out wearisome details about an all-night sitting in the House of Commons,[208] and a small panic on the Stock Exchange.[209] At four o'clock the evening papers came in, and Lord Arthur disappeared into the library with the PALL MALL, the ST. JAMES'S, the GLOBE, and the ECHO, to the immense indignation[210] of Colonel Goodchild, who wanted to read the reports of a

---

[204] SO *overspecific/specific; normal/abnormal*; LM *none*; SI *Herr Winckelkopf details the cost of the bomb*; TA *Herr Winckelkopf*; NS *irr*; LA *irr*.

[205] SO *art/bombing; good/bad*; LM *reasoning from false premises (making bombs is a craft like any other)*; SI *cotext*; TA *Herr Wincklekopf*; NS *irr*; LA *irr*.

[206] SO *overspecific/specific; normal/abnormal*; LM *none*; SI *Herr Winckelkopf details the cost of the bomb*; TA *Herr Winckelkopf; LAS; narrator(?)*; NS *irr*; LA *irr*.

[207] SO *anarchists/friends; normal/abnormal*; LM *reasoning from false premises*; SI *invitation*; TA *Herr Wincklekopf; LAS*; NS *irr*; LA *irr*.

[208] SO *wearisome/significant; normal/abnormal*; LM *reasoning from false premises*; SI *LAS is expecting news of the explosion*; TA *LAS*; NS *irr*; LA *irr*.

[209] SO *wearisome/significant; normal/abnormal*; LM *reasoning from false premises*; SI *LAS is expecting news of the explosion*; TA *LAS*; NS *irr*; LA *irr*.

[210] SO *immense indignation/minor upset; normal/abnormal*; LM *none*; SI *Colonel Goodchild's irritation at not being able to read his favorite paper*; TA *Colonel Goodchild*; NS *irr*; LA *irr*.

8.5. CHAPTER V

speech he had delivered that morning at the Mansion House, on the subject of South African Missions, and the advisability of having black Bishops in every province, and for some reason or other had a strong prejudice against the EVENING NEWS.[211] None of the papers, however, contained even the slightest allusion to Chichester, and Lord Arthur felt that the attempt must have failed. It was a terrible blow to him,[212] and for a time he was quite unnerved. Herr Winckelkopf, whom he went to see the next day was full of elaborate apologies, and offered to supply him with another clock free of charge, or with a case of nitro-glycerine bombs at cost price.[213] But he had lost all faith in explosives, and Herr Winckelkopf himself acknowledged that everything is so adulterated nowadays,[214] that even dynamite can hardly be got in a pure condition. The little German, however, while admitting that something must have gone wrong with the machinery, was not without hope that the clock might still go off, and instanced the case of a barometer that he had once sent to the military Governor at Odessa, which, though timed to explode in ten days, had not done so for something like three months. It was quite true that when it did go off, it merely succeeded in blowing a housemaid to atoms, the Governor having gone out of town six weeks before, but at least it showed that dynamite, as a destructive force, was, when under the control of machinery, a powerful, though a somewhat unpunctual[215] agent. Lord Arthur was a little consoled[216] by this reflection, but even here he was destined to disappointment,[217] for two days afterwards, as he was going upstairs, the Duchess called him into her boudoir, and showed him a letter she had just received from the Deanery.

'Jane writes charming letters,' said the Duchess; 'you must really read her last. It is quite as good as the novels Mudie sends us.'

Lord Arthur seized the letter from her hand. It ran as follows:-
THE DEANERY, CHICHESTER, 27TH MAY.

---

[211] SO *verbose/to the point; normal/abnormal*; LM *none*; SI *narrator provides too much detail irrelevant to the plot*; TA *narrator*; NS *irr*; LA *irr*. Of course this may be a completely subjective impression on the part of this reader that the amount of detail about Colonel Goodchild's speech is in violation of the maxim of quantity.

[212] SO *blow/no blow; good/bad*; LM *reasoning from false premises*; SI *LAS bombing attempt failed*; TA *LAS*; NS *irr*; LA *irr*. Note also the (possible) pun with *blow*.

[213] SO *bombs/merchant goods; normal/abnormal*; LM *reasoning from false premises*; SI *Herr Winckelkopf tries to make up to LAS for the failed bombing*; TA *Herr Winckelkopf*; NS *irr*; LA *irr*.

[214] SO *adulterated/pure; good/bad*; LM *none*; SI *explanation of the bomb's failure to explode*; TA *Herr Winckelkopf*; NS *irr*; LA *irr*. Another instance of the "stereotypical grumbling" strand (cf. 201) applied, quite successfully, to dynamite.

[215] SO *puctual/deadly; normal/abnormal*; LM *reasoning from false premises*; SI *Barometer explodes late*; TA *Herr Wincklekopf*; NS *irr*; LA *irr*. Not a punch line, as the jab, is a metanarrative commentary by Herr Winckelkopf, outside of the embedded narrative.

[216] SO *consoled/alarmed; normal/abnormal*; LM *reasoning from false premises*; SI *failure of attempted bombing*; TA *LAS*; NS *irr*; LA *irr*.

[217] SO *disappointment/success; normal/abnormal*; LM *reasoning from false premises*; SI *failure of attempted bombing*; TA *LAS*; NS *irr*; LA *irr*.

CHAPTER 8. "LORD ARTHUR SAVILE'S CRIME" BY OSCAR WILDE

My Dearest Aunt,

Thank you so much for the flannel for the Dorcas Society, and also for the gingham. I quite agree with you that it is nonsense their wanting to wear pretty things,[218] but everybody is so Radical[219] and irreligious[220] nowadays,[221] that it is difficult to make them see that they should not try and dress like the upper classes. I am sure I don't know what we are coming to.[222] As papa has often said in his sermons, we live in an age of unbelief.[223]

We have had great fun over a clock that an unknown admirer[224] sent papa last Thursday. It arrived in a wooden box from London, carriage paid, and papa feels it must have been sent by some one who had read his remarkable sermon, 'Is Licence Liberty?' for on the top of the clock was a figure of a woman, with what papa said was the cap of Liberty on her head. I didn't think it very becoming myself, but papa said it was historical,[225] so I suppose it is all right. Parker unpacked it, and papa put it on the mantelpiece in the library, and we were all sitting there on Friday morning, when just as the clock struck twelve, we heard a whirring noise, a little puff of smoke came from the pedestal of the figure, and the goddess of Liberty fell off, and broke her nose on the fender![226] Maria was quite alarmed, but it looked so ridiculous, that James and I went off into fits of laughter, and even papa was amused. When we examined it, we found it was a sort of alarm clock, and that, if you set it to a particular hour, and put some gunpowder and a cap under a little hammer, it went off whenever you wanted. Papa said it must not remain in the library, as it made a noise, so Reggie carried it away to the schoolroom, and does nothing but have small explosions all day long.[227] Do you think Arthur would like one for a wedding

---

[218] SO *nonsense/logical; normal/abnormal;* LM *none;* SI *Jane's comment on the desire of poor people to have pretty clothes;* TA *Jane;* NS *irr;* LA *irr.*

[219] SO *Radical/moderate (?); normal/abnormal;* LM *none;* SI *Jane's comment on the desire of poor people to have pretty clothes;* TA *Jane;* NS *irr;* LA *irr.*

[220] SO *irreligious/religious; normal/abnormal;* LM *none;* SI *Jane's comment on the desire of poor people to have pretty clothes;* TA *Jane;* NS *irr;* LA *irr.*

[221] SO *nonsense, radical, irreligious/sensible, moderate, religious; good/bad;* LM *none;* SI *Jane's comments;* TA *Jane;* NS *irr;* LA *irr.* Another instance of the "stereotypical grumbling" strand applied, this time to charities; the closeness in the text to the previous instance of the strand applied to dynamite is clearly not casual.

[222] SO *doesn't know/knows; good/bad;* LM *none;* SI *Jane's comments;* TA *Jane;* NS *irr;* LA *irr.* Another instance of the "stereotypical grumbling" strand.

[223] SO *belief/unbelief; good/bad;* LM *none;* SI *Jane's comments;* TA *Jane;* NS *irr;* LA *irr.* Another instance of the "stereotypical grumbling" strand, which establishes a sub-strand of Jane's grumbling, which has the peculiarity that she seems to be merely repeating her father's complaints. Jabs 218 to 223 set up a comb strand with "Jane" as TA.

[224] SO *admirer/assassin; actual/non-actual;* LM *none;* SI *receipt of clock;* TA *Dean of Chichester;* NS *irr;* LA *irr.*

[225] SO *becoming/historical; good/bad;* LM *none;* SI *description of the clock;* TA *Jane;* NS *irr;* LA *irr.*

[226] SO *noble/clumsy; good/bad;* LM *none;* SI *explosion of the clock;* TA *Liberty (?);* NS *irr;* LA *irr.*

[227] SO *small/large explosion; good/bad;* LM *missing link (small explosions will not kill anyone);* SI

8.5. CHAPTER V

present?[228] I suppose they are quite fashionable in London.[229] Papa says they should do a great deal of good,[230] as they show that Liberty can't last, but must fall down.[231] Papa says Liberty was invented at the time of the French Revolution.[232] How awful it seems!

I have now to go to the Dorcas, where I will read them your most instructive letter. How true, dear aunt, your idea is, that in their rank of life they should wear what is unbecoming.[233] I must say it is absurd, their anxiety about dress,[234] when there are so many more important things in this world, and in the next. I am so glad your flowered poplin[235] turned out so well, and that your lace[236] was not torn. I am wearing my yellow satin,[237] that you so kindly gave me, at the Bishop's on Wednesday, and think it will look all right. Would you have bows[238] or not? Jennings says that every one wears bows now,[239] and that the underskirt should be frilled.[240] Reggie has just had another explosion, and papa has ordered the clock to be sent to the stables. I don't think papa likes it so much as he did at first, though he is very

---

description of Jane's brother's (?) games with the "bomb"; TA *LAS;Herr Wincklekopf*; NS *irr*; LA *irr*.

[228] SO *bomb/present; good/bad*; LM *reversal (LAS who sent the bomb may get an explosive clock too)*; SI *Jane's narration*; TA *LAS/Jane*; NS *irr*; LA *irr*.

[229] SO *bomb/fashion; good/bad*; LM *reasoning from false premises*; SI *Jane's narration*; TA *Jane*; NS *irr*; LA *irr*. Note the strand involving Jane and clothing.

[230] SO *do good/kill; good/bad*; LM *reasoning from false premises*; SI *Jane's narration*; TA *Jane/Dean of Chichester*; NS *irr*; LA *irr*.

[231] SO *allegory/reality; normal/abnormal*; LM *reasoning from false premises*; SI *Dean of Chichester's interpretation of bomb as allegory*; TA *Dean of Chichester*; NS *irr*; LA *irr*.

[232] SO *abstract/concrete; normal/abnormal*; LM *none*; SI *Jane's naration*; TA *Jane*; NS *irr*; LA *irr*. This ends the "liberty" strand.

[233] SO *social class/clothing; normal/abnormal*; LM *none*; SI *Jane's comments (see 218)*; TA *Jane/LAS's mother (the Duchess)*; NS *irr*; LA *irr*.

[234] SO *anxiety about clothing/no anxiety; normal/abnormal*; LM *none*; SI *Jane's comments*; TA *Jane/LAS's mother (the Duchess)*; NS *irr*; LA *irr*. The level 0 narrator establishes the peripheral strand "fixation with clothing."

[235] SO *about clothing/not about clothing; normal/abnormal*; LM *self contradiction*; SI *Jane's comments*; TA *Jane*; NS *irr*; LA *irr*. Note how, immediately after chastising the poor for the excessive interest in clothing, Jane proceeds to make several remarks about clothing. Naturally, the fact that Jane is part of the nobility allows us to read a certain aspect of social satire in the strand.

[236] SO *about clothing/not about clothing; normal/abnormal*; LM *self contradiction*; SI *Jane's comments*; TA *Jane*; NS *irr*; LA *irr*.

[237] SO *about clothing/not about clothing; normal/abnormal*; LM *self contradiction*; SI *Jane's comments*; TA *Jane*; NS *irr*; LA *irr*.

[238] SO *about clothing/not about clothing; normal/abnormal*; LM *self contradiction*; SI *Jane's comments*; TA *Jane*; NS *irr*; LA *irr*.

[239] SO *about clothing/not about clothing; normal/abnormal*; LM *self contradiction*; SI *Jane's comments*; TA *Jane*; NS *irr*; LA *irr*. The strand "clothing" is here complicated by the insertion of the "fashion" theme.

[240] SO *about clothing/not about clothing; normal/abnormal*; LM *self contradiction*; SI *Jane's comments*; TA *Jane*; NS *irr*; LA *irr*.

flattered[241] at being sent such a pretty and ingenious toy. It shows that people read his sermons,[242] and profit by them.[243]

Papa sends his love, in which James, and Reggie, and Maria all unite, and, hoping that Uncle Cecil's gout is better, believe me, dear aunt, ever your affectionate niece,

JANE PERCY.

PS. - Do tell me about the bows.[244] Jennings insists they are the fashion.

Lord Arthur looked so serious and unhappy over the letter, that the Duchess went into fits of laughter.

'My dear Arthur,' she cried, 'I shall never show you a young lady's letter again! But what shall I say about the clock? I think it is a capital invention, and I should like to have one myself.'[245]

'I don't think much of them,'[246] said Lord Arthur, with a sad smile, and, after kissing his mother, he left the room.

When he got upstairs, he flung himself on a sofa, and his eyes filled with tears. He had done his best[247] to commit this murder, but on both occasions he had failed, and through no fault of his own.[248] He had tried to do his duty,[249] but it seemed as if Destiny herself had turned traitor.[250] He was oppressed with the sense of the barrenness of good intentions,[251] of the futility of trying to be fine.[252] Perhaps, it would be better to break off the marriage altogether. Sybil would suffer, it is true, but suffering could not really mar a nature so noble as hers. As for himself, what did it matter? There is always some war in which a man can die, some cause to which a

---

[241] SO *flattered/alarmed; normal/abnormal;* **LM** *reasoning from false premises;* **SI** *Dean of Chichester has received what he takes to be a gift;* **TA** *Dean of Chichester;* **NS** *irr;* **LA** *irr.*

[242] SO *read/not read; good/bad;* **LM** *false reasoning;* **SI** *explanation for the sending of the anonymous "gift";* **TA** *Dean of Chichester;* **NS** *irr;* **LA** *irr.*

[243] SO *profit/not profit; good/bad;* **LM** *false reasoning;* **SI** *explanation for the sending of the anonymous "gift";* **TA** *Dean of Chichester;* **NS** *irr;* **LA** *irr.*

[244] SO *about clothing/not about clothing; normal/abnormal;* **LM** *self contradiction;* **SI** *Jane's comments;* **TA** *Jane;* **NS** *irr;* **LA** *irr.* The final instance of the "fashion" strand.

[245] SO *bomb/present; normal/abnormal;* **LM** *reversal (see 228);* **SI** *Duchess likes the description of the toy/bomb;* **TA** *Duchess/LAS;* **NS** *irr;* **LA** *irr.*

[246] SO *dislike/failure; normal/abnormal;* **LM** *double entendre;* **SI** *LAS is disappointed as his bombing attempt failed;* **TA** *LAS/Duchess (unaware of double entendre);* **NS** *irr;* **LA** *irr.*

[247] SO *do his best/murder; good/bad;* **LM** *reasoning from false premises;* **SI** *cotext;* **TA** *LAS;* **NS** *irr;* **LA** *irr.* The central strand returns.

[248] SO *fault/no fault; normal/abnormal;* **LM** *reasoning from false premises;* **SI** *cotext;* **TA** *LAS;* **NS** *irr;* **LA** *irr.*

[249] SO *duty/murder; good/bad;* **LM** *reasoning from false premises;* **SI** *cotext;* **TA** *LAS;* **NS** *irr;* **LA** *irr.*

[250] SO *traitor/faithful, no murder/murder; normal/abnormal;* **LM** *reasoning from false premises;* **SI** *cotext;* **TA** *LAS;* **NS** *irr;* **LA** *irr.*

[251] SO *good intentions/murder; good/bad;* **LM** *reasoning from false premises;* **SI** *cotext;* **TA** *LAS;* **NS** *irr;* **LA** *irr.*

[252] SO *good/bad;* **LM** *reasoning from false premises;* **SI** *cotext;* **TA** *LAS;* **NS** *irr;* **LA** *irr.*

8.5. CHAPTER V

man can give his life, and as life had no pleasure for him, so death had no terror. Let Destiny work out his doom. He would not stir to help her.

At half-past seven he dressed, and went down to the club. Surbiton was there with a party of young men,[253] and he was obliged to dine with them. Their trivial conversation and idle jests did not interest him, and as soon as coffee was brought he left them, inventing some engagement in order to get away. As he was going out of the club, the hall-porter handed him a letter. It was from Herr Winckelkopf, asking him to call down the next evening, and look at an explosive umbrella,[254] that went off as soon as it was opened. It was the very latest invention, and had just arrived from Geneva. He tore the letter up into fragments. He had made up his mind not to try any more experiments. Then he wandered down to the Thames Embankment, and sat for hours by the river. The moon peered through a mane of tawny clouds, as if it were a lion's eye, and innumerable stars spangled the hollow vault, like gold dust powdered on a purple dome. Now and then a barge swung out into the turbid stream, and floated away with the tide, and the railway signals changed from green to scarlet as the trains ran shrieking across the bridge. After some time, twelve o'clock boomed from the tall tower at Westminster, and at each stroke of the sonorous bell the night seemed to tremble. Then the railway lights went out, one solitary lamp left gleaming like a large ruby on a giant mast, and the roar of the city became fainter.

At two o'clock he got up, and strolled towards Blackfriars. How unreal everything looked! How like a strange dream! The houses on the other side of the river seemed built out of darkness. One would have said that silver and shadow had fashioned the world anew. The huge dome of St. Paul's loomed like a bubble through the dusky air.[255]

As he approached Cleopatra's Needle he saw a man leaning over the parapet, and as he came nearer the man looked up, the gas-light falling full upon his face.

It was Mr. Podgers, the cheiromantist! No one could mistake the fat, flabby face, the gold-rimmed spectacles, the sickly feeble smile, the sensual mouth.

Lord Arthur stopped. A brilliant idea[256] flashed across him, and he stole softly up behind. In a moment he had seized Mr. Podgers by the legs, and flung him into the Thames. There was a coarse oath, a heavy splash, and all was still. Lord Arthur looked anxiously over, but could see nothing of the cheiromantist but a tall hat, pirouetting in an eddy of moonlit water. After a time it also sank, and no trace

---

[253] Most likely a gay flag.

[254] SO *explosive umbrella/umbrella*; LM *reasoning from false premises*; SI *cotext*; TA *LAS/Herr Winckekopf*; NS *irr*; LA *irr*. We note here a peculiar substrand "everyday objects turned into bombs" (barometer, clock, umbrella). The domain of everyday objects is made to overlap with that of bombing. The effect is of course humorous but resonates also with other strands in the text which involve the bringing together of unrelate domains (consider the "terrorist as friend" strand or many of the strands associated with Lady Windermere).

[255] Serious relief. One could argue that the description is too overblown to be intended to be taken straightforwardly. If so, this would be a series of stylistic jabs.

[256] SO *brilliant idea/murder; good/bad*; LM *reasoning from false premises*; SI *cotext*; TA *LAS/ Podgers*; NS *irr*; LA *irr*.

of Mr. Podgers was visible. Once he thought that he caught sight of the bulky misshapen figure striking out for the staircase by the bridge, and a horrible feeling of failure[257] came over him, but it turned out to be merely a reflection, and when the moon shone out from behind a cloud it passed away. At last he seemed to have realised the decree of destiny. He heaved a deep sigh of relief,[258] and Sybil's name came to his lips.

'Have you dropped anything, sir?' said a voice behind him suddenly.

He turned round, and saw a policeman with a bull's-eye lantern.

'Nothing of importance,[259] sergeant,' he answered, smiling,[260] and hailing a passing hansom, he jumped in, and told the man to drive to Belgrave Square.

For the next few days he alternated between hope and fear. There were moments when he almost expected Mr. Podgers to walk into the room, and yet at other times he felt that Fate could not be so unjust[261] to him. Twice he went to the cheiromantist's address in West Moon Street, but he could not bring himself to ring the bell. He longed for certainty, and was afraid of it.

Finally it came. He was sitting in the smoking-room of the club having tea, and listening rather wearily to Surbiton's account of the last comic song at the Gaiety, when the waiter came in with the evening papers. He took up the ST. JAMES'S, and was listlessly turning over its pages, when this strange heading caught his eye:

SUICIDE OF A CHEIROMANTIST.

He turned pale with excitement, and began to read. The paragraph ran as follows:

Yesterday morning, at seven o'clock, the body of Mr. Septimus R. Podgers, the eminent cheiromantist, was washed on shore at Greenwich, just in front of the Ship Hotel. The unfortunate gentleman had been missing for some days, and considerable anxiety for his safety had been felt in cheiromantic circles.[262] It is supposed that he committed suicide under the influence of a temporary mental derangement, caused by overwork, and a verdict to that effect was returned this afternoon by the coroner's jury. Mr. Podgers had just completed an elaborate treatise on the subject of the Human Hand, that will shortly be published, when it will no doubt attract much attention. The deceased was sixty-five years of age, and does not seem to have left any relations.

---

[257] SO *failure/murder; good/bad*; LM *reasoning from false premises*; SI *cotext*; TA *LAS*; NS *irr*; LA *irr.*

[258] SO *relief/regret; normal/abnormal*; LM *reasoning from false premises*; SI *cotext*; TA *LAS*; NS *irr*; LA *irr.*

[259] SO *important/unimportant; good/bad*; LM *reasoning from false premises*; SI *LAS wants to hide his murder*; TA *Podgers; policeman*; NS *irr*; LA *irr.* Note that LAS considers Podgers "unimportant." The disregard of the lower class is echoed by the remarks of Jane and others.

[260] SO *smile/murder; normal/abnormal*; LM *reasoning from false premises*; SI *LAS wants to hide his murder*; TA *Podgers; policeman*; NS *irr*; LA *irr.*

[261] SO *just/unjust; good/bad*; LM *reasoning from false premises*; SI *cotext*; TA *LAS*; NS *irr*; LA *irr.*

[262] SO *cheiromantic circles/social circles; normal/abnormal*; LM *none*; SI *embedded narrator treats cheiromantists as a social group*; TA *cheiromantists; embedded narrator*; NS *irr*; LA *irr.*

8.6 CHAPTER VI

Lord Arthur rushed out of the club with the paper still in his hand, to the immense amazement[263] of the hall-porter, who tried in vain to stop him, and drove at once to Park Lane. Sybil saw him from the window, and something told her that he was the bearer of good news. She ran down to meet him, and, when she saw his face, she knew that all was well.

'My dear Sybil,' cried Lord Arthur, 'let us be married to-morrow!'

'You foolish boy! Why, the cake is not even ordered!'[264] said Sybil, laughing through her tears.

8.6 CHAPTER VI

WHEN the wedding took place, some three weeks later, St. Peter's was crowded with a perfect mob of smart people. The service was read in the most impressive manner by the Dean of Chichester,[265] and everybody agreed that they had never seen a handsomer couple than the bride and bridegroom. They were more than handsome, however - they were happy. Never for a single moment did Lord Arthur regret all that he had suffered[266] for Sybil's sake, while she, on her side, gave him the best things a woman can give to any man - worship, tenderness, and love. For them romance was not killed by reality. They always felt young.

Some years afterwards, when two beautiful children had been born to them, Lady Windermere came down on a visit to Alton Priory, a lovely old place, that had been the Duke's wedding present to his son; and one afternoon as she was sitting with Lady Arthur under a lime-tree in the garden, watching the little boy and girl as they played up and down the rose-walk, like fitful sunbeams, she suddenly took her hostess's hand in hers, and said, 'Are you happy, Sybil?'

'Dear Lady Windermere, of course I am happy. Aren't you?'

'I have no time to be happy,[267] Sybil. I always like the last person who is introduced to me; but, as a rule, as soon as I know people I get tired of them.'

'Don't your lions satisfy you, Lady Windermere?'

'Oh dear, no! lions are only good for one season. As soon as their manes are cut, they are the dullest creatures going.[268] Besides, they behave very badly, if you are

---

[263] SO *surprise/immense amazement; normal/abnormal*; LM *exaggeration*; SI *LAS exits the club*; TA *hall-porter*; LAS; NS *irr*; LA *irr*.

[264] SO *marriage/cake; normal/abnormal*; LM *none*; SI *Sybil believes that a cake is indispensable for a wedding*; TA *Sybil*; NS *irr*; LA *irr*.

[265] SO *read service/die; good/bad*; LM *reversal*; SI *Dean of Chichester reads the service of LAS's weddign after LAS tried to blow him up*; TA *Dean of Chichester*; LAS; NS *irr*; LA *irr*.

[266] SO *suffer/not suffer; good/bad*; LM *reasoning from false premises*; SI *cotext*; TA *LAS; Podgers*; NS *irr*; LA *irr*.

[267] SO *time/no time; normal/abnormal*; LM *none*; SI *cotext*; TA *Lady Windermere*; NS *irr*; LA *irr*.

[268] Not a jab line, as far as I can determine. The extended metaphor is complex: Lady Windermere's lions are young men who are lionized. They "last only one season" because, as Lady Windermere explained

really nice to them. Do you remember that horrid Mr. Podgers? He was a dreadful impostor.[269] Of course, I didn't mind that at all,[270] and even when he wanted to borrow money I forgave him, but I could not stand his making love to me.[271] He has really made me hate cheiromancy. I go in for telepathy now. It is much more amusing.'[272]

'You mustn't say anything against cheiromancy here, Lady Windermere; it is the only subject that Arthur does not like people to chaff about. I assure you he is quite serious over it.'

'You don't mean to say that he believes in it, Sybil?'

'Ask him, Lady Windermere, here he is'; and Lord Arthur came up the garden with a large bunch of yellow roses in his hand, and his two children dancing round him.

'Lord Arthur?'

'Yes, Lady Windermere.'

'You don't mean to say that you believe in cheiromancy?'

'Of course I do,' said the young man, smiling.

'But why?'

'Because I owe to it all the happiness of my life,'[273] he murmured, throwing himself into a wicker chair.

'My dear Lord Arthur, what do you owe to it?'

'Sybil,'[274] he answered, handing his wife the roses, and looking into her violet eyes.

---

above, she tires of them after she gets to know them. This is probably what "cutting their manes" means (unless it is another gay flag). So, Lady Windermere seems to be saying: once I get to know well the young men I lionize I lose interest in them.

[269] SO *impostor/authentic; good/bad*; LM *none*; SI *Lady Windermere knew that Podgers could not predict the future*; TA *Podgers; LAS*; NS *irr*; LA *irr*. Compare this revelation with Lady Windermere's remark to Podgers that he should not tell LAS that he is engaged to Sybil "because that appeared in the Morning Post" a month before, which of course reveals how Podgers knows about the people whose hand he "reads."

[270] SO *mind/not mind; normal/abnormal*; LM *none*; SI *Lady Windermere knew that Podgers was an impostor*; TA *Lady Windermere; Podgers*; NS *irr*; LA *irr*.

[271] "Make love" acquired its modern meaning of "have intercourse with" only later. It originally mean "flirt." Note that Lady Windermere tolerates fraudulence and an ettempt at borrowing money, but cannot tolerate Podgers' flirting with her. It is reasonable to assume that the difference lies in the fact that this would bring Podgers on an equal footing with Lady Windermere, i.e., would violate the noble/commoner opposition upon which Lady Windermere's semantic system is built. We will say more on Lady Windermere's complex semiotic universe.

[272] SO *amusing/not amusing; normal/abnormal*; LM *none*; SI *Lady Windermere prefers telepathy to cheiromancy*; TA *Lady Windermere*; NS *irr*; LA *irr*.

[273] SO *happiness/murder; good/bad*; LM *reasoning from false premises*; SI *cotext*; TA *LAS*; NS *irr*; LA *irr*.

[274] SO *Sybil/no Sybil; good/bad*; LM *reasoning from false premises*; SI *LAS believes that he would not have gotten to live with Sybil if he had not killed Podgers*; TA *LAS*; NS *irr*; LA *irr*.

8.6. CHAPTER VI

'What nonsense!' cried Lady Windermere. 'I never heard such nonsense in all my life.'[275]

---

[275] SO *sense/nonsense; normal/abnormal;* **LM** *reasoning from false premises;* **SI** *Lady Windermere evaluates LAS's words;* **TA** *LAS;* **NS** *irr;* **LA** *irr.* Lady Windermere closes the narrative exposing LAS's faulty reasoning which has been the central strand of the narrative. This brings about a question about her peculiar semiotic standing. We have seen above LAS's reversed moral universe, in which murder is a duty, etc. Lady Windermere's universe yields no such straightforward reductions. Lady Windermere seems to exist in a semiotic universe which allows the copresence of opposites: her pianists look like poets, and viceversa; her indiscretions look like innocence; she does not have a personality, but enjoys its privileges; she knows Podgers is a fraud, but treats him as a genuine fortune teller. In her house, a "medley" of people meet (see the opening scene), and the starting point of the central strand is determined at her instigation. In sum, Lady Windermere is the *locus* of a contradiction, which the (implied) narrator exploits for humor. The fact that she is a member of the nobility and that she sets the limits of acceptable contradictions (medleys) at the blurring of the lines between nobility and commoners, does introduce a limit to the free-for-all of associations, in which opposites may coexist, but only to exclude a domain from the process. It is tempting, knowing what we know about Wilde's biographical data to read a specific authorial intent in this aspect. Be that as it may, the entire text reflects this paradoxical stance: if Podgers is a fraud, as Lady Windermere believes, how could he correctly predict that LAS was going to kill someone? In fact, as we saw, it is possible that Podgers sees his own death. If Podgers is not a fake, why is Lady Windermere convinced he is?

It was a great temptation to title this chapter W, for Windermere. W being a letter almost exactly between S and Z. *Le hasard fait parfois bien les choses.* I was held in check by the fact that I felt that the influence of Barthes was all too obvious in this chapter.

Chapter 9

Further Perspectives

It seems fitting to conclude this book by dedicating a few words, even more tentative than the rest of the text, to the quantitative analysis of LASC, made possible by the combination of the method presented in the text and by machine-treatment of texts. The remainder of the chapter will sum up some of the central points of the discussion, in a more traditional ending.

9.1 A quantitative look at LASC

The availability of a medium-size text analyzed in the detail of the previous chapter allows us a novel approach to humorous text, namely to investigate the distribution patterns of jab lines within the text itself.

To do so, the text of LASC was segmented in 100 words chunks and the number of jab lines within each chunk of text was tallied.[1] Overall, there are 253 (jab/punch) lines in LASC, over a text of about 12,500 words. If the lines were distributed randomly this would give us a line/text ratio of 50.81.[2]

Consider the graphical representation of the results of the segmentation described above, in fig. (9.1). Several observations present themselves. LASC begins with the highest peaks of lines (chunks 2 and 4) and by and large the first 700 words (chunks 1-7) are those which present the highest line/text ratio (17.95)[3], the second closest

---

[1] This was done using the Unix editor Emacs, so no particular precision is assumed in the word count algorithm. Since the size of the chunks is absolutely arbitrary, it seems irrelevant to be too particular about their exact boundaries. Few jab lines fell very close to the boundaries. Those which did were adjudicated using a purely mechanical procedure: if the end of the jab line was after the 100-word chunk marker, the jab line was counted as belonging to the second chunk.

[2] "Line/text ratio" is defined as the number of words divided by the number of jab lines. Lower scores have higher line/text ratios. A score of 1 would mean that every word is a jab line.

[3] A score close to 18 means that, on average, every 18 words there's a jab line. Counting the need to set up, this is amazing. In Attardo (1998: 249) I pointed out that the beginning of the Mary Tyler Moore

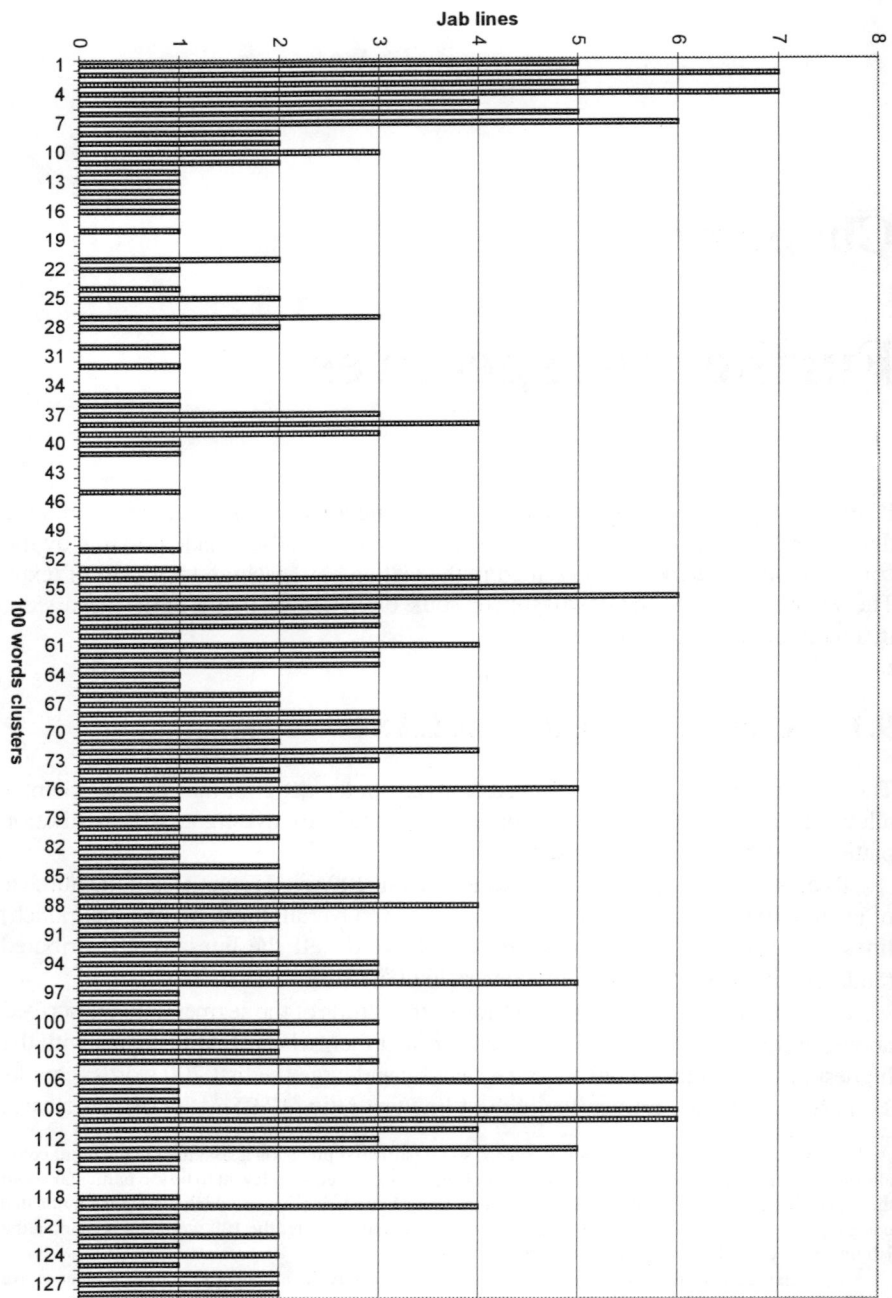

Figure 9.1: *LASC segmentation chart*

9.1. A QUANTITATIVE LOOK AT LASC

high-density area is between chunks 106-113, where the ratio is 21.87. The third section of text is a largish stretch between chunks 54 and 72, where the ratio is 32.35. The text does not maintain those levels of humor throughout. In the analysis I pointed at instances of "serious relief" and, even assuming that all the potential "gay flags" and parodic targets which I have recorded as questionable in their humorous intent are indeed jab lines, there are stretches of text without much humor: the most obvious ones are the reading of Lord Arthur Savile's hand by Podgers (chunks 19-36) with a ratio of 113.33 (i.e., over six times less funny than the introductory section) and the murder of Podgers (114-118) with 133.33. Needless to say, the section beginning after Lord Arthur Savile rushes out of the party until he makes up his mind (41-52) would obviously rank as the least funny (ratio of 366.67).

If we observe the overall pattern of the distribution, we see a "wave" disposition: the introduction with high ratio of jabs is followed by a low ratio passage (Podgers reading Lord Arthur Savile's hand). Another set of peaks (54-76) is followed by most of ch. IV (77-84) without more than 2 jabs per chunk (ratio 63.64). It seems that this may be the first clue at capturing that most elusive quality of texts: timing. The text seems to pace itself: after a virtuoso display of verbal fireworks, follows a slower paced section, or to put it differently, stretches of text with high line/text ratios are followed by stretches of text with significanlty lower ratios, thus creating an effect of alternance.

Another significant pattern is that peaks (i.e., high jab line concentrations) do not occur in isolation. They are usually preceded and/or followed by relatively high concentration chunks. Once more, it is too early to say whether this is a peculiarity of this text, of Wilde's style, or a general phenomenon. We can gather some interesting conclusions if we compare the distribution of lines in LASC to the distribution in Peacham's MDMT: given the different types of source texts, MDMT was segmented according to the original pagination, which therefore cannot be compared directly to the analysis in 100-words chunks. However, the relatively uniform distribution of the lines is fairly clear. Virtually every page has between one and three instances of humor, with very few pages lacking any line. Contrast this with Wilde's vast range of variation (between seven lines per 100-word chunk and zero and one gets a clear idea of the differences in style, of course, but also in narrative organization (the picaresque novel being organized in a sequence of episodes, which encourages the regular distribution of the lines). In general, it is too early to elaborate further on these data, especially given the fact that virtually no comparison data are available. Nonetheless, it is clear that potentially, the type of analyses that we have sketched here can be very interesting in establishing factual comparisons across texts (of the same author, of different authors, etc.).

If we turn to consider strands, i.e., organized clusters of jabs, we find a fairly obvious generalization, whereby target strands occur in relation to the presence of the targeted character in the plot, cf. section (5.3.3). The same can be said for

---

show analyzed gave a ratio of about 28. This should give an idea of Wilde's skill.

the SO-based strands, where we noted a strand based on HOMICIDE/MURDER VS. SOMETHING ELSE, and the BOMB VS. DAILY OBJECT strand highlighted in the text, which occur obviously only in relation to the introduction of the respective topics in the plot. In this sense, we can say that the humor is parasitic to the development of the plot, notwithstanding what we said about humorous plots (5.5).

As far as other strands go, we note a very central strand (97 instances) which include the LMs "faulty reasoning" and "reasoning from false premises" which are closely linked with the main story line in which Lord Savile decides to murder someone so as to be able to marry Sybil. Out of the 97 jabs with those LMs, 59 are targeted at Lord Arthur. For comparison, the next TA for frequency in the LM strand is Lady Clementina (9 instances), followed by Lady Windermere (6), the police/Scotland Yard (6), Winckelkopf (5), Podgers and the Dean of Chichester (4). Therefore, we can safely say that there is a central strand in LASC which associates faulty reasoning of some sort and Lord Arthur Savile. Other strands in LASC were discussed in section (5.3.3) and elsewhere and are not repeated here.

9.2 General Conclusions

Besides presenting an updated version of the GTVH, we have tried to present an analytical approach towards humorous texts such that it can account for their humorous nature, presupposing only a semantic/pragmatic analysis of the text. To do so we have broadened the GTVH, along the lines of Attardo (1996, 1997a/b, 1998, 2000) and also going in new directions.

Considering the specific aspects of "longer" texts, the most significant innovations of the approach described in this book are the following:

- introduction of the jab line: this allows us to account for the different functions of humor in a narrative, according to their position, as well as to account for diffuse disjunction;

- attention towards the linear nature of the texts (the "vector" approach): this aspect of my approach distinguishes it from Chlopicki's original approach and in general from "mainstream" narratological/semiotic approaches;

- the importance of configurations of jab and punch lines;

- the concept of strand;

- the concept of central vs. peripheral strand: this concept allows me to model the interesting aspects of the "shadow opposition" idea, while maintaining the general vector approach;

- humorous plots: this is the least developed aspect of the work, but a most promising one;

- a continuum of text-types linking jokes to longer texts: by showing that no qualitative jump exists bewteen the two types of texts, I establish both the legitimacy of extending the GTVH to longer texts and highlight the necessity of the extension at the same time.

Considering humor theory at large, the update of the GTVH is incremental but contains several noteworthy aspects: the work on local antonymy is one of them but the most significant one is probably the incorporation of psycholinguistic and cognitive science concerns about the processing of the humorous text. Originally, these came from the need to handle some phenomena such as bridges, but the revision of the theory with an increased attention to mental representations and the text world representations is applicable to humor theory at large, not just to long texts.

The attention towards the distribution of humor in the text is a significant innovation of this approach. As we have seen, it may be considered both at a detailed level (bridges/combs) or at a global, textual level (line/text ratios). Based on what I believe to be the first ever analysis of a text the size of LASC it was possible to point out a "wave" pattern in the distribution of the humor. It is very dangerous to generalize from a corpus of one or two texts, so it is not clear whether this is a general fact, something applicable to Wilde's production, or something unique to the specific text. The comparison with MDMT seems to rule out the first option (the null hypothesis, so to speak), but here too it is too early to say. Be that as it may, the interest of this method is unquestionable. It remains to be seen if it will yield significant results for humor research and for narratological studies.

9.3 Limitations of the Model

The first, obvious, limitation of the model I have discussed in the book is that it does not apply as readily to non-narrative texts as well as to non-texts. While the latter is certainly a small problem, as it is even arguable that there are no non-semiotic cases of humor, contra Morreall (1983), the former is a serious problem, that would prevent the application of the model to non-narrative texts, such as plays. However, as the application to the CBTD example shows, what is technically a non-narrative text shares enough features with a common narrative that the difference may be safely ignored, in some cases. This is not to say that this is true at large of all non-narrative texts, of course. To my mind, the biggest problem is that there seems to be a lack of examples of non-narrative texts that do not fall under the SSTH's purview already (e.g., puns, one-liners, etc.). In other words, since most readily available non-narrative humorous texts do fall under the GTVH, it is difficult to find materials to study contrastively.

The GTVH's background of the model is all too apparent. From that theory all sorts of weaknesses have been inherited. The LM is still the weak link in the chain, but ongoing research promises to put an end to that situation (Attardo *et al.* forth., Hempelmann 2000, Di Maio 2000.) The SI KR remains very vague and in dire need of some theoretical work. The TA slot needs to be refined. At this point, it often ends up being a repository for anyone who may be targetable in the joke. In the SO domain, the concept of "local antonymy" needs further work.

Possibly the biggest problem for the GTVH is its informal character. I believe some steps forward towards that goal have been made in this book, but it is clear that the theory is far from being completely formalized. On the other hand, it would be unrealistic to expect an axiomatized theory of humor, at a time when there does not exist a complete syntactic description of any language, let alone a semantic analyzer capable of describing the meaning of a sentence. In this sense, I stand by the claim in Raskin and Attardo (1994) that computational (i.e., formal) treatment of humor requires a complete treatment of language. Hackers have a term for this: they say that the problem is "AI complete."

There are of course a number of issues that have not been addressed: timing, despite a valiant attempt (Norrick 2000), still remains a weak spot in the linguistics of humor. So do the macro aspects of humorous texts, despite the attention I dedicate to them in this book. There is need to have some serious, concerted work on the narratology of humor. For example, it remains difficult to capture the differences between a funny story and a story with lots of humor in it, except for the plots that are humorous in and of themselves, of course (cf. 5.5). Finally, the psycholinguistics of humor is seriously wanting: I attempted to show that the model used in this book is broadly compatible with the construction-integration model of Kintsch (1998). There is need of research addressing the degree of this match, as well as some basic data, for example, how long does the resolution of incongruity take? Is a text with unresolved incongruities harder to process than one in which all incongruities get resolved? We can only hope that further work will help our understanding.

Primary Sources

Allais, Alphonse. 1989. Han Rybeck ou le coup de l'étrier. *Oeuvres anthumes.* Paris: R. Laffont.

Allen, Woody. 1975. The Kugelmass Episode. *Side Effects.* New York: Random House. 41-55. Joint edition with *Without Feathers* and *Getting Even.* New York, NY: Random House. 1989.

Eco, Umberto. 1981. *Il nome della rosa.* Milano: Bompiani.

Lloyd, David. Chuckles Bites the Dust. *The Mary Tyler Moore Show.* (Written: June 5, 1975; revised: August 20, 1975; filmed: August 22, 1975. Prod. #5009.) Rpt. in *The Big Book of Jewish Humor.* William Novak and Moshe Waldoks, (eds.) New York: Harper & Row, 1981.

Peacham, Henry. *A Merry Discourse of Meum and Tuum.* In Angela Locatelli. 1998. *Il doppio e il picaresco: un caso paradigmatico nel Rinascimento inglese.* Milano: Jaca Book.

Peacock, Thomas Love. 1997. *Headlong Hall.* Columbia, SC: Camden House.

— 1992. *Nightmare Abbey.* Oxford: Woodstock.

Poe, Edgar Allan. 1982. *The System of Dr. Tarr and Dr. Fethers.* In *The Complete Poems and Stories of Edgar Allan Poe.* New York, Alfred A. Knopf.

Sexton, Anne. 1981. *Transformations.* In *The Complete Poems.* Boston: Houghton Mifflin.

Voltaire. 1987. *Candide.* OEuvres. Paris: Fernand Nathan.

Wilde, Oscar. 1995.*Lord Arthur Savile's Crime.* In *The Complete Oscar Wilde.* New York: Crescent Books.

Works Cited

Abelson, Robert P. 1981. Psychological status of the script concept. *American Psychologist*. 36:7. 715-729.

Alexander, Richard. 1984. Verbal humor and variation in English: Sociolinguistic notes on a variety of jokes. *Beiträge zur Fremdsprachenvermittlung aus dem Konstanzer Sprachlerinstitut* (SLI). 14. 53-63.

Andor, Jozsef. 1985. On the psychological relevance of frames. *Quaderni di Semantica*. 6:2. 212-221.

Attardo, Salvatore. 1986. *Per una sintesi della ricerca linguistica sul comico*. Tesi di laurea. Unpublished Doctoral dissertation. Milan, Italy: Catholic University of Milan.

— 1988. Trends in European humor research: towards a text model. *HUMOR*. 1:4. 349-369.

— 1989. Type-jokes and token-jokes. In Victor Raskin and Shaun F.D. Hughes, (eds.) *WHIMSY* VII. Tempe, AZ/West Lafayette, IN: International Society for Humor Studies. 271-274.

— 1992. Intentionality and communication: The case of joking and humorous interaction. Unpublished paper presented at the Seminar on Humor and Communication, Speech Communication Association National Meeting, October 28th, 1992, Chicago, IL.

— 1993. Review of Chiaro (1992). *HUMOR*. 6:3. 325-334.

— 1994. *Linguistic Theories of Humor.* Berlin: Mouton de Gruyter.

— 1996. Humor theory beyond jokes: The treatment of humorous texts at large. In Joris Hulstijn and Anton Nijholt, (eds.) *Automatic Interpretation and Generation of Verbal Humor. IWCH'96*. Enschede: University of Twente. 87-101.

— 1997. Mécanismes linguistiques de l'humour d'Alphonse Allais dans "Han Rybeck ou le coup de l'étrier." In Jean-Marc Defays and Laurence Rosier, (eds.) *Alphonse Allais écrivain.* Actes du premier colloque international Alphonse Allais. Saint Genouph: A.G. Nizet. 77-87.

— 1997b. A rejoinder to Chlopicki. *HUMOR.* 10:3. 347-348.

— 1997c. The semantic foundations of cognitive theories of humor. *HUMOR.* 10:4. 395-420.

— 1998. The analysis of humorous narratives. *HUMOR.* 11:3. 231-260.

— 2000. Irony as relevant appropriateness. *Journal of Pragmatics.* 32(2000). 793-826.

— 2000b. The analysis of humorous literary texts: The case of register humor. *Stylistyka.* IX. 37-44.

— 2000c. Irony markers and functions: Towards a goal-oriented theory of irony and its processing. *Rask.* 12. 3-20.

— In preparation. Metahumor.

— In preparation b. *Theoretical Pragmatics.*

Attardo, Salvatore, Donalee H. Attardo, Paul Baltes, and Marnie J. Petray. 1994. The linear organization of jokes: statistical analysis of two thousand texts. *HUMOR.* 7:1. 27-54.

Attardo, Salvatore and Jean-Charles Chabanne. 1992. Jokes as a text type. *HUMOR.* 5:1. 165-176.

Attardo, Salvatore, Christian F. Hempelmann and Sara DiMaio. In preparation. Script oppositions and logical mechanisms: modeling incongruities and their resolutions.

Attardo, Salvatore and Victor Raskin. 1991. Script theory revis(it)ed: joke similarity and joke representation model. *HUMOR.* 4:3-4. 293-347.

Aubouin, Elie. 1948. *Technique et psychologie du comique.* Marseilles: OFEP.

Bal, Mieke. 1977. *Narratologie: essais sur la signification narrative dans quatre romans modernes.* Paris: Klincksieck.

— 1985. *Narratology: introduction to the theory of narrative.* Trans. Christine van Boheemen. Toronto: University of Toronto Press.

Bally, Charles. 1909. *Traite de stylistique Française.* Heidelberg: Winter. 2nd ed. 1921.

Barbe, Katherina. 1995. *Irony in Context*. Amsterdam: Benjamins.

Barthes, Roland. 1970. *S/Z*. Paris: Seuil.

Bartlett, Frederick C. 1932. *Remembering*. Cambridge: Cambridge University Press. Rpt. 1977.

Bateson, Gregory. 1955. A theory of play and fantasy. *A.P.A. Psychiatric Research Reports*. 2. 39-51. Rpt. in *Steps to an Ecology of Mind*. New York: Ballantine, 1972.

Berrendonner, Alain. 1981. *Elements de pragmatique linguistique*. Paris: Minuit.

Bower, Gordon H., John B. Black and Terrence J. Turner. 1979. Scripts in memory for text. *Cognitive Psychology*. 11. 177-220.

Braester, Marlena. 1992. Du 'signe ironique' à l'énoncé ironique. *Semiotica* 92:1/2. 75-86.

Bremond, Claude. 1973. *Logique du récit*. Paris: Seuil.

Burns, Bryan. 1985. *The Novels of Thomas Love Peacock*. London: Croom Helm.

Butler, Marilyn. 1979. *Peacock Displayed: A Satirist in His Context*. London: Routledge & K. Paul.

Caffi, Claudia. 1994. Pragmatic presupposition. In R. E. Asher, (ed.) *The Encyclopedia of Language and Linguistics*. Oxford: Pergamon. 3320-3327.

Caradec, François. 1994. *Alphonse Allais*. Paris: Belfond.

Carston, Robyn. 1981. Irony and Parody and the Use-Mention Distinction. *The Nottingham Linguistic Circular*. 10:1, 24-35.

— 1988. Implicature, explicature and truth-throretic semantics. In Ruth M. Kempson, (ed.) *Mental Representations*. Cambridge: Cambridge University Press. 155-181.

Cawley, Robert Ralston. 1971. *Henry Peacham: His Contribution to English Poetry*. University Park, PA: Pennsylvania State University Press.

Chafe, Wallace L. 1977. Creativity in verbalization and its implication for the nature of stored knowledge. In Roy O. Freedle, (ed.) *Discourse Production and Comprehension*. Norwood, NJ: Ablex. 41-56.

Champion, Laurie. 1992. Allens "The Kugelmass Episode." *Explicator*. 51. 61.

Charney, Maurice. 1978. *Comedy High and Low: An Introduction to the Experience of Comedy*. New York: Oxford University Press.

Charniak, Eugene. 1972. Towards a model of children's story comprehension. Cambridge: Artificial Intelligence Laboratory, MIT.

Chatman, Seymour. 1978. *Story and Discourse: Narrative Structure in Fiction and Film.* Ithaca: Cornell University Press.

Chen, Rong. 1990. Verbal Irony as Implicature. Unpublished PhD, Ball State University, Muncie, IN.

Chiaro, Delia. 1992. *The Language of Jokes: Analysing Verbal Play.* London/New York: Routledge.

Chlopicki, Wladyslaw. 1987. An Application of the Script Theory of Semantics to the Analysis of Selected Polish Humorous Short Stories. Unpublished M.A. thesis. West Lafayette, IN: Purdue University.

— 1997. An approach to the analysis of verbal humor in short stories. *HUMOR*. 10:3. 333-347.

— 2000. Linguistic analysis of humour in short stories. *Stylistyka*. IX. 513-524

Chomsky Noam. 1965. *Aspects of the Theory of Syntax.* The Hague: Mouton.

Cigada, Sergio. 1969. *Sull'autonomia dei valori fonetici nella poesia.* Milan: Vita e pensiero.

Clark, Herbert H. 1977. *Psychology and Language: An Introduction to Psycholinguistics.* New York: Harcourt Brace Jovanovich.

— 1996. *Using Language.* Cambridge: Cambridge University Press.

Clark, Herbert H. and Thomas B. Carlson. 1982. Hearers and speech acts. *Language*. 58:2. 332-373.

Cleese, John and Connie Booth. 1988. *The Complete Fawlty Towers.* New York: Pantheon Books.

Clements, William M. 1969. The types of the Polack joke. *Folklore Forum. A Bibliographic and Special Series.* N.3. 22.

Collins, Allan, John Seely Brown, and Kathy M. Larkin. 1978[1980]. Inference in text understanding. In Rand J. Spiro, Bertram C. Bruce, and William F. Brewer, (eds.) *Theoretical Issues in Reading Comprehension.* Hillsdale, NJ: Lawrence Erlbaum Associates. 385-407.

Corblin, Francis. 1995. *Les formes de reprise dans le discours: Anaphores et chaines de reference.* Rennes: Presses Universitaires de Rennes.

Coseriu, Eugenio. 1975. Vers une typologie des champs lexicaux. *Cahiers de lexicologie.* 27. 30-51.

Davies, Catherine E. 1984. Joint joking: Improvisational humorous episodes in conversation. In Claudia Brugman, Monica Macaulay, Amy Dahlstrom, Michele Emanatian, Birch Moonwomon, O'Connor, (eds.) *Proceedings of the Tenth Annual Meeting of the Berkeley Linguistics Society* Berkeley: University of California. 360-371.

Davies, Christie. 1990. *Ethnic Humor Around the World.* Bloomington: Indiana University Press.

Dawson, Carl. 1968. *Thomas Love Peacock.* London: Routledge & Kegan.

— 1970. *His Fine Wit: A Study of Thomas Love Peacock.* Berkeley: University of California Press.

de Beaugrande, Robert Alain and Wolfgang Ulrich Dressler. 1981. *Einführung im die Textlinguistik.* Tübingen: Niemeyer.

Defays, Jean-Marc. 1992. *Jeux et enjeux du texte comique: stratégies discursives chez Alphonse Allais.* Tübingen: Niemeyer.

Defays, Jean-Marc and Laurence Rosier, (eds.) 1997. *Alphonse Allais écrivain.* Nizet: Saint-Jenouph.

Dews, Shelly, Joan Kaplan, and Ellen Winner. 1995. Why not say it directly? The social functions of irony. *Discourse Processes.* 19. 347-367.

Dews, Shelly, and Ellen Winner. 1995. Muting the meaning: A social function of irony. *Metaphor and Symbolic Activity.* 10:1. 3-19.

Di Maio, Sara. 2000. *A Structured Resource for Computational Humor.* Unpublished Doctoral dissertation. Siena, Italy: University of Siena.

Dixon, Barbara. 1989. Structure, tone and style in Garrison Keillor's *Lake Wobegon Days.* In Victor Raskin and Shaun F.D. Hughes, (eds.) *WHIMSY.* VII. Tempe, AZ/West Lafayette, IN: International Society for Humor Studies. 113-114.

Douglas, Mary. 1968. The social control of cognition: Some factors in joke perception. *Man.* N.S. 3. 361-376. Rpt. in *Implicit Meanings.* London: Routledge. 1975.

Doyle, Arthur Conan. 1950. *The Adventures of Sherlock Holmes.* Edgar W. Smith, (ed.) New York: Heritage Press.

Dundes, Alan. 1987. *Cracking Jokes: Studies of Sick Humor Cycles and Stereotypes.* Berkeley: Ten Speed Press.

Eco, Umberto. 1979. *Lector in fabula.* Milan: Bompiani.

— 1992. *Interpretation and Overinterpretation.* Stefan Collini, (ed.) Cambridge: Cambridge University Press. (With Richard Rorty, Jonathan Culler, Christine Brooke-Rose.)

Eco, Umberto and Thomas Sebeok, (eds.) 1983. *The Sign of Three: Dupin, Holmes, Peirce.* Bloomington: Indiana University Press.

Emmott, Catherine. 1997. *Narrative Compehension: A discourse perspective.* Oxford: Clarendon.

Ericsson, K. Anders and Walter Kintsch. 1995. Long-term working memory. *Psychological Review* 102:2. 211-245.

Fauconnier, Gilles. 1985. *Mental Spaces: Aspects of Meaning Construction in Natural Language.* Cambridge, MA: MIT Press.

— 1997. *Mappings in Thought and Language.* Cambridge: Cambridge University Press.

Feldman, Jerome. 1975. Bad-mouthing frames. In Roger Schank and J.L. Nash-Webber, (eds.) *Theoretical Issues in Natural Language Processing: An Interdisciplinary Workshop in Computational Linguistics, Psychology, Linguistics [and] Artificial Intelligence, 10-13 June 1975, Cambridge, MA.* Cambridge, MA: Yale University, Mathematical Social Sciences Board, 1975.

Fellbaum, Christiane, (ed.) 1998. *Wordnet: An Electronic Lexical Database.* Cambridge, MA: MIT Press.

Fillmore, Charles. 1975. An alternative to checklist theories of meaning. C. Cogen et al., (eds.) *Proceedings of the Annual Meeting of the Berkeley Linguistics Society.* Berkeley: Berkeley Linguistics Society. 123-131.

— 1985. Frames and the semantics of understanding. *Quaderni di Semantica.* 6:2. 222-254.

Fishman, Joshua. 1972. The relationship between micro- and macro- sociolinguistics in the study of who speaks what language to whom and when. In J.B. Pride and Janet Holmes, (eds.) *Sociolinguistics.* Harmondsworth: Penguin.

Forabosco, Giovannantonio. 1992. Cognitive aspects of the humor process: the concept of incongruity. *HUMOR.* 5:1. 45-68.

Fowler, Roger. 1986. *Linguistic Criticism.* Oxford: Oxford University Press.

Freedman, Matt and Paul Hoffman. 1980. *How Many Zen Buddhists Does it Take to Screw in a Lightbulb?* New York: St. Martin's Press.

Freud, Sigmund. 1905. *Der Witz und seine Beziehung zum Unbewussten.* Leipzig: Deuticke. English trans. *Jokes and Their Relation to the Unconscious.* New York: Norton. 1960.

Gaskill, David. 1988. Victor Raskin's semantic theory of humor applied to certain Cotton Mather texts. In Don L.F. Nilsen and Alleen Pace Nilsen, (eds.) *WHIMSY.* VI. Tempe, AZ/West Lafayette, IN: International Society for Humor Studies. 154-155.

Gazdar, Gerald. 1979. *Pragmatics: Implicature, Presupposition, and Logical Form.* New York: Academic Press.

Giora, Rachel. 1995. On irony and negation. *Discourse Processes.* 19. 239-264.

— 1997. Understanding figurative and literal language: The graded salience hypothesis. *Cognitive Linguistics.* 7. 183-206.

— 1998. Irony. In Jef Verschueren, Jan-Ola Östman, Jan Blommaert, and Chris Bulcaen, (eds.) *Handbook of Pragmatics.* Amsterdam: J. Benjamins. 1-21.

Giora, Rachel, Ofer Fein and Tamir Schwartz. 1998. Irony: Graded salience and indirect negation. *Metaphor and Symbol.* 13:2. 83-101.

Giora, Rachel and Ofer Fein. 1999. Irony comprehension: The graded salience hypothesis. *HUMOR.* 12:4. 425-436.

— Under review. Irony, context and salience.

Goffman, Erving. 1974. *Frame Analysis.* New York: Harper and Row.

— 1981. *Forms of Talk.* Philadelphia: University of Pennsylvania Press.

Greenbaum, Andrea. 1999. Stand-up comedy as rhetorical argument: an investigation of comic culture. *HUMOR.* 12:1. 33-46.

Grice, H. Paul. 1989. *Studies in the Way of Words.* Cambridge, MA: Harvard University Press.

Guiraud, Pierre. 1976. *Les jeux de mots.* Paris: Presses Universitaires de France. 2nd ed. 1979.

Guntheroth, Kurt. 1990. Canonical Collection of Light Bulb Jokes. Posting on rec.humor 6 Jul 1990. (e-mail kurt@tc.fluke.COM).

Haiman, John. 1990. Sarcasm as theater. *Cognitive Linguistics.* 1:2. 181-205.

Hay, Jennifer. 2000. Functions of humor in the conversations of men and women. *Journal of Pragmatics.* 32:6.

— Forthcoming. The Pragmatics of Humor Support. *HUMOR.*

Hempelmann, Christian F. 2000. *Incongruity and Resolution of Humorous Narratives: Linguistic Theory and the Medieval Bawdry of Rabelais, Bocaccio, and Chaucer.* Unpublished M.A. thesis. Youngstown, OH: Youngstown State University.

Hockett, Charles Francis. 1973. Jokes. In M. Estellie Smith, (ed.) *Studies in Linguistics in Honor of George L. Trager.* The Hague: Mouton. 153-178. Rpt. in *The View from the Language: Selected Essays, 1948-1974..* Athens: University of Georgia Press. 1977. 257-289.

Hofstadter, Douglas, and Liane Gabora. 1989. Synopsis of the workshop on humor and cognition. *HUMOR.* 2:4. 417-440.

Holcomb, Christopher. 1992. Nodal humor in comic narrative: a semantic analysis of two stories by Twain and Wodehouse. *HUMOR.* 5:3. 233-250.

Holmes, Janet. 1973. Linguistic humor: It's not the way you tell it. *Te Reo.* 16. 1-7.

Johnson-Laird, Philip N. 1983. *Mental models : towards a cognitive science of language, inference, and consciousness.* Cambridge, MA: Harvard University Press.

— 1986. Reasoning without logic. In Terry Myers, Keith Brown and Brendon McGonigle, (eds.) *Reasoning and Discourse Processes.* London: Academic Press. 13-49.

Jolles, André. 1930. *Einfache Formen.* T übingen: Niemeyer. [3rd ed. 1968]

Jorgensen, Julia. 1996. The functions of sarcastic irony in speech. *Journal of Pragmatics.* 26:5. 613-634.

Josephson, John R., and Susan G. Josephson. 1994. *Abductive Inference. Computation, Philosophy, Technology.* Cambridge: Cambridge University Press.

Karman, Barbara. 1998. *Postmodern Power Plays: A Linguistic Analysis of Postmodern Comedy.* Unpublished M.A. thesis. Youngstown, OH: Youngstown State University.

Karttunen, Lauri. 1973. Presuppositions of compound sentences. *Linguistic Inquiry.* 4. 169-193.

Katz, Jerrold J. and Jerry A. Fodor. 1963. The structure of a semantic theory. *Language.* 39:1. 170-210.

Kerman, Judith B. 1980. The light-bulb jokes: Americans look at social action processes. *Journal of American Folklore.* 93. 454-58.

Kintsch, Walter. 1998. *Comprehension: A Paradigm for Cognition.* Cambridge: Cambridge University Press.

Kintsch, Walter and Suzanne M. Mannes. 1987. Generating scripts from memory. In Elke van der Meer and Joachim Hoffmann, (eds.) *Knowledge-Aided Information Processing.* Amsterdam: Elsevier. 61-80.

Koch, Walter A. 1989. *The Well of Tears.* Brockmeyer: Bochum.

Kolek, Leszek S. 1985. Towards a poetics of comic narratives: notes on the semiotic structure of jokes. *Semiotica.* 53: 1-3. 145-163.

— 1989. Bricks and blocks, or how jokes make up comic narratives. In Victor Raskin and Shaun F.D. Hughes, (eds.) *WHIMSY.* VII. Tempe, AZ/West Lafayette, IN: International Society for Humor Studies. 132-133.

Kosslyn, Stephen Michael. 1996. *Image and Brain: The Resolution of the Imagery Debate.* Boston: MIT Press.

Kreuz, Roger J., Debra L. Long, and Mary B. Church. 1991. On being ironic: pragmatic and mnemonic implications. *Metaphor and Symbolic Activity.* 6:3. 149-162.

Kuhn, Thomas S. 1962. *The Structure of Scientific Revolution.* International Encyclopedia of Unified Science. Volumes I and II: Foundations of the Unity of Science. Chicago: University of Chicago. 2nd ed., 1970.

Labov, William. 1972. *Sociolinguistic Patterns.* Philadelphia: University of Pennsylvania Press.

Lakoff, George, and Mark Johnson. 1981. *Metaphors We Live By.* Chicago: Chicago University Press.

Langacker, Ronald W. 1991. *Concept, Image, and Symbol: The Cognitive Basis of Grammar.* Berlin: Mouton de Gruyter.

Lefort, Bernard. 1992. Structure of verbal jokes and comprehension in young children. *HUMOR.* 5:1-2. 149-163.

— 1999. Le discours comique et sa réception: les cas des histoires drôles. In Jean-Marc Defays and Laurence Rosier, (eds.). *Approches du discours comique.* Liège: Mardaga. 113-120.

Lehrer, Adrienne and Eva Feder Kittay. 1992. *Frames, Fields, and Contrasts: New Essays in Semantic and Lexical Organization.* Hillsdale, NJ: Lawrence Erlbaum Associates.

Levinson, Stephen C. 1983. *Pragmatics.* Cambridge: Cambidge University Press.

Lew, Robert. 2000. Dowcip jezykowy w swietle najnowszych jezykoznawczych teorii humoru. [The linguistic joke in the light of current linguistic theories of humor.] *Stylistyka.* IX. 127-136.

Lewis, David. 1979. Scorekeeping in a language game. *Journal of Philosophical Logic.* 8. 339-359.

Locatelli, Angela. 1998. *Il doppio e il picaresco: un caso paradigmatico nel Rinascimento inglese.* Milan: Jaca.

Lovell, Terry. 1982. A genre of social disruption. In BFI Dossier No. 17. *Television Sitcom.* London: British Film Institute.

Madden, Lionel. 1967. *Thomas Love Peacock.* London: Evans Bros.

Mandler, Jean Matter. 1984. *Stories, Scripts, and Scenes: Aspects of Schema Theory.* Hillsdale, NJ: Lawrence Erlbaum Associates.

Mansfield, Katherine. 1920. *Bliss and Other Stories.* New York: Alfred A. Knopf.

Marcush, George. 1996. Web page http: www.crc.ricoh.com/marcush/lightbulb

Marino, Matthew. 1989. Fabliau scripts. In Victor Raskin and Shaun F.D. Hughes, (eds.) *WHIMSY.* VII. Tempe, AZ/West Lafayette, IN: International Society for Humor Studies. 44-46.

McDonough, Craig. 1997. *The Information-Conveying Ability of Humorous Texts: An Analysis of "Semantic Objects."* Unpublished M.A. thesis. Youngstown, OH: Youngstown State University.

Mettinger, Arthur. 1994. *Aspects of Semantic Opposition in English.* New York: Oxford University Press. 160-1.

Mills, Howard. *Peacock: His Circle and His Age.* Cambridge: Cambridge University Press, 1969.

Mizzau, Marina. 1984. *L'ironia.* Milan: Feltrinelli.

Morin, Violette. 1966. L'histoire drôle. *Communications.* 8. 102-119. Rpt. in *L'analyse structurale du recit. Communications.* 8. Paris: Seuil. 1981.

Morreall, John. 1983. *Taking Laughter Seriously.* Albany, NY: State University of New York.

Muecke, Douglas C. 1978. Irony markers. *Poetics.* 7, 363-375.

Müller, Ralph. 1999. Theorie der Pointe. Untersuchungen am Beispiel der Anekdote. Unpublished Lizentsiatarbeit. University of Freiburg, Switzerland.

Mulvihill, James. 1987. *Thomas Love Peacock.* Boston: Twayne Publishers.

Nelms, Jody, Diana Boxer and Salvatore Attardo. 2000. The least disruption principle: Sarcasm revisted. Paper presented at the Conference on Pragmatics and Language Learning. Urbana-Champaign (IL). April 13-15, 2000.

Norrick, Neal. 1989. Intertextuality in humor. *HUMOR.* 2:2. 117-139.

— 1993. *Conversational Joking: Humor in Everyday Talk.* Bloomington: Indiana University Press.

— 1993b. Repetition in canned jokes and spontaneous conversational joking. *HUMOR.* 6:4. 385-402.

— 2000. On the conversational performance of narrative jokes: Towards an account of timing. *HUMOR.* In press.

Oring, Eliot. 1989. Between jokes and tales: on the nature of punch lines. *HUMOR.* 2:4. 349-364.

— 1999. Joke as gloss. Paper presented at the Conference of the International Society for Humor Studies. June 29-July 3, 1999. Oakland, CA.

Paivio, Allan. 1986. *Mental Representations: A Dual Coding Approach.* Oxford: Clarendon Press.

Palmer, Jerry. 1987. *The Logic of the Absurd.* London: British Film Institute.

— 1994. *Taking Humor Seriously.* London: Routledge.

Paolillo, John C. 1998. Gary Larson's *Far Side*: Nonsense? Nonsense!. *HUMOR.* 11:3. 261-290.

Peirce, Charles S. 1931-36. *Collected Papers.* Cambridge: Cambridge University Press.

Peeters, Bert. 2000. *The lexicon-encyclopedia interface.* Amsterdam/New York : Elsevier.

Prince, Gerald. 1973. *A Grammar of Stories.* Den Haag: Mouton.

— 1987. *A Dictionary of Narratology*. Lincoln: University of Nebraska Press.

Quillian, M. Ross. 1967. Word concepts: a theory and simulation of some semantic capabilities. *Behavioral Science.* 12. 410-430. Rpt. in Ronald J. Brachman and Hector J. Levesque, (eds.) *Readings in Knowledge Representation.* San Mateo, CA: Morgan Kaufmann. 1985. 97-118.

Raskin, Victor. 1981. Script-based lexicon. *Quaderni di Semantica.* 2:1. 25-34.

— 1985. *Semantic Mechanisms of Humor.* Dordrecht/Boston/Lancaster: D. Reidel.

— 1985b. Jokes. *Psychology Today.* 19. 24-39. Italian trans. Umorismo. *Psicologia Contemporanea.* 1986. 12: 74. 2-9.

— 1985c. Script-based sematics: a brief outline. *Quaderni di Semantica.* 6:2. 306-313.

— 1986. Language, linguistics and humor. In Don L.F. Nilsen and Alleen Pace Nilsen, (eds.) *WHIMSY.* IV. Tempe, AZ/West Lafayette, IN: International Society for Humor Studies. 144-146.

—. 1986b. Script-based semantics. In Donald G. Ellis and William A. Donohue, (eds.) *Contemporary Issues in Language and Discourse Processes.* Hillsdale, NJ: Lawrence Erlbaum Associates. 23-61.

Raskin, Victor and Salvatore Attardo. 1994. Non-literalness and non-bona-fide in language: An approach to formal and computational treatments of humor. *Pragmatics and Cognition.* 2:1. 31-69.

Rimmon-Kenan, Shlomith. 1983. *Narrative Fiction: Contemporary Poetics.* London/New York: Methuen.

Ronen, Ruth. 1994. *Possible Worlds in Literary Theory.* Cambridge: Cambridge University Press.

Ruch, Willibald, Salvatore Attardo and Victor Raskin. 1993. Towards an empirical verification of the General Theory of Verbal Humor.*HUMOR.* 6:2. 123-136.

Rutter, Jason. 1997. Stand-up as Interaction: Performance and Audience in Comedy Venues. Unpublished Ph.D. dissertation. Salford, UK: University of Salford.

Sage, Lorna, ed. *Peacock: The Satirical Novels.* London: Macmillan.

Sachs, J.S. 1967. Recognition memory for syntactic and semantic aspects of connected discourse. *Perception and Psychophysics.* 2. 437-442.

— 1974 Memory in reading and listening to discourse. *Memory and Cognition.* 2. 95-100.

Sacks, Harvey. 1974. An analysis of the course of a joke's telling in conversation. In Richard Bauman and Joel Scherzer, (eds.) *Explorations in the Ethnography of Speaking.* Cambridge: Cambridge University Press. 337-353, 467, 490. 2nd ed., 1989.

Sala, Michele. 2000. *Humor, Nonsense, and Absurd: The Linguistic Analysis of Non-Serious Narratives.* Unpublished M.A. thesis. Youngstown, OH: Youngstown State University.

Schaffer, Rachel R. 1982. Vocal Clues for Irony in English. Unpublished Ph.D. dissertation. Columbus, OH: Ohio State University.

Schank, Roger C. 1975. *Conceptual Information Processing.* Amsterdam: North Holland.

Schank, Roger C., and Robert P. Abelson. 1977. *Scripts, Plans, Goals and Understanding.* New York: Wiley.

Searle, John R. 1979. *Expression and Meaning: Studies in the Theory of Speech Acts.* Cambridge: Cambridge University Press.

— 1983. *Intentionality.* Cambridge: Cambridge University Press.

Seuren, Pieter A. M., 1985. *Discourse semantics.* Oxford, Blackwell.

— 1994. Accommodation and presupposition. In R.E. Asher, (ed.) *The Encyclopedia of Language and Linguistics.* Oxford: Pergamon Press. 15-16.

Shepard, Roger N. 1980. *Internal Representations: Studies in Perception Imagery and Cognition.* Montgomery, VT: Bradford.

Shieber, Stuart M. 1986. *An Introduction to Unification-Based Approaches to Grammar.* Stanford: CSLI.

Smith, Neil V., (ed.) 1982. *Mutual Knowledge.* London: Academic Press.

Sperber, Dan, and Deirdre Wilson. 1986. *Relevance: Communication and Cognition.* Cambridge, MA: Harvard University Press.

Talbot, Mary M. 1994. Relevance. In R. E. Asher, (ed.) *The Encyclopedia of Language and Linguistics.* Oxford: Pergamon Press. 3524-3527.

Tannen, Deborah. 1985. Frames and schemas in interaction. *Quaderni di Semantica.* 6:2. 326-335.

Thomason, R. H. 1990. Accomodation, meaning and implicature: Interdisciplinary foundations for pragmatics. In Philip R. Cohen, Jerry Morgan and Martha E. Pollack, (eds.) *Intentions in Communication*. Cambridge, MA: MIT Press, 1990. 325-363.

Toolan, Michael J. 1988. *Narrative: A Critical Linguistic Introduction*. London: Routledge.

Ungerer, Friedrich and Hans-Jorg Schmid. 1996. *An Introduction to Cognitive Linguistics*. London/New York: Longman.

Van Dijk, Teun A. 1973. A note on linguistic macro-structures. In Abraham P. Ten Cate and Peter Jordens, (eds.) *Linguistische Perspektiven, Referate des VII Linguistischen Kolloquiums, Nijmegen, 26-30 September 1972*. Tübingen: Niemeyer.

— 1980. *Macrostructures*. Hillsdale, NJ: Lawrence Erlbaum Associates.

Van Dijk, Teun A. and Walter Kintsch. 1983. *Strategies of Discourse Comprehension*. London: Academic.

Van Doren Stern, Philip. 1945. Introduction. In *Edgar Allan Poe, selected and edited, with an introduction and notes, by Philip Van Doren Stern*. New York: The Viking Press. Rpt. 1973.

Vigliotti, Cynthia. 1998. The subversive function of humour in Anne Sexton's *Transformations*. Unpublished paper.

— Forthcoming. Never telling the same story twice: The subversive function of humour in Anne Sexton's *Transformations*.

Vogel, Susan. 1989. *Humor: A Semiogenetic Approach*. Bochum: Brockmeyer.

Webster's Third New International Dictionary of the English Language, unabridged. 1971. Philip B. Gove, (ed.) Springfield, MA: G & C Merriam Co.

Wenzel, Peter. 1988. Joke. In Walter Koch, (ed.) *Simple Forms: An Encyclopedia of Simple Text-Types in Lore and Literature*. Bochum: Brockmeyer. 123-130.

— 1989. *Von der Struktur des Witzes zum Witz der Struktur: Studien zur Technik der Pointierung*. Heidelberg: Winter.

Wilson, Thomas. 1997. This is *Sports Center*: Confirming the Russian doll theory. Unpublished paper. Youngstown State University. Available online at http://cc.ysu.edu/šattardo/wilson.html

Young, Alan R. 1979. *Henry Peacham*. Boston: Twayne Publishers.

Yus, Francisco. forthcoming. Humor and the search for relevance. Journal of Pragmatics. Special issue on Humor and Pragmatics.

Zajdman, Anat. 1991. Contextualization of canned jokes in discourse. *HUMOR*. 4:1. 23-40.

Zhao, Yan. 1987. The Information Conveying Aspect of Jokes. Unpublished M.A. thesis. West Lafayette, IN: Purdue University.

— 1988. The Information Conveying Aspect of Jokes. *HUMOR* 1: 3. 279-298.

Ziv, Avner. 1984. *Personality and Sense of Humor.* New York: Springer.

Index

1001 Nights, 90

45 Mercy Street, 134

A Merry Discourse of Meum and Tuum (MDMT), ix, 90, 127, 142–147, 205, 207
A Modest Proposal, 113
abduction, 16, 57
Abelson, Robert P., 2–4, 54, 56
Acadèmie française, 153
accomodation, 49, 53, 57
accumulation (stylistic effect), 107
AI, 2, 3, 8, 53, 208
Alexander, Richard, 104, 105
Alexis, Paul, 152, 153
All My Pretty Ones, 134
Allais, Alphonse, ix, x, 82, 86, 95, 96, 100, 127, 149, 150, 153–155
allegory, 18
Allen, Woody, ix, 59, 64, 83, 94, 104, 105
alliteration, 85
allusion, 18, 78, 87, 101, 152
amalgamation rules, 9
ambiguity, 14, 18, 23
    cross-categorial, 14
anachronism, 148, 149, 153
anachronistic juxtaposition, 136
analogy, 136, 137
Andor, Jozsef, 2, 3
antonymy, 8, 18, 19, 53, 114
    contextual, 19
    encyclopedic, 19
    lexical, 18, 19, 53
    local, 18, 19, 43, 53, 122, 124, 207, 208
    non-systemic, 18
    systemic, 18
appropriateness, 52, 115–117, 123
    contextual, 114, 116, 149
Art of Living in London, the, 142
Attardo, Salvatore, vii–x, 1, 7, 17–19, 21–23, 25–27, 29, 32, 33, 37–39, 41, 42, 44, 47–49, 61, 64, 66, 69, 70, 79, 82–86, 88, 92, 93, 103–105, 108, 109, 111–113, 116, 117, 119, 122–124, 150, 203, 206–208
Aubouin, Elie, 25
audience, 31–33
Austen, Jane, 45
authorial aside, 100
    comment, 97, 108, 109, 150
    cues, 81
Awful Rowing Toward God, the, 134
axiological system, 114

background assumption, 50
Bal, Mieke, 32, 33, 88
Bally, Charles, 104
Barbe, Katherina, 121
Bartlett, Frederick C., 2
Bateson, Gregory, 2
bathtub placement, 88, 91
Baudolino, 148
Becque, Henri, 152, 153
Berrendonner, Alain, 114, 122

INDEX

Blazing Saddles, 45, 94
blooper, 91
Book of Folly, the, 134
Booth, Connie, 99
Borges, Jorge Luis, 31
Bower, Gordon H., 54, 57, 59
Braester, Marlena, 114
Bremond, Claude, 80, 88
bridge, 29, 56, 58–60, 63, 64, 87, 88, 139, 140, 143, 207
bridging, 16, 53, 57
Brooks, Mel, 94
Brothers Grimm, 134
Brown, Steven, x
Burns, Bryan, 105
Bush, George, 26
Butler, Marilyn, 105
Byron, Lord, 106

Caffi, Claudia, 51, 52
Candide (CAND), ix, 83, 100, 103, 107, 123
Canterbury Tales, 90
Captain Cap, 150
Caradec, François, 150, 154
Carlson, Thomas B., 117
Carston, Robyn, 49, 121
Casadonte, Donald, x
catastrophe
    see *dénouement*, 42
Cawley, Robert R., 142
Chabanne, Jean Charles, viii, 23, 32, 61
Chafe, Wallace L., 2
Champion, Laurie, 83
character frame, 39
Charney, Maurice, 85
Charniak, Eugene, 2
Chatman, Seymour, 80
Cheers, 87
Chen, Rong, 121
Chiaro, Delia, 65, 66
chiasmus, 26, 59

Chlopicki, Wladyslaw, x, 20, 37–39, 59, 64, 83, 85, 103, 206
Chomsky, Noam, 30
Chuckles Bites the Dust (CBTD), ix, 28, 32, 35, 81, 82, 87, 91, 101, 127, 128, 207
Cigada, Sergio, 19
Cinderella, x, 127, 134–137, 139
citation, 87
Clair, René, 98
Clark, Herbert, 116
Clark, Herbert H., 52, 53, 117
Cleese, John, 99
Clements, William M., 22, 70
Coach and Sedan, 142
coexistence of senses, 17
coincedence (narrative mechanism), 99
Collins, Allan, 54
collocation, 14, 104
comb, 29, 63, 87, 88, 136, 139, 140, 143, 207
combinatorial
    explosion, 9, 15, 50, 107
    rules, 9, 14, 17, 21
comedy
    crazy, 45
    physical, 107
    realistic, 45
    romantic, 40
    sentimental, 40
    slapstick, 93, 109, 110
    stand-up, 59, 61–63, 91
comical confusion, 104
common ground, 51–53, 116
competence, 30, 45
Compleat Gentleman, the, 142
conceptual dependency, 56
conceptual integrator, 18, 19
connector, 18
connotation, 104, 105
constancy under negation, 50
construction-integration model, 16, 49,

208
context, 116
Corblin, Francis, 96
Cosenza, Giovanna, 111
Coseriu, Eugenio, 18
CP, *see* Principle of Cooperation
Cratylism, 25
Crotchet Castle, 105
culminatore semantico, 19

daemon (see also *script*), 53
Davies, Catherine E., x, 67
Davies, Christie, x, 24
Dawson, Carl, 105
de Beaugrande, Robert Alain, 115
de Sade, Donatien A.F., 31
de Saussure, Ferdinand, 30
Death Notebooks, the, 134
Decameron, 90
decontextualization, 62
Defays, Jean-Marc, x, 150, 154
deixis, 31
Dews, Shelly, 120–122
Di Maio, Sara, 20, 26, 207
dialogic style, 63
Dickens, Charles, 93
disambiguation, 9
disjunction
    diffuse, viii, 29, 99, 103, 104, 206
    humorous, 29
disjunctor, 17, 83, 101, 103, 104, 122
    discrete, 103
    dissipated, 39
Dixon, Barbara, 37
Douglas, Mary, 20
Dressler, Wolfgang, 115
Dundes, Alan, 70
dénouement, 42

Eco, Umberto, ix, 8, 16, 31, 95, 96,
    98, 127, 146, 148, 149, 153
Emma, 45
Emmott, Catherine, 57

epilogue, 135, 136
episodic narrative, 90
equifinal action, 4
Ericsson, K. Anders, x, 58
Euclidean laws, 48
euphemism, 123
event, 80, 81, 89, 92, 97, 98
exotism, 153, 154

fabula, 80, 92–94, 96–98, 142, 148, 150
    disruption of, 98
    humorous, 97, 98
    serious, 98
Fall of the House of Usher, the, 93
false analogy (LM), 25, 26
Far Side, 25
Fauconnier, Gilles, 57, 58, 113
Fawlty Towers, 99
Feldman, Jerome, 54
Fellbaum, Christiane, 11
Feuille d'Album, 93, 94
Feydeau, Georges, 86
figure/ground, 26
figure/trajector, 19
Fillmore, Charles, 2, 4
fin de siècle, 151, 153
Fisher, Benjamin F., 93
Fishman, Joshua, 104
flashback, 92
Fludernik, Monika, 32
Fodor, Jerry A., 5, 9, 115
following (of inferences), 50
Foraboco, Giovannantonio, x, 69
foregrounding, 19
formal theory, 2
frame
    change model, 43
    opposition, 43
    semantics, 5
frame (Goffman), 58
frame (see also *script*), 2, 18, 48, 49, 53, 54, 70, 75

INDEX

frame of reference
    breaking, 43
    establishing, 43
framing device, 136
free behaviors, 5
Freedman, Matt, 22
Freud, Sigmund, 25
Frye, Northrop, 45

Gabora, Liane, 25
garden path phenomena (LM), 25
Gaskill, David, 37
Gazdar, Gerald, 51
General Theory of Verbal Humor (GTVH), vii, viii, 17, 22, 23, 27–29, 34, 35, 43, 60, 63, 68, 69, 71–73, 75, 76, 79, 93, 96, 100, 101, 135, 137, 206–208
generative linguistics, 2
genre, 23, 44, 45, 62, 66, 78, 92, 98
Gergits, Julia, x
Gibbs, Raymond H., 118
Giora, Rachel, x, 113, 114, 122, 124
goal, 4
Goffman, Erving, 2, 58, 67
Gorbachev, Mikhail, 26
graded informativeness requirement, 122
graph, 7, 139
    sub-, 7
graph theory, 19, 25
Greenbaum, Andrea, 63
Greimas, Algirdas J., 43, 97
Grice, H. Paul, 15, 16, 21, 31, 48, 49, 51, 69, 108, 111, 112, 114–117, 120
Grosse, Carl, 110
ground/landmark, 19
Gryll Grange, 105
GTVH, 73
Guglielmo di Baskerville, 153
Guiraud, Pierre, 17
Guntheroth, Kurt, 70

Haiman, John, 104, 118, 119
Han Rybeck (HRCI), ix, x, 80, 82, 84, 100, 101, 127, 128, 150–153, 155, 157
hapax-bridge, 29, 84, 88
Hay, Jennifer, x, 68
Headlong Hall (HEHA), ix, 97, 105, 107–109
Hempelmann, Christian F., x, 42, 128, 207
Herring, Susan, x
histoire drôle, vii
Hockett, Charles F., 103
Hoffman, Paul, 22
Hofstadter, Douglas, 25
Holcomb, Christopher, 41, 42
Holmes, Janet, 104
Horrid Mysteries, 110
Hulstijn, Joris, ix
humor
    absurd, 25
    computational treatment of, ix
    deadpan, 118
    dramatic, 23
    duetting, 67
    farcical, 44, 110
    hyperdetermined, 99–101
    intertextual, 70, 87
    involuntary, 33
    level of, 42
    meta-, 70, 100
    non-communicative, 32
    non-narrative, 23
    nonsense, 25
    of action, 109
    Polish, 38
    register, viii, 44, 83, 100, 103–106, 108–110, 122–124
    self-deprecating, 97
    support, 67, 68
    visual, 23
humorous disruption, 98

husteron-proteron, 150
hyperdetermination, 29, 100, 109, 110, 123, 124, 154
    punctual, 100, 101
    textual, 100, 101
hyponymy, 8

ideal reader (see also *model reader*), 30, 31, 34, 148
idealization, 30, 34
idiom, 49
Il nome della rosa (ROSE), ix, 98, 127, 148, 149, 153
Il pendolo di Foucault, 148
Imitation of Jesus Christ, 31
implicature, 9, 15, 16, 51–53, 60, 112, 113, 115, 116, 132
    flouting, 113
    scalar, 15
    strongly backed, 51
    weakly backed, 51
inappropriateness, 103, 115–117, 124, 125
    contextual, 116, 117
    relevant, 124
incongruity, 53, 105, 108, 132, 135, 136, 153, 208
    lexical, 53
    resolution of, 25, 208
    sentence-level, 53
incongruity-resolution
    model, 25
    theory (IR), 45, 63, 64
indirect negation, 122
inference, 9, 15, 16, 21, 49–51, 55, 57, 75, 111–113, 116, 143
    inferential chain, 101, 143
    inferential explosion, 9, 15, 107
    inferential process, 74, 75, 111, 114
    inferential tree, 51
    probabilistic, 51
infinite regression, 52

informativeness, 18
intent
    authorial, 31
    hearer, 31, 33
    speaker, 31, 33
interference, 5
interpolation, 57
intersubjective verification, 34
intertextuality, 45, 61, 71, 72, 74, 75, 78, 85, 87, 101, 148, 149, 154
intonation, 119
    ironical, 119
intuition, 33, 34
irony, viii, ix, 85, 103, 104, 110–125
    assumption of, 114
    clues of, 64
        auditory, 35
        linguistic, 35
        visual, 35
    factor, 118
    humorous, 122
    interpretation of, 110
    marker, 110, 118, 119
    negation, 124
    recognition of, 110, 112, 114
    rhetorical function of, 121
    situational, 134
    unintentional, 117
    value of, 112, 114
ISA, 8
isotopy, 86
Isotopy Disjunction Model (IDM), 17, 43, 83

jab line, 23, 27, 29, 33, 42, 59, 63, 64, 79, 81–91, 99, 101, 103, 104, 127–130, 132, 139, 143, 145, 146, 148, 149, 152–155, 203, 205, 206
    intertextual, 131
    non-antagonistic, 83
    non-essential, 83

INDEX

visual, 129
wave pattern, 205, 207
Jeeves, 86
Johnson, Mark, 49
Johnson-Laird, Philip N., 57, 58
joke
    canned, 61–64, 68, 70, 78, 85
    capping, 65, 66
    clustering, 68
    communicative function of, 49
    complex, 90
    contests, 65
    conversational, 61–63, 68, 70, 85
    cycle, 61, 69, 71–73, 75, 78
    doctor's wife, 17, 21, 24, 43, 143, 146
    elaborate, 90
    folk taxonomy of, 68, 69
    frame, 71, 72, 74, 75
    instantiation, 72
    intertextual, 84, 87
    knock-knock, 85
    light bulb, 22, 26, 70–76
    meta-, 70, 75–78
    narrative, 23, 61, 62
    non-intertextual, 87
    one-liner, 207
    onomastic, 97
    para-, 70, 74, 75, 78
    perlocutionary goal of, 33
    Polish, 27
    prop, 24
    referential, 23
    second generation, 70, 74, 75
    similarity, 22, 68, 69
    situational, 78
    structure, 40
    telling, 61, 62, 65, 66
    third generation, 70, 75
    ur-, 25
    verbal, 23
    vertical integration of, 40
joking
    footing, 67
    joint, 67, 68
    theme, 67
Jolles, André, 43, 45
Jorge da Burgos, 153
Jorgensen, Julia, 122
Josephson, John R., 16
Josephson, Susan G., 16
justification, 25

Karman, Barbara, x, 24
Karttunen, Lauri, 50
Katz, Jerrold J., 5, 9, 115
Keillor, Garrison, 37
Kerman, Judith B., 70
Kintsch, Walter, 7, 16, 17, 49, 51, 54, 56–59, 208
Kittay, Eva Feder, 2
knowledge
    encyclopedic, 5, 6, 18, 51, 100
    lexical, 5, 6
    mutual, 51, 52
    of the world, 18
    representation
        non-monotonic, 48
    structure, 56
Knowledge Resource (KR), 22–27, 29, 68, 71–74, 78, 153, 207
    hierarchical organization of, 73
    hierarchy of, 25, 27, 28
Koch, Walter A., 42
Kolek, Leszek S., 37, 39, 40
Kosslyn, Stephen M., 58
Kotthoff, Helga, x
KR, *see* Knowledge Resource
Kreuz, Roger J., 122
Kugelmass Episode, the (KUGE), ix, 83
Kuhn, Thomas S., 20

L'affaire Blaireau, 150
L'isola del giorno prima, 148

L1 acquisition, 6
LA, *see* Language
La revue illustrèe, 153
Labiche, Eugene, 98
Labov, William, 80
Lacan, Jaques, 96
Ladri di saponette, 94
Lake Wobegone Days, 37
Lakoff, George, 49
Langacker, Ronald W., 19
Language (LA), 22, 23, 27, 28, 67, 69, 71, 73–77, 127
langue, 30
Le journal, 150, 153
Le matin, 153
Le parapluie de l'escouade, 150
Least Disruption Principle (LDP), 69, 111–113
Lefort, Bernard, 70
Lehrer, Adrienne, 2
Leibnizian philosophy, 124
Levinson, Stephen C., 50, 51
Lew, Robert, 23
Lewis, David, 53
lexematic handle, 3, 6–8, 10, 54, 56
lexeme, 3, 5, 7, 11, 14, 19, 49, 53, 55, 104
lexical analysis, 38
lexicon, 5, 6, 8, 10, 14
line, 29, 33, 34, 79, 82–84, 87, 88, 205
    distribution, 205
    intertextual, 29
line/text ratio, 203, 205, 207
literary theory, 23, 33, 34, 37, 42
Live or Die, 134
LM, *see* Logical Mechanism
local logic, 25, 69
Locatelli, Angela, 142
Logical Mechanism (LM), ix, 22, 25–29, 68, 69, 73, 75, 76, 93, 127, 135–137, 155, 206, 207

Lord Arthur Savile's Crime (LASC), ix, 10, 34, 80, 82, 84–86, 89, 96, 97, 101, 106, 127, 128, 142, 155, 203–207
Loti, Pierre, 151, 153, 154
Love Poems, 134
Lovell, Terry, 44, 45, 98

macroproposition, 51, 56
macrorules, 56
    construction, 56
    deletion/selection, 56
    generalization, 56
macrostructure, 56, 57, 97
Madden, Lionel, 105
Madonna, 25
main storyline, 82, 90, 92, 206
Mandler, Jean M., 2, 59
Mannes, Suzanne, 7
Mansfield, Katherine, 93
Manzoni, Alessandro, 96
Marcush, George, 70
Marino, Matthew, 37
Mary Tyler Moore Show, the, ix, x, 127, 128
maxim, 112, 116
    manner, 108, 111
    quality, 108, 115
    quantity, 15, 31, 108
    relevance, 16, 69, 108, 113, 114, 116, 124, 125
    violation of, 31, 113
McDonough, Craig, x, 15
meaning, 5, 9, 14, 15, 18, 22, 31, 34, 43, 49, 50, 57, 58, 60, 111, 112
    antiphrastic, 114
    inferential, 48
    intended, 111, 112, 114
    ironical, 111, 115
    lexical, 3, 49
    literal, 48, 49, 51, 60, 111, 112
Mele, Franco, x, 33

Melincourt, 105
Memoirs of Percy Bysse Shelley, 105
mental image, 58
mental model, 57, 58
    cynematic, 58
    dynamic, 58
    spatial, 58
    temporal, 58
mental representation, 207
    non-propositional, 58
    propositional, 58
mental space, 57–59, 113
metahumor, 45
metaphor, 18, 49
    frozen, 49
Mettinger, Arthur, 18
minimal story, 80
Minsky, Marvin, x
Mizzau, Marina, 122
modality, 53
mode factivity, 111, 113
model reader (see also *ideal reader*), 31, 96, 149
Monti, Mauro, 94
More the Merrier, the, 142
Morin, Violette, vii, viii, 88
Morreall, John, 207
Muecke, Douglas C., 118
Mueller, Ralph, 42
Mulvihill, James, 105
Murphy Brown, 89
mutual mainfestness, 52
Müller, Ralph, 45

narrative, vii, viii, 16, 23, 26, 28, 29, 32, 38–45, 63, 69, 76, 79–83, 86, 88–92, 94–101, 104, 109, 110, 128, 131, 142, 146, 150, 151, 154, 155, 205–207
    bipartite structure, 43
    central, 150
    central complication of, 97–99, 150
    comic, 40, 44
    complex, 82
    digression, 82
    disruption of, 92, 94, 96, 98, 99
    embedded, 79–81, 85, 91, 92, 128, 133, 150, 156
    excursus, 82, 100, 150, 154, 155
    frame, 29, 45, 75, 76, 99
    frame breach, 76–78
    humorous, viii, 30, 37, 40, 44, 45, 88, 89, 98, 99, 109
    level, 81, 82
    location, 42
    loup-phoque, 154
    macro-, 80–82, 86, 91, 93
    meta-, 28, 81, 92, 94, 96, 136, 142, 150
        commentary, 151, 154–156
        disruption, 99
    micro-, 80, 81, 88, 90, 92, 93, 103, 129
    minimal, 80
    naturalistic, 99, 100
    non-comic, 44
    non-humorous, 29, 44, 88, 89, 109
    parasitic, 150, 155
    pointed, 43
    realist, 44, 45, 94, 98
    simplex, 23, 81, 90
    tripartite arrangement, 150
    tripartite structure, vii, 43
Narrative Strategy (NS), 22, 23, 27, 28, 68, 73–76, 78, 127, 136, 137, 140
narrativity, 22
narratology, viii, 32, 33, 42, 43, 80, 88, 92, 206–208
narrator, 80–82, 96, 134, 142, 151, 152, 154, 155
    actual, 80
        explicit, 80
        implicit, 80

implied, 80, 151
meta-, 82
Nelms, Jodi, x, 69, 113
network of concept, 54
Newton, J.F., 105, 106
Nichetti, Maurizio, 94
Nielsen, Don L.F., x
Nightmare Abbey (NIAB), ix, 96, 97, 105, 106, 109, 110
Nijholt, Anton, ix, x
noble savage, 154
nodal point, 41, 42
node, 7, 8
    lexical, 7
    semantic, 7
non-bona fide (NBF), 21, 25
Norrick, Neal, x, 66, 70, 85, 208
novel, viii, 40, 48, 70, 83, 89, 97, 105, 106, 110, 127, 148, 149, 153
    detective, 43
    exotic, 153
    naturalistic, 151, 153
    picaresque, 90, 142, 205
    Romantic, 97
NS, *see* Narrative Strategy

Odyssey, the, 71
Oeuvres anthumes, 150
Oeuvres postumes, 150
orientalism, 154
Oring, Eliot, 62, 82, 92

Paivio, Allan, 58
Palmer, Jerry, 44, 45, 94, 98, 99, 149
Pangloss, Dr., 123
Paolillo, John, x, 25
parallelism, 135–137
parallelization, 135
paraphrase, 22, 23
parody, 71, 87, 91, 97, 100, 110, 151, 153, 156, 205
    intertextual, 76, 77
    non-ridiculing, 71

parole, 30
partially ordered sets, 25
Pas de bile, 150
Peacham, Henry, ix, 127, 142, 144–146, 205
Peacock, Thomas Love, ix, 96, 97, 103, 105–110
peak (of lines), 205
Peeters, Bert, 6
Peirce, Charles S., 8
perceptibility, 42
performance, 30, 45
periphrasis, 109
perlocutionary goal, 33
phraseme, 49
picaresque, 45
Pirandello, Luigi, 98
plan, 4
play frame, 58
plot, viii, 29, 38, 44, 45, 48, 80, 83, 92–94, 97–100, 109, 142, 149 150, 205, 206, 208
    comic, 44
    humorous, 29, 45, 92, 206
    metanarrative, 94
    non-comic, 44
Poe, Edgar Allan, ix, 38, 93, 109
poetry, viii, 33, 34
pointe, 42–44
pointierung, 44
Pope, the, 26
Popperian epistemology, 6
possible world, 57, 101
presupposition, 15, 49–53, 56, 111
    pragmatic, 49, 51–53
    presuppositional basis, 49
Prince, Gerald, 32, 80
Principle of Cooperation, 16, 21, 48, 49, 51, 69, 111–116, 121
prologue, 134–136
Promessi sposi, 96
proposition, 49, 50, 52, 53, 56

psycholinguistics, 7, 16, 47, 58, 60, 91, 207, 208
psychology, 2, 19, 25
pun, 17, 23, 25, 56, 77, 85, 100, 104, 136, 150, 207
   alliterative, 39
   onomastic, 100, 151–153, 156
   topographical, 100
punch line, viii, 23, 27, 29, 41–43, 59, 79, 81–84, 86, 87, 89–94, 97–101, 103, 108, 109, 127, 128, 143, 146, 150, 154, 155, 203, 206
   final, 89, 91
   non-final, 29
Purple Rose of Cairo, the, 94
Pêcheur d'Islande, 151, 153

quantitative analysis, viii, 203
Quillian, M. Ross, 8

Raskin, Victor, x, 1–6, 8, 9, 15, 17–22, 25, 27, 37–39, 41, 43, 54, 78, 83, 146, 208
realistic illusion, 80, 98, 113, 149
recycling, 62
reflexive intention, 117
register, 104, 105, 107–110, 123, 124
reincorporation, 63
release
   theory of humor, 45
Relevance Theory, 43, 51
relief
   comic, 89
   serious, 89, 205
Remembering Needleman, 105
repetition, 85–87, 153
Rhododaphne, 105
riddle, 23
Rimmon-Kenan, Shlomith, 32
Ronen, Ruth, 57
Rosier, Laurence, x, 150
Ruch, Willibald, x, 22, 25, 68, 73

Russel's theory of types, 52
Rutter, Jason, 62–64

Sachs, J.S., 58, 59
Sage, Lorna, 105
Saint Theresa, 31
Sala, Michele, x
saliency, 19
   hierarchy, 19
   perceptual, 19
sarcasm, 104
satire, 109, 110, 124
scenario see also *script*, 2
scene selection, 4
Schaffer, Rachel R., 111
Schank, Roger C., 2, 4, 54, 56
schema (see also *script*), 2, 53, 54
Scott, Sir Walter, 97
script, 1–10, 15, 17–22, 24, 25, 38, 39, 41–43, 48, 49, 51, 53–57, 59, 62, 71, 72, 83, 85, 86, 92, 101, 103, 104, 108, 132, 143, 146
   competing, 21
   complex, 4, 54
   dynamic model, 6, 54
   explicit presentation of, 7
   hierarchical organization of, 4, 54
   hierarchy of, 4
   implicit presentation of, 7
   individualizing, 54
   inferential, 7, 54–57
   internalized, 74
   lexical, 3, 6–8, 54–57, 59, 108
   macro-, 4, 38, 48, 51, 54, 56, 57, 94, 98
   main, 38, 56
   meta-, 4
   mythical, 18, 24
   non-lexical, 8
   overlap, 1, 17, 18, 26, 38, 39, 43, 101, 103, 104
   path, 4, 5

psychological reality of, 3
restricted knowledge of, 6
static model, 6, 7, 54
sub-, 54
track, 5
underspecified, 4
variation within, 4
weak, 2, 4
Script Opposition (SO), ix, 1, 20, 22,
     23, 25–29, 37–39, 41, 42,
     67, 69, 72–76, 84–86, 93,
     98, 101, 107, 123, 127, 135,
     141, 142, 151–153, 206, 208
   binary, 38, 39
   distant, 41
   local, 41, 42
   paradigmatic, 39
   surface, 38
Searle, John R., 116
Sebeok, Thomas, 16
segmentation, 81, 92
Seinfeld, 86
self-parody, 93
self-reference, 52
semantic
   apex, 19
   axis, 18
   field, 18
   network, 6–8, 17
   theory, 9
Semantic Script Theory of Humor (SSTH),
     viii, 1, 8, 17–22, 25, 26, 35,
     37–39, 41–43, 53, 60, 63,
     78, 79, 98, 100, 101, 104,
     108, 207
   expansionist approach, 37, 38
   revisionist approach, 37, 41
semiotics, 32, 42, 206
set theory, 19
setup-incongruity-resolution (SIR), 39,
     43, 66, 93
Seuren, Pieter A.M., 53

Sexton, Anne, ix, x, 82, 127, 134–137
shadow opposition, 38, 39, 85, 206
Shelley, Percy Bysse, 105, 106
Shepard, Roger N., 58
Shieber, Stuart M., 9
short story, viii, 37–40, 43, 103, 109,
     150
SI, *see* Situation
Side Effects, 105
signifier, 23, 29
simile, 136, 137, 151
sitcom
   tag, 91
   teaser, 91
Situation (SI), 22, 24, 25, 27, 28, 68,
     73–76, 78, 127, 128, 136,
     207
situation model, 57, 58
Six Characters in Search of an Author, 98
Skowron, Justyna, x
slot-filler pair, 7, 19
Smith, Neil V., 52
SO, *see* Script Opposition
space builder, 57
Spaceballs, 94, 95
Sperber, Dan, 16, 51, 52, 119, 120
stack, 29, 34, 79, 86, 87, 101, 141,
     142
stereotype, 23, 24
Sterne, Laurence, 94
Stock, Oliviero, x
storage area, 47–49, 54, 55, 92, 100,
     101
strand, 29, 34, 42, 48, 79, 83–88, 100,
     101, 135–137, 139–143, 148,
     149, 151–154, 205, 206
   central, 84, 86, 141–143, 206
   strong, 142
   weak, 142
   intertextual, 83, 141
   one-instance, 87

INDEX

peripheral, 84, 85, 206
    sub-, 84, 135, 136, 151, 152
    textual, 83
subcategorization rules, 14, 21
surface memory, 59
surface structure, 47, 58, 59, 71
synonymy, 8, 22, 108
    near, 108
syntactic rules, 21
syntagm, 14
System of Dr. Tarr and Dr. Fethers, the (TSTF), ix, 38, 93
szuzjet, 80

TA, *see* Target
tag, 92
Talbot, Mary M., 52
Tannen, Deborah, 3
Target (TA), 22–24, 27, 28, 68, 73–76, 78, 84, 127, 137, 205, 206, 208
    ideological, 24
teleological system, 114
text, 32
    conversational, 28
    dramatic, 28
    humorous, viii, 29, 30, 32, 33, 59
    intermediate, viii
    literary, 59
    long, viii, 207
    macro-, 61, 78
    meta-, 96
    narrative, 28, 33, 43, 79, 81
    non-humorous, 18, 90
    non-literary, 59
    non-narrative, 28, 40, 79, 81, 207
    well-formed, 9, 17
text world (TW), 48, 53, 57, 59, 80, 113
text world representation (TWR), 57, 58, 149, 153, 207
textbase, 16, 49, 56, 57

textual analysis
    paradigmatic, 38
textual linguistics, 22
textual processing, 16, 47, 56
thematic affinity, 68, 69, 86
Thomason, R.H., 53
tinge theory, 120, 121
To Bedlam and Part Way Back, 134
Toolan, Michael J., 32, 80
toponym, 152
tragic theater, 98
Transformations (TRAN), ix, 34, 80, 82, 84, 101, 127, 128, 134, 141, 142
translation, 22
travesty, 87
trigger, 104, 123
    diffuse, 103
    dissipated, 38, 39, 103, 104
    script-switch, 17, 18, 101, 103
Tristram Shandy, 94
TW(R), *see* Text World (Representation)

Ulysses, 71
Un chapeau de paille d'italie, 98
Un drame bien parisien, 95, 96
understatement, 108
unification, 9

valeur argumentative (argumentative value), 114
Van Dijk, Teun A., 56, 57
Van Doren Stern, Philip, 93
vector, 29, 34, 79, 81, 89, 101, 128, 139, 155, 206
Viaud, Julien, 153
Vigliotti, Cynthia, x, 134, 139, 141
Vogel, Susan, 42, 43
Voltaire, ix, x, 100, 103, 123, 124, 149

weights, 19

Wenzel, Peter, x, 42–45, 93, 94
Wilde, Oscar, viii, ix, 10, 15, 34, 82, 86, 96, 97, 127, 142, 155, 163, 205, 207
Wilson, Deidre, 16, 51, 52
Wilson, Deirdre, 119, 120
Wilson, Thomas, 29, 86, 141
Winner, Ellen, 120, 121
Wittgenstein, Ludwig, 148
Wodehouse, P.G., 86, 89
Wordnet, 11
Words for Dr. Y, 134

Xau, Fernand, 152, 153

Young, Alan R., 142
Yus, Francisco, x, 43

Zajdman, Anat, x, 62
Zhao, Yan, 24
Ziv, Avner, 25, 69
Zola, Emile, 153